DATE DUE

~~JE 11 '03~~			
~~AP 27 05~~			
~~JE 15~~ 05			

DEMCO 38-296

Catering
Menu
Management

Catering
Menu
Management

Nancy Loman Scanlon, CFE

John Wiley & Sons, Inc.

New York • Chichester • Weinheim • Brisbane • Singapore • Toronto

Library of Congress Cataloging-in-Publication Data

Scanlon, Nancy Loman.
    Catering menu management / Nancy Loman Scanlon.
        p.   cm.
    Includes bibliographical references and index.
    ISBN 0-471-54615-1 (alk. paper)
        1. Caterers and catering–Management.   2. Menus.   I. Title.
    TX921.S33   1992
    642'.4–dc20   91-41558

Printed in the United States of America
10 9 8 7 6 5 4 3

For D.A. Weiland
In recognition of his consistent persistence
to produce a book that effectively communicates
management information. His immeasurable contributions
to this book and support to my efforts are very gratefully acknowledged.

Contents

Preface

In 1991 the foodservice industry was predicted to generate $16 billion in additional foodservice sales opportunities within an industry that initially represented $250 billion in sales. The segments of the industry that were expected to experience this growth opportunity were those that offer some form of takeout or delivery service. In addition, those foodservice businesses that provided facilities and services that were convenient and time-conserving were expected to be warmly received by the public.

Surveys conducted by the Bureau of Foodservice Research indicate that banquet and catering facilities at all levels and styles of foodservice operations will see major gains in the 1990s. Hotel catering services continue to expand as food and beverage management develops new concepts and continues to keep pace with trends in special functions and entertainment. Institutional foodservices are increasingly expanding catering services to accommodate the demand for meeting- and conference-related foodservice and social functions. Club management is responding to increased member needs for both on- and off-premise catering services. Contract feeders for business and industry accounts have seen marked increases in the demands for executive dining and catering services. Full service restaurants are experiencing continued growth in takeout and home delivery business as customers turn to upscale and midrange restaurants to provide quality, prepared foodservice. One of the fastest-growing segments of the takeout and off-premise catering service industry consists of retail food outlets such as charcuteries and delicatessens.

According to *Restaurant & Institutions Magazine* "the foodservice industry in 1992 is estimated to have overall industry sales in excess of $256 billion. Food cooked away from home now accounts for 45 percent of all dollars spent on food and may account for half of all food dollars by the year 2000." The magazine identifies caterers, for the purpose of its research, as individuals whose primary business is catering. This does not, however, include catering services provided by hotels, restaurants, contract feeding programs, country clubs, and retail food outlets. The 1991 Commercial Market Summary Forecast prepared by the Bureau of Foodservice Research has identified 5,430 foodservice businesses whose *primary* business is catering, representing a growth of 7.5 percent since 1990. These operations alone generated over $2,742,000,000 in 1991.

Catering Menu Management has been developed in response to the need by both foodservice professionals and educators for menu management information that is specifically directed toward the needs of catering-related businesses. The variety of settings in which catering services can be offered creates a wide range of opportunities for every style of foodservice operation to take advantage of this high-growth segment in the industry. The information presented in this book on how to incorporate catering services into an ongoing business is important to the successful development of this source of increased revenues.

Catering menu management requires an understanding of menu development and menu pricing. Identifying target markets, developing customer profiles, and analyzing the competition are just some of the important keys to successfully creating a menu program that responds to customer and community needs. Accurate pricing concepts that reflect customer needs and perceived values for catering menus are necessary for ongoing business development.

For those catering businesses offering such services, well-managed beverage programs, both nonalcoholic and alcoholic, can be highly profitable and contribute significantly to the success the business. Customer relations are an extremely important consideration for any foodservice business offering alcoholic beverage service. In addition, both servers and managers must have a thorough understanding of current laws and regulations concerning alcohol.

Creative design and presentation of function menus, special function packages, and conference and convention menu programs also contribute to the success of a catering business. Catering menus should create market-oriented presentations.

The ongoing success of a catering-related business is dependent on the installation and continued practice of various food and beverage operational controls. These controls are put in place to ensure that established standards of quality, service, and presentation are met on a daily basis. In addition, cost controls monitor the financial well-being of the business, providing checkpoints and reports by which management can evaluate operations on a daily and weekly basis. To that end, computerized foodservice management programs can have a significant impact on the success of a catering business. The application of institutional software programs for volume feeding to retail, contract, and institutional catering operations can dramatically enhance overall profitability.

Finally, marketing is an important aspect of every catering operation. As customer demands increase for services to which catering facilities can respond, corresponding marketing efforts will need to be developed. The ability of caterers to adapt to these demands by developing an extensive product line and a broad range of services will determine how well they can take advantage of the changing way in which the general public is eating out.

Catering
Menu
Management

1

Historical Banqueting

The history of modern banqueting was not recorded in detail until the Middle Ages (1000–1500 A.D.); written records from the ancient Greek and Roman periods concentrated primarily on the types of foods eaten rather than on records of the menus for entire meals. There does exist, however, a collection of recipes dating from approximately 42 B.C. to 37 A.D. titled *Cookery and Dining In Imperial Rome.* Concentrating on the dining habits of ancient Rome, this collection of recipes includes the familiar dishes "Sole in White Wine and Asparagus" as well as a number of now–unknown items such as "Sea-Scorpion with Turnips and Dasheens" (a root vegetable). The origins of popular twentieth-century food items are found in such recipes as Baian Seafood Stew, in which minced poached oysters, mussels, scallops, and sea nettles are combined with toasted nuts, rue, celery, pepper, coriander, cumin, raisin wine, broth, reduced wine, and oil. This seafood stew is similar to the basic recipe for bouillabaisse, a staple of the modern cuisine of southern France.

Greek banqueting featured the hors d'oeuvre trolley, on which were served a number of dishes featuring small portions of different food items. Garlic (boiled or roasted), sea urchins, cockles, sturgeon, and sweet wine sop were among the dishes offered. A fifth-century Roman feast elaborated on this concept beginning:

> With a drink of heated wine with honey, to be followed by fresh eggs, quarters of beef, mutton, and pork, all highly seasoned with pepper, pickles, caraway, and poppy seeds, saffron, aromatic balsam, honey, and salt. There was also boar meat with a garniature of cooked apples, deer, roebuck, hare, and even urus, a wild buffalo.
>
> Everything was tasted, from grasshopper to ostrich, from dormouse to wild boar. The whole world was put to gastronomical use, by both soldiers and travellers. Guinea fowl and truffles were brought from Africa, and rabbits from Spain and pheasants from Greece and peacocks from Asia. The number of courses of the banquet gradually rose to twenty and more. A kind of herald announced the merits of such dishes as were worthy of special attention. Nothing was neglected which could sharpen the appetite, hold the attention, and prolong the pleasures of the table. There must always be actors, singers, mimes, clowns and everything that could add to the pleasure of people who had been invited to gather for the sole purpose of being amused.[1]

The Banqueting Hall

The modern banqueting menu was founded during the medieval period of European history. The outline of thirteenth-century meal service followed these instructions for the serving of dishes set down by Bartholomaeus Anglicus, Parisian professor of theology:

> At feasts, first meat is prepared and arrayed, guests be called together, forms and stools be set up in the hall, and tables, cloths, and towels be ordained, disposed and made ready. Guests be set with the lord in the chief place of the board before

the guests wash their hands. First knives, spoons and salt be set on the board, and then bread and drink and many divers messes. The guests are gladdened with lutes and harps. Now wine and messes of meat are brought forth and departed. At the last cometh fruit and spices, and when they have eaten, cloths and relief (trestles) are borne away, and guests wash and wipe their hands again. The grace is said, and guests thank the Lord. Then, for gladness and comfort, drink is brought yet again.[2]

Food preparation methods included roasting and boiling or stewing, following the pattern seen in Figure 1–1.

The three-course menu outline containing as many as 25 dishes for each course became the standard for menu planning used well into the nineteenth century.

Elaborate preparations and rituals accompanied banquets of the medieval period. At feasts in honor of Richard II of England in 1387 the head table was placed on a raised platform with long tables set parallel to the main table. The king was provided with an arm chair while the other guests sat on backless benches or *banquettes*. The use of these banquettes for seating was the origin of the term *banquet*.

It is ten thirty, about half an hour before dinner is to be served. The marshal raises his rod in the sunlit hall and commands the ewerer to set three linen cloths on the high borde. Meanwhile, ushers and grooms arrange subordinate tables with cloths, napkins and surnapes. At each setting the ushers place a trencher, a mazer cup, and a spoon . . .

Suddenly clarions echo throughout the hall announcing the arrival of the king and honored guests.[3]

Following the ceremony in which the king's trencher (a plate, cut from stale bread) was prepared and drinking water tested, the meal commenced.

As the Latin grace is chanted in unison, a procession of trusted servants emerges from the kitchen, each carrying a resplendent creation prepared by the chefs. Hidden under ornate silver covers are the multitude of delicacies that Richard will sample on this day.[4]

In Figure 1–2, a three-course banquet menu served in Paris in 1393 details the mixture of sweets, sours, and spices found in each menu course.

The banqueting menu for the marriage feast of Henry IV of England and Joan of Navarre in 1403 featured a *sotelte* with each course. Soteltes were food sculptures and showpieces molded or sculpted into animals, figures, or representatives of crowns and coats of arms. The elaborate *pièces montées* of the eighteenth and nineteenth centuries were later versions of the sotelte.

Renaissance Europe

The three-course medieval menu format was used for a sixteenth century banquet held to honor Elizabeth of Austria on her entry into Paris in 1571.

Figure 1–1   *Medieval feasting. (Source: Harrison, The Kitchen in History, p. 30.)*

FIRST COURSE

Miniature Pastries Filled With Cod Liver or Beef Marrow

Cameline Meat Brewet
(pieces of meat in a thin cinnamon sauce)

Beef Marrow Fritters

Eels in a Thick Spicy Pureé

Loach in a Cold Green Sauce Flavored with Spices and Sage

Large Cuts of Roast or Boiled Meat

Saltwater Fish

Fritters

Roast Bream and Darioles

Sturgeon

Jellies

SECOND COURSE

"The best roast that may be had"

Freshwater Fish

Broth with Bacon

Meat Tile
(satuéed chicken or veal in a spiced sauce
of pounded crayfish tails, almonds and toasted bread)

Capon Pasties and Crisps

Bream and Eel Pasties

Blank Mang (blanmanger)

THIRD COURSE

Frumenty

Venison

Lampreys with Hot Sauce

Sweets and Confections

Spiced Wine and Wafers

Figure 1–2   *Three-course menu, 1393. (Source:* Tannahill, *Food in History,* 1988, pp. 185–60.)

Because the occasion fell on a religious "fish day," the main menu was limited to fish or shellfish dishes. Figure 1–3 outlines the purchasing requirements for those items.

During the same period in England the two-course menu for a summer dinner for 50 included the items shown in Figure 1–4.

4 Large salmon

10 large turbots

18 brill, 18 mullet, 18 gurnad

50 crabs

18 trout

9 large and 8 small pike

9 shad

3 creels* of large smelts

2 creels of oysters in the shell

2 creels of oysters removed from shell

1 creel of mussels

200 pickled herring

200 smoked herring

12 lobsters

24 cuts of salted salmon

50 pounds of whale

200 cod tripes

200 fat young lampreys

200 fat crayfish

12 yard long carps

50 foot long carps

18 full grown lampreys

1000 frog legs

*A creel is a wicker receptacle for fish and an acknowledged measurement.

Figure 1–3 *Purchasing requirements, banquet for Elizabeth of Austria, 1571.* (*Source:* Tannahill, *Food in History*, 1973, pp. 224, 226.)

FIRST COURSE

Capons

Pike

Partridges

Wild Ducks

Quails

A Florentine of Puft-paste

A Forced boyld Meate

Hash of Venison

Swan

A Fawne with Pudding in his Belly

A Bustard

Chicken Pie, Potato Pie

SECOND COURSE

Kid

Carp

Heron

Trout

A Hartichoake Pie

Soust Pigge

Gull

Partridge

Salmon

Sturgeon

Dried Neatestongue

Gooseberry Tart

Figure 1–4 *English summer menu for 50. (Source:* Tannahill, *Food in History,* 1973, p. 222.)

Eighteenth-Century Banqueting

By 1727 the banquet menu format had been abridged to two main course settings, with the third course reduced to fruits, nuts, and cheese served with appropriate ports. Menus in the American colonies were mirroring the English menus of the period in the mid-1700s, as seen in Figure 1–5.

The eighteenth-century menu underwent a metamorphosis to become the banquet menu of the twentieth century. The menu in Figure 1–6 details the items served in two courses by the Duke de Richelieu to members of the Hanoverian Court. The duke was limited to serving only meat-based menu items due to a shortage in his food supplies.

FIRST COURSE

Soup

Ragoût of Breast of Veal

Roast Venison

Boiled Leg of Lamb with Cauliflower

Served with smaller dishes of Stewed Eels

Stewed Carp

A Pupon of Pigeons

A Roast Pig

SECOND COURSE

Four Partidges and Two Quails

Lobsters

Almond Cheesecakes and Custards

With smaller dishes of

Four pocket and Lamb Testicles

Apricot Fritters

Sturgeon

Fried Sole

Green Peas

Potted Pigeons

Figure 1–5 *American Colonies menu, 1700s. (Source:* Tannahill, *Food in History,* 1973, p. 334.)

FIRST COURSE

Tureen of Garbure Gratinée

Palate of Beef à la Sáinte-Menehould

Kidneys with Fried Onion

Tripe à la Poulette with Lemon Juice

Rump of Beef with Root Vegetables

Oxtail with Chestnut Purée

Civet of Tongue à la Bourguignonne

Paupiettes of Beef a l'estouffade with Pickled Nastertium Buds

Filet of Beef Braised with Celery

Beef Rissoles with Hazelnut Purée

Beef Marrow on Toast

SECOND COURSE

Roast Sirloin

Endive Salad with Ox Tongue

Beef à la Mode with White Jelly

Cold Beef Gâteau with Blood and Jurançon Wine

Glazed Turnips

Beef Bone Marrow Pie with Breadcrumbs and Candy Sugar

Beef Stock Aspic with Lemon Rind and Pralines

Purée of Artichoke Hearts with Beef Stock and Almond Milk

Fritters of Beef Brain in Seville Orange Juice

Beef Jelly with Alicante Wine and Verdun Mirabelles

Figure 1–6 *Richelieu menu.* (Source: Montagné, *The New Larousse Gastronomique*, 1961, p. 586.)

Nineteenth-Century Menu Revisions

By 1867 the menu format contained a sharp reduction in the number of menu items offered and a separation of items into distinct menu categories. The menu in Figure 1–7 for example, was served at the Café Anglais in Paris in 1867.

The classical banquet menu evolved into a nine-course format made up as follows:

FIRST COURSE:	Soup
SECOND COURSE:	Hot hors d'oeuvre
THIRD COURSE:	Cold hors d'oeuvre
FOURTH COURSE:	Intermediate fish course
FIFTH COURSE:	Intermediate meat, poultry, or game course
SIXTH COURSE:	Entrée
SEVENTH COURSE:	Rôt (poultry, game, or beef)
EIGHTH COURSE:	Salad
NINTH COURSE:	Entremets (dessert)

Source: Montagné, *The New Larousse Gastronomique*, 1961, p. 587.

An interpretation of this menu format appears in Figure 1–8, a menu developed by Toulouse-Lautrec for a banquet party in Paris in 1896. It is interesting to note that the third course is imported trout from Lake Michigan in the United States. Some of the menu items are noted only by course, whereas others are specifically named. The seventh course, sweet, would have been a fruit tart. The eighth course, dessert, would have been fruit. Missing from this menu is the traditional cheese course that, when served, precedes the sweet course.

European menu presentation continued to influence the United States. The banquet dinner in Figure 1–9 was given in 1866 for President Andrew Johnson at Delmonico's restaurant in New York City.

Native American Feasts

Feasting is an American tradition dating back to the social ceremonies of many of the Native American tribes. Early written records of naturalists and explorers such as John Bartram and George Catlin provide a fascinating glimpse of the use of food in ceremonies in Native American societies. A ceremonial feast called a *potlatch* was held by tribes in the American Northwest to mark important occasions such as a marriage or the succession to a chieftainship.

SOUPS

Impératrice—Fontanges

INTERMEDIATE COURSE

Soufflé à Reine

Filet of Sole à la Vénitienne

Collops of Turbot au Gratin

Saddle of Mutton with Breton Purée

ENTRÉES

Chickens à la Portugaise

Hot Quail Pâté

Lobster à la Parisienne

Champagne Sherbets

RÔTS

Duckling à la Rouennaise

Canapés of Bunting

FINAL COURSE

Aubergines à l'Espagnole

Asparagus

Cassolettes Princesse

Iced Bombe

Fruit

WINES

Madère Retour des Indes 1846

Sherry 1821

Château-Yqem 1847

Chambertin 1846

Château-Margaux 1847

Château-Latour 1847

Château-Lafite 1848

Figure 1–7 *Café Anglais menu, 1867. (Source:* Montagné, *The New Larousse Gastronomique,* 1961, p. 586.)

Oxtail Soup

Hors d'oeuvre

Lake Michigan Trout

Haunch of Venison on a Purée of Chestnuts

Foie Gras in a Crust

Salad

Sweet Course

Dessert

Grand Table Wine—Vouvray, Corton

Figure 1–8 *Toulouse-Lautrec menu, 1896. (Source:* Toulouse-Lautrec and Joyant, *The Art of Cuisine, 1966, p. 159.)*

The rules of the potlatch required the host to provide, as a sign of conspicuous wealth, the best quality foods available in quantities too great to be eaten by the number of invited guests.

> He was also expected to give away a fortune in gifts.... At a single Kwakiutl potlatch, the guests...were gratified with eight canoes, six slaves, fifty-four elk skins, two thousand silver bracelets, seven thousand brass bracelets, and thirty-three thousand blankets.[5]

George Catlin was served the following feast by the Mandan plains tribe:

> The simple feast which was spread before us consisted of three dishes only, two of which were served in wooden bowls, and the third in an earthen vessel.... The last contained a quantity of *pem-i-can* and marrow-fat; and one of the former held a fine brace of buffalo ribs, delightfully roasted; and the other was filled with a kind of paste or pudding, made of the flour of the *"pomme blanche,"* as the French call it, a delicious turnip of the prairie, finely flavored with the buffalo berries which are...used with divers dishes in cooking, as we in civilized countries use dried currents, which they very much resemble.[6]

Prerevolutionary American cuisine and the patterns in which meals were served primarily followed English custom. The menu pattern for formal meals, as shown in Figure 1–5, was offered in two courses, each a complete meal in itself. Figure 1–10 details a banquet meal that would have been served in Providence, Rhode Island at the home of wealthy shipping traders during the early 1700s.

Major port cities along the eastern seaboard were the scene of feasts and revelries in support of a variety of causes and occasions during the 1800s.

	POTAGES	
Amontillado	Consommé Châtelaine	Bisque aux Quenelles
	HORS D'OEUVRE	
	Timbales de Gibier à Vénitienne	
	POISSONS	
Hechheimerberg	Saumon Livonien	Paupiettes de Kingfish
	RELEVÉS	
Champagne	Selle d'Agneau aux Concombres	
	Filet de Boeuf á la Pocahontas	
	ENTRÉES	
Châteaux-Margaux '48	Suprême de Volaille Dauphine	
	Ballottines de Pigeon Lucullus	
	Filets de Caneton Tyrolienne	
	Côtelettes à la Maréchale	
	Ris de Veau Montgomery	
	Boudins à la Richelieu	
	Sorbet à la Dunderberg	
	RÔTS	
Clos de Vougeot	Bécassines Bardées	
	Ortolans Farcis	
	ENTREMETS DE LÉGUMES	
	Petits Pois à l'Anglaise	Tomates Farcies
	Aubergines Frites	Artichauts Barigoule
	ENTREMETS SUCRÉS	
Tokai Impérial	Pêches à la New York	Mille-feuilles Pompadour
	Abricots Siciliens	Gâteau Soleil
	Macédoine de Fruits	Moscovites aux Oranges
	Bavarois aux Fraises	Galée Californienne
	Créme aux Amandes	Meringues Chantilly
	Beausejour au Malaga	Biscuits Glacés aux Pistaches
Madère Faquart	FRUITS ET DESSERTS	
	PIÈCES MONTÉES	
	Monument de Washington	Fontaine des Aigles
	Temple de la Liberté	Trophée Nationale

Figure 1–9 *Delmonico's menu, 1866. (Source: Cannon and Brooks, The President's Cookbook, 1968, p. 263.)*

A DINNER FOR JUNE

FIRST COURSE

*Asparagus Soup, remove**

Leg of Grass Lamb boiled with capers, carrots, and turnips

Boiled Potatoe Pudding

Venison Pasties

Rice Pellaw

Forced Cock's Combs

SECOND COURSE

White Fricassée of Rabbit

Salamagundi

Ragoo of French Beans with Carrot Force

Water-Soakey

Pear Pie

Followed by

Cheese and grapes

*Remove indicates the the tureen was removed after the soup service and replaced by the meat platters.

Figure 1–10 *Providence banquet meal, 1700s. (Source: The Rhode Island Historical Society, Providence, Rhode Island.)*

General Nathanael Greene wrote to General James Varnum of his visit to Philadelphia in 1779:

> Luxury and dissipation is very prevelant. When I was in Boston last Summer I thought luxury very predominant there: but they were no more to compare with than now prevailing in Philadelphia, than an Infant Babe to a full grown Man. I dine'd at one table where there was a hundred and Sixty dishes: and at several others not far behind.[7]

In the South during this same period a dinner at Shirley Hall plantation in Virginia was described:

> His service is all of silver and you drink your porter out of silver goblets.... The finest Virginia hams, and saddle of mutton, Turkey, then canvas back duck, beef, oysters.... Then comes the sparkling champagne, after that dessert, plum pudding, tarts, ice cream, peaches preserved in Brandy.... then the table is cleared and on comes the figs, almonds and raisens, and the richest Madeira, the best Port and the softest Malmsey wine I ever tasted.[8]

Presidential Banqueting

The Washington presidency was the first opportunity that America had to entertain world politicians. The format for meals followed the three-course meal pattern popular at the time. Figure 1–11 shows the place setting for each of the courses outlined in Figure 1–12. These elaborate settings were repeated for each course.

The menu in Figure 1–12, from Martha Washington's cookbook, illustrates the elaborateness of the first two courses of dinner. The third course was offered after the tablecloth had been removed. Decanters of port, cheeses, nuts and fruit were placed on the table. Menus from this period indicate the diversity and availability of food products in the Mid-Atlantic area as well as Washington's eagerness to present them to his guests.

> "The food served at the president's table from 1789 to the end of Washington's second term in 1797, indicates the new nation's dependence on the land. Game, fowl, meats, plantation-grown fruits and vegetables, fish from local rivers or the Atlantic reveal the abundance of the land. Spliced through the menus are the remnants of Washington's English heritage—puddings, cream trifles, a taste for port and wine."[9]

Thomas Jefferson greatly influenced the development of banqueting styles in America. Following his years as minister plenipotentiary to the court of Louis XVI, Jefferson imported many of the traditions, foods, and wines of the European table to his Virginia home, Monticello. As president of the United States, Jefferson established a pattern of elegant banquets featuring French cuisine and the best available wines.

> Never before had such dinners been given in the President's house, nor such a variety of the finest and most costly wines. In his entertainments republican simplicity was united with epicurian delicacy; while the absence of splendor, ornament and profusion was more than compensated by the neatness, order and elegant simplicity that pervaded the whole establishment.[10]

A summary of dinners from November 5, 1804, to February 22, 1805 totals forty dinners, with 564 guests. The banqueting style that Jefferson brought to America was termed *cuisine bourgeoise*, a simplification of the heavy three-course meals held over from the Middle Ages and used throughout Europe through the eighteenth century (see Figure 1–13).

Similar to the twentieth-century modifications to French cuisine, known as *la nouvelle cuisine*, these changes were a reaction against the rich stocks and sauces and theatrical pièces montées of the eighteenth century. This cuisine appealed to Jefferson's preference for simplistic elegance.

Jefferson's contributions to American cuisine include ice cream, vanilla, pasta, and tomatoes. Vanilla flavoring was a new ingredient for American cookery appearing in the recipe for vanilla ice cream written by Jefferson. Pasta had been incorporated into French cuisine from Italy by the time of his stay in Paris. His notes call it *macaroni*, now known as a tubular pasta. Further investigation shows, however, that he was actually referring to the

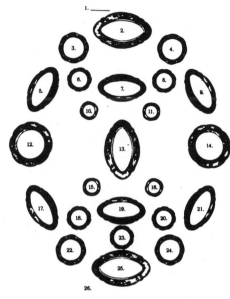

Key to First Course
1. Transparent Soup-remove for
2. fish
3. Pigeons Comfort
4. Fricassee of Chicken
5. French Dip
6. Haricot
7. Sauteed Pheasant
8. Calf's Sweetbreads
9. Torrent of Veal
10. Kidney Beans
11. Broccoli
12. Boilit Turkey
13. Mock Turtle
14. Small Ham
15. Bottled Peas
16. Sallat
17. Sheeps Rumps & Kidneys in Rice
18. Larded Oysters
19. House Lamb
20. Ox Pallets
21. Sweet Breads A la Royal
22. Florentine of Rabbits
23. Beef Olives
24. Ducks a la Mode
25. Hare Soup-remove for
26. Haunch of Venison

Figure 1–11   *Eighteenth-century place settings.*

FIRST COURSE

Small Chicken Patties	Soup Purée	Pork Cutlets
Red Cabbage Stewed	(replaced by salmon)	Sauce Robert
Boiled Chickens	Shoulder of Mutton in Epigram	Mashed Potatoes
Plain Butter	Ham	Boiled Turkey
Shrimp Sauce	Beef Tremblongue	French Beans Fricasseed
Dressed Greens	Soup Santea	Celery Sauce
	(replaced by Stewed Carp)	Oyster Loaves
	Scotch Collops	

SECOND COURSE

Maids of honor	2 Wild Ducks	Rhenish Cream
Asparagus à la Pettit Poi	Lambs Tails (au Béchamel)	Prawns
Sauce	Hare Roasted	Sauce
2 Teal	Sweetbreads (à la Dauphin)	Plovers
Crayfish	3 Partridges	Sauce
Sauce		Chardoons
Fruit in Jelly		Fricasseed Birds
		Custards

Figure 1–12   *Martha Washington's menu.* (*Source:* Cannon and Brooks, *The President's Cookbook,* 1968, p. 9.)

Gazpacho

Tio Pepe Sherry

Hot Devill'd Crab

Roast Leg of Lamb   Conserve of Currants

Château Latour

Saffron Rice   Green Peas with Mint   Corn Pudding

Asparagus Vinaigrette

Montrachet

Cheese Mold   Beaten Biscuits

Strawberry Meringues Chantilly

Pedro Ximenez

Nuts and Candied Fruits

Coffee   Brandy

Figure 1–13 *Jefferson menu. (Source:* Rysary and Leighton, A *Treasury of White House Cooking,* 1972, p. 184.)

pasta cut now known as spaghetti. The tomato, meanwhile, had been taken from Central America and popularized in Southern Europe. Jefferson brought the fruit and its seeds back to Monticello for cultivation.

Jefferson's fascination with French cuisine extended to the equipment used to prepare and serve it. On his return to Monticello from France the following inventory was added to the plantation books. Jefferson's kitchen could have matched a French caterer in its supply of specialized cooking and baking ware. Jefferson purchased in Paris the necessary accompaniments to French cuisine:

silver service
pewterware
dishes for hors d'oeuvres
porcelain cups
saucers
plates
soup tureens and bowls
serving platters and casseroles
crystal goblets
wine tumblers
decanters
a tea urn and coffee pot

For the kitchen he included:

28 round saucepans—19 saucepan covers
frying pans

food warmers
chocolate molds
ice molds
pie pans
spoons, ladles
cleavers, knives
pair of kitchen scales[11]

By 1825 the John Quincy Adams family occupied the White House. The following describes a *levee*, or reception, held in 1829.

> Gentlemen and ladies both attend, arrive about eight and leave about ten. The company is treated with coffee, tea and a variety of cakes, jellies, ice-cream, and white and red wine, mixed and unmixed, and sometimes other cordials and liquors, and frequently with West Indian fruit; all of which are carried about the rooms amongst the guests, upon large trays by servants dressed in livery.[12]

Like Thomas Jefferson, John Tyler favored informality blended with fine cuisine. A gala ball held in the White House in 1845, near the end of Tyler's presidency, contained

> enormous bouquets of flowers filling the rooms and side tables loaded with every imaginable delicacy. The atmosphere radiated luxury and extravagance. The evening was a huge success and much talked of for years to come. There were many parties given during the holiday season for Washington officaldom. Always the tables were laden with substantial and varied foods. Roast ham, a saddle of venison or some other heavy roast, roast wild ducks, or other poultry was in evidence. Enormous supplies of home-made cakes and puddings were on hand. Punch, madeira, and the ubiquitous champagne were ready. Such galas usually began around eight o'clock and ended at eleven.[13]

James Buchanan brought the formal elegance of European society back to the White House, enlisting a French caterer named Gautier to reign over the White House kitchen. The purchasing requirements for the inaugural ball on March 4, 1857, to which 5,000 guests were invited, are listed in Figure 1–14.

President Lincoln's second inaugural ball in 1865 was not to be overshadowed by the ongoing Civil War. The menu in Figure 1–15 for the inaugural supper reflects the diverse cuisine styles of the first one hundred years of the American Presidency, combining the nation's bounty of foods so evident at Washington's table, with influences of French cuisine.

At the turn of the century the formal seven-course French menu in Figure 1–16 was served on the occasion of a state dinner such as pictured in Figure 1–17.

Diverse influences in menu planning created changes in the White House kitchen from one administration to another. In 1877 President Grant served the menu in Figure 1–18 to President-elect and Mrs. Rutherford Hayes. A combination of American foods served in the classical French dinner format accompanied by appropriate wines with each course, this menu embodies the marriage of American cuisine and traditional French dining customs.

Sixty Saddle of Mutton

Eight Rounds of Beef

Seventy five Hams

Foure Saddles of Venison

Four Hundred Gallons of Oysters

Five Hundred Quarts of Chicken Salad

One Hundred Twenty Five Tongues

Five Hundred Quarts of Jellies

Twelve Hundred Quarts of Ice Cream in Assorted Flavors

Cake Pyramid: Four Feet High

Decorated with the Flags of 31 States and the Territories

Figure 1–14 *Buchanan inaugural ball menu: purchasing requirements. (Source: Cannon and Brooks, The President's Cookbook, 1968, p. 221.)*

President Franklin Roosevelt served the informal American cuisine menu in Figure 1–19 to General Charles de Gaulle for a working lunch in 1944. In marked contrast to this simple style is the very formal French menu in Figure 1–20 served by President Nixon to the President of France and Madame Pompidou in 1970.

The one individual besides Thomas Jefferson who significantly influenced the White House style of banqueting was Jacqueline Kennedy. Her personal interest in the quality and style of cuisine and service for White House functions changed the pattern that had been carried out by previous presidencies. Mrs. Kennedy, like Jefferson, dramatically changed the menu format, reducing the number of courses from seven to four or a maximum of five as seen in Figure 1–21. The emphasis on simple elegance that marked Jefferson's banqueting style came full circle in one hundred and sixty-five years with the efforts of Jacqueline Kennedy to imbue a similar style to the White House of the early 1960s. This change reflected current dining trends and reduced the overall dining time, allowing more time for the evening entertainment that became a hallmark of the Kennedy presidency (see Figure 1–22).

Summary

Modern banqueting has its roots in the traditions of the Greeks and Romans. The Greeks introduced the hors d'oeuvre course, to which the Romans added up to twenty courses as they furthered the development of the banquet feast. From this twenty-course format evolved the three-course medieval menu, offering as many as twenty-five menu items with each course.

STEWS

Oyster Stew

Terrapin Stew

Pickled Oysters

BEEF

Roast Beef

Filet de Boeuf

Beef à la Mode

Beef à l'Anglaise

VEAL

Roast Leg of Veal

Fricandeau

Veal Malakoff

POULTRY

Roast Turkey

Boned Turkey

Roast Chicken

Grouse

Quail

Venison Pâtés

Pâté of Duck en Gelée

Pâté de Foie Gras

Smoked Hams

Tongue en Gelée

Tongue Plain

SALADS

Chicken

Lobster Ornamental Pyramids

DESSERTS

Nougat

Orange

Caramel with Fancy Cream Candy

Coconut

Macaroon

Chocolate

Cakes and Tarts

Almond

Sponge

Belle Alliance

Dame Blanche

Macaroon Tart

Tarte à la Nelson

Tarte à la Orléans

Tarte à la Portugaise

Tarte à la Vienne

Jellies and Creams

Calf's Foot and Wine Jelly

Charlotte Russe

Charlotte à la Vanille

Blanc Mange

Crème Napolitaine

Crème à la Nelson

Crème Chateaubriand

Crème à la Smyrna

Crème à la Nesselrode

Bombe à la Vanille

Ice Cream Vanilla

Lemon White Coffee

FRUIT ICES

Strawberry, Orange, Lemon

Grapes, Almonds, Raisins

Coffee & Chocalate

Figure 1–15 *Lincoln's inaugural ball menu, 1865. (Source:* Cannon and Brooks, *The President's Cookbook,* 1968, p. 235.)

STATE DINNER AT WHITE HOUSE

Blue Points.

POTAGES.

Potage tortue á l'Anglaise Consommé Printaniére Royale.

HORS D'OEUVRES.

Canapé á la Russe   Timbales á Talleyrand.

Ranenthaler Berg.

POISSONS.

Saumon, Sauce Hollandaise.   Grenadines de Bass.

Pommes de Terre Duchese.   Cucumber Salade.

Ernest Jeroy.

RELEVÉS.

Seile d' Agneau, Sauce Menthe.   Filet de Boeuf á la Richelieu.

Chateau Margause.

ENTREES.

Ris de Veau á la Perigneux.   Cotelettes d'Agneau d'or Maison

Terrapin á la Maryland.

Punch Cardinal.   Clas de Vuguet.

RÔTI.

Canvas Back Duck.

ENTREMETS.

German Asparagus.   Petite Peis.

Golde au Champagne.   Flombieré aux Framboise.

Pudding Diplomate.

Café.   Liqueurs.

Fruits.   Fromage.

Figure 1–16 *State dinner menu. (Source:* Ziemann and Gilette, *The White House Cookbook,* 1906, p. 481.)

Figure 1–17 *State dinner print. (Source: Amy La Follette Jensen, The White House and Its Thirty-Three Families, New York: McGraw-Hill, 1962, p. 151.)*

	Consommé Impérial
	Bisque de Grevisse
Sherry	Woodcock Patties*
	Salmon
White Wine	Roast of Beef
	Breast of Pheasant
	Crawfish Pudding
	Goose Livers
Roman Punch	Turkey
	Artichokes
	Canvasback Duck
Red Wine	Sweet Warm Dish**

*Woodcock is a small game bird that was common to the Eastern coast of the United States.
**A form of dessert pudding

Figure 1–18 *President Grant's menu, 1877. (Source: Cannon and Brooks, The Presidents' Cookbook, 1968, p. 279.)*

Jellied Bouillon

Boiled Chicken   *Currant Jelly*

Asparagus   *Duchess Potatoes*

Parsleyed Carrots

Tossed Salad

Vanilla Ice Cream   *Crushed Raspberries*

Angel Food Cake

Coffee

Figure 1–19   *Roosevelt–de Gaulle luncheon menu, 1944. (Source: Rysary and Leighton, A Treasury of White House Cooking, 1972, p. 140.)*

The menu format revisions of the late eighteenth and nineteenth centuries transformed the three primary courses with multiple dishes into a series of nine courses, each featuring an individual menu item. These revisions were incorporated into menus throughout Europe and America in a variety of formats.

The history of American banqueting begins with the feasts of the Native Americans. The menu formats of early colonial American feasts were primarily influenced by England. French cuisine and menu formats intially threaded their way through the colonies via English recipes and customs. The emigration of the French royalists during the French Revolution accelerated the assimilation of both French cuisine and menus into American banqueting

Le Salmon Lafayette

Le contre-filet de Boeuf aux Cèpes

Les Pommes Nouvelles

Les Asperges Fraîches Hollandaise

La Laitue de Kentucky

Le Fromage de Camembert

Le Melon Glacé à la Vigneronne

Les Petits Fours

Figure 1–20   *President Nixon's menu for President Pompidou. (Source: Rysary and Leighton, A Treasury of White House Cooking, 1972, p. 107.)*

DINNER

Almaden   Vol-au-Vent Maryland
Pinot Blanc

Château   Gigot d'Agneau aux flageolets
Haut-Brion   Tomates grillé
1953   Épinards à la crème

                        Mousse aux Concombres
Cuvée Dom
Pérignon Brut
1952   Bombe Glace Caribienne

The White House
Tuesday, November 7, 1961

Figure 1–21   *Kennedy menus. (Source:* Lincoln, *The Kennedy White House Parties,* 1967, p. 11.)

DINNER

Inglenook
Pinot
Chardonnay

Boston sole Diplomate

Roast sirloin of beef Chevreuse

Château
Corton-Grancey
1959

String beans with almonds
Braised endive

Galantine of chicken
Green salad

Dom
Pérignon
1955

Charlotte Plombière

The White House
Tuesday, October 1, 1963

Figure 1–21 *(continued)*

Figure 1–22 *Kennedy concert. (Source:* Lincoln, *The Kennedy White House Parties,* 1967, pp. 154–55.)

customs. Thomas Jefferson greatly aided the development of American banqueting during his years in the White House. His simplification of the menu and emphasis on wines were major elements of a style of banqueting that would continually appear during the next one hundred and sixty-five years of White House functions. During the presidency of John Kennedy, banquets were enhanced by the contributions of Jacqueline Kennedy. Like Jefferson, she preferred menus that emphasized a style of simple elegance, concentrating on a high quality of food and service.

The records tracing the development of the banquet menu through the centuries provide a rich and exciting chronicle of food items, recipes, and traditions. Many of these food items and recipes have endured as part of our contemporary food customs.

Endnotes

1. Apicius, *Cooking and Dining in Imperial Rome,* ed. Joseph Dommers, Vehling (New York: Dover, 1977)
2. Jean Anthélme Brilate–Savarin, *The Physiology of Taste,* ed. M.F.K. Fisher (San Francisco: North Point Press, 1986), pp. 287–290.
3. Lorna J. Sass, *To the King's Taste* (New York: Metropolitan Museum of Art, 1975), pp. 29, 30.

4. Ibid. p. 31.
5. Waverly Root, and Richard de Rochemont, *Eating In America* (New York: William Morrow & Co. Inc., 1976), p. 36.
6. Ibid. p. 37.
7. Richard K. Showman et al., eds., *The Papers of General Nathanael Greene*. Volume III, *October 1778 to May 1779* (Chapel Hill: University of North Carolina Press, 1983), p. 223.
8. Root and Rochemont, *Eating in America*, p. 95.
9. Poppy Cannon and Patricia Brooks, *The President's Cookbook* (Funk & Wagnalls, 1968), p. 9.
10. Marie Thomas Kimball, *Thomas Jefferson's Cookbook* (New York: G.P. Putnam's Sons, 1972), p. 184.
11. Jack McLaughlin, *Jefferson & Monticello* (New York: Henry Holt & Co., 1988), p. 230.
12. Cannon and Brooks, *The President's Cookbook* (1968), p. 112.
13. Ibid. p. 170.

2

Styles of Catering Operations

Catering operations exist in a wide variety of foodservice facilities. From fine dining establishments to delicatessens, catering services are meeting the increased need for pre-prepared foodservice demanded by an American public that finds the time available for food preparation shrinking.

Forward-thinking foodservice businesses are incorporating catering services into their operations in recognition of this expanding market. Off-premise catering and takeout services offer an excellent avenue for increasing revenue with minimal costs.

This chapter will summarize the ways in which catering services have been incorporated into foodservice operational styles, providing operators with techniques and methods for expanding their businesses. The categories of foodservice operations to be reviewed are:

1. Full service restaurants
2. Hotel food and beverage facilities
3. Catering halls
4. Independent caterers
5. Country clubs
6. Contract feeding
7. Charcuteries and delicatessens

Services in a foodservice operation refer to the opportunities management makes available to the customer to purchase food, beverage, entertainment, and ancillary services. Services include:

1. Table food services
2. Packaged takeout food services
3. Beverage services
4. Entertainment services
5. Business meeting services
6. Conference and convention services
7. Contract feeding services

Full Service Restaurants

Full service restaurants have the opportunity to offer a variety of catering services to their customers. However, before any decision is made to offer these services, five important factors should be considered:

1. Location
2. Customer profile
3. Restaurant style or concept

4. Restaurant facilities
5. Cuisine and menu offerings

Additional material on identifying and developing these factors is discussed in Chapter Three, Catering Foodservice Development.

Location

The proximity of the restaurant to office complexes and centralized business areas will determine whether the focus of the catering services should be on business or social catering.

Businesses in the 1990s are no longer concentrated in the central urban districts. The growth of office parks in suburban locations provides an ideal customer base for catering both business functions and in-office lunches. A significant factor in developing the market for business catering is that service is generally required during time periods in the business week, when restaurants are usually slow.

Both urban and suburban restaurants can successfully develop social catering business. Suburban locations are generally more appropriate for social catering to private homes, clubs, churches, and other facilities. Delivery to urban locations can pose security and logistical problems creating additional costs for transportation and service help.

Population density also affects the volume of anticipated catering business. Restaurants situated in rural areas with low population density cannot expect an immediate high volume of catering business. Areas of high-density population yield a variety of catering opportunities that steadily increase in volume through referrals and reputation.

The location of the physical restaurant building plays a role in the type of catering services offered. Storage facilities, expansion possibilities, and access to major transportation routes are factors in catering service production.

Customer Profile

A restaurant targets its current average customer for catering services. Customers should be classified as business or social catering clients and designated by income bracket. Accordingly, the type of functions for which customers need catering services must coincide with the restaurant's capabilities.

Style or Concept

The style, theme, and/or concept of the restaurant must be taken into consideration when planning catering services. Off-premise catering services do not necessarily have to match those offered by the restaurant. On-premise catering services must, however, blend with the overall style or concept.

Facilities

Restaurant facilities are a major factor in providing on-premise catering. The percentage of catering services to restaurant services that can be offered at any one time depends on the size and flexibility of the physical plant. Small private parties are often incorporated into the general dining room area. Large parties must, however, be given facilities that are separated from the general public. The restaurant floor plan in Figure 2–1 outlines flexible catering space for a full service restaurant operation. This restaurant has a private dining room and bar facility complete with dance floor that can also be used as restaurant dining room area for busy time periods and holidays. Flexible facilities such as these allow a restaurant to maximize revenues.

Many restaurants offering in-house catering schedule large parties such as weddings, anniversaries, luncheons, and dinners on days and times when the restaurant is not otherwise open. Thus sometimes catering business must be refused because sufficient facilities are not available. When such refusals become too frequent management will need to decide how the restaurant will balance its future development of catering versus full service dining services.

Kitchen facilities play a major part in determining when and how catering service demands can be met. Kitchen equipment must be flexible, allowing for large portion production at the same time as à la carte restaurant service. The cooking load and holding capacity of ovens and auxiliary equipment is important if a kitchen is to be used to its full capacity during busy times.

Storage and refrigeration facilities determine the amount of food products immediately available at any given time. The cost of waste from food spoilage due to lack of refrigerator and freezer space could dilute the profit from additional catering business. A further discussion regarding equipment capabilities for catering services is found in Chapter Four.

Cuisine and Menu

The primary cuisine and menu offerings of a restaurant constitute one of the most important considerations for on-premise catering. As discussed earlier, off-premise catering services do not necessarily need to be the same as those offered by the restaurant for full service dining.

Purchasing and production requirements are crucial to the successful development of catering services. On-premise catering must offer menu items that duplicate the established menu program as closely as possible in order to enhance production capabilities. Surrounding items such as vegetables and starches are the most effective area of the menu to duplicate. Kitchen production is more efficient when the number of surrounding menu items is limited. Profitable and effective purchasing for catering functions requires that the ingredients for menu items be the same or similar to those on the restaurant

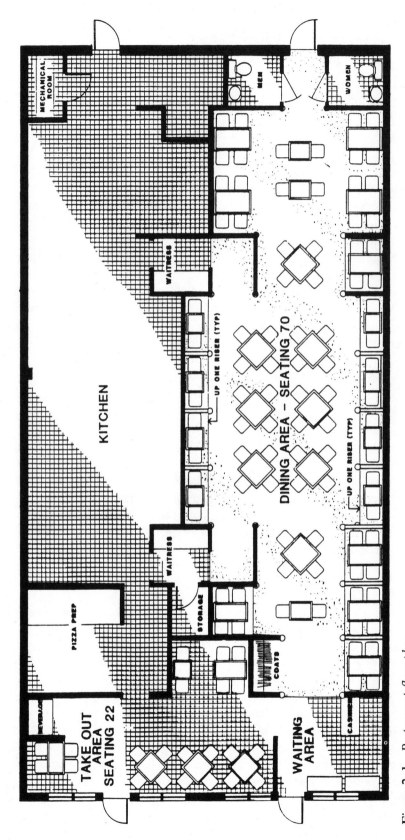

Figure 2–1   Restaurant floor plan.

34

menu. This allows the purchasing agent to place orders for maximum volume pricing and quality.

Off-Premise Catering

The decision to participate in off-premise catering requires a restaurant operation to thoroughly review its resources. A successful in-house catering service can lull management into thinking that off-premise catering services will not be much more difficult to handle.

Several problems must be anticipated regarding the facilities in which final production and off-premise service takes place. During in-house functions, service staff can often work between parties and the dining room, filling in where needed, and the kitchen staff can function as usual, planning ahead to handle increased production loads. However, a separate staff has to be assigned to service off-premise functions, including at least one member of the production staff working only on that function and therefore unavailable to the restaurant for the time period involved. Equipment as well as food needs to be transported both to and from the function location. Hot food and cold food must be kept at specific temperatures to prevent food spoilage. A refrigerator truck may be necessary at certain times of the year. Transportation routes and problems with traffic congestion must be considered in the timing of the delivery.

Subcontractors may be necessary for equipment such as tables, chairs, dishes, glassware, linens, dance floors, and even tents. The extent to which the restaurant commits to a full service catering business determines the amount of extra work required to handle the business. Planning for off-premise catering requires attention to detail. Contingency plans for bad weather, delays in food transportation, and failure of on-site equipment to function should be set in place ahead of time so that problems can be dealt with expediently when they arise. Additional costs are incurred when solutions to these situations are not planned in advance. Contract prices must include these contingencies or management will find that costs are higher than the fees charged.

Takeout

Takeout service is the most profitable way for restaurants and catering services to increase revenues without increasing costs in the 1990s, because takeout service does not require extra seating or service personnel. Kitchen production does not need to be altered or extra staff added to handle large increases in volume for short time periods. Takeout does not require the additional expenses incurred by table service for glassware, linens, flowers, menus, and entertainment. Disposable containers, plastic flatware, and a carrying container are the basic requirements. Successful takeout does, however, require planning so that customers will receive menu items in satisfactory condition. The takeout menu should be developed from the restaurant menu.

Hotel Food and Beverage Facilities

The hotel food and beverage department provides food-related guest facilities and services throughout a hotel or resort property. These can include the following:

1. Full service restaurant
2. Coffee shop
3. Catering
4. Room service
5. Recreation food services

Food items for these combined food services are produced from a central kitchen, with the exception of large hotel facilities where satellite kitchens provide auxiliary production and service areas. An executive chef supervises production for all areas, consulting with the manager of each area individually.

Of the five food service areas, catering affords the possibility for the greatest profit, in addition to providing much-needed cash flow during periods when room sales are slow. Hotel catering services are usually classified as business, convention/conference, or social. The volume of catering service available in a hotel is based on the size and number of facilities that can be used for private functions as well as the availability of production and service staff and related equipment.

The primary catering market for a hotel is based on three factors:

1. Location
2. Hotel facilities
3. Customer profile

Location

The location of a hotel determines the demand for *in-house* catering. In-house catering is defined as guest-related foodservice functions associated with business meetings, conferences, or conventions.

A hotel with a remote location focuses its catering efforts on the businesses and meetings booked into the hotel. Resort locations often provide additional opportunities for catering services at sports facilities throughout the property.

A hotel with a suburban or downtown location can expect to develop a large volume of *outside* catering business, both business-related and social, in addition to conferences and conventions. The Chicago Hilton, located in downtown Chicago, breaks down its annual catering business into the following percentages:

65% Conference/Convention

35% Outside Social

Facilities

The amount of combined catering business that can be handled at any one time in a hotel is based primarily on the number and size of the facilities available. The major function rooms are usually referred to as the ballroom areas. These are complemented by a series of meeting rooms, some adjacent to the main ballroom area and some located in other areas of the hotel. The diagrams in Figure 2–2 show the variety of facilities available at the Four Seasons Hotel in Philadelphia, Pennsylvania.

The main facility is a ballroom that seats 380 for dining. Adjacent to that room is a foyer that seats 80 and a terrace that accommodates 125 for receptions. Private meeting rooms are found on both the main level and other locations throughout the hotel. The formal function space is broken down into 9 separate rooms that can seat a total of 712 guests at any one time.

Customer Profile

The customer profile for hotel catering services is made up of both business and social clientele. Customers who use the hotel as a location for a two- or three-day meeting consider meal functions as part of the total meeting package. This arrangement not only enables them to work within a budget that covers the entire project, but also fits with their approach to planning catering functions, which considers the success of the complete meeting rather than one individual function. The catering manager is generally given the responsibility of creating a menu plan for the entire program and has little client involvement once prices have been agreed upon.

The target for outside catering services is a customer who reflects the social, business, and economic profile of the local community. Hotel catering services attract a wide base of customers with a broad range of requests. Customers who plan functions on a regular basis for businesses are familiar with the catering services and staff of the hotel. Their needs are often easy to identify and provide for. Customers who plan social functions on a one-time basis, however, need more personal guidance throughout much of the planning stage. Pricing is a major concern for this customer group.

Catering Halls

A catering hall is a facility dedicated to private parties with an on-site production kitchen and staff. These facilities can offer a wide range of both in-house and off-premise catering services. The major factors that influence the market for a catering hall are:

1. Style or concept
2. Facilities
3. Customer profile

CONFERENCE & BANQUET FACILITIES

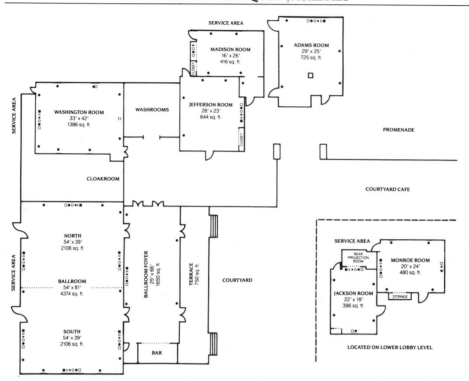

Meeting Room	Dimensions	Ceiling Height	Square Feet	U-Shape	Dining	Reception	Conference	School Room	Theatre
LOBBY LEVEL									
Ballroom	54' × 81'	13'6"	4374	—	380	500	—	260	600
North	54' × 39'	13'6"	2106	63	190	250	—	135	300
South	54' × 39'	13'6"	2106	63	190	250	—	135	300
Foyer	25' × 66'	10'6"	1650	—	80	200	—	—	—
Terrace	—	—	750	—	—	125	—	—	—
Washington Room	33' × 42'	10'	1386	45	120	150	45	80	150
Adams Room	29' × 25'	11'6"	725	24	50	80	24	40	70
Jefferson Room	28' × 23'	10'	644	23	50	50	24	45	60
Madison Room	16' × 26'	9'6"	416	—	15	—	14	—	—
LOWER LOBBY LEVEL									
Monroe Room	20' × 24'	10'	480	23	40	60	24	30	40
Jackson Room	22' × 18'	10'	396	19	30	50	20	20	30
FLOORS 3–8									
Boardrooms (2)	25' × 16'	—	400	—	10-12	—	10-12	—	—
Boardrooms (3)	26' × 14'	—	364	—	12-15	—	12-15	—	—

■ TELEPHONE JACK   ● OUTLET   ○ TELEVISION   ◆ MICROPHONE   □ AUDIO INPUT   ◇ REMOTE CONTROL FOR REAR SCREEN PROJECTOR

ONE LOGAN SQUARE, PHILADELPHIA, PENNSYLVANIA, 19103, (215) 963-1500, TELEX 00-831805, FAX (215) 963-9507

Figure 2–2   *Four Seasons Hotel floor plans. (Courtesy of Four Seasons Hotel, Philadelphia, PA.)*

Style or Concept

Catering halls such as that pictured in Figure 2–3 offer customers a self-contained private function space independent of a hotel or restaurant. Many catering halls specialize in social functions such as weddings and plan the design of the landscaping and building to accent the theme of the function. This design is also often aimed at a particular segment of the customer market, depending on location of the hall and the density and ethnic breakdown of the surrounding population.

Catering halls can also specialize in large functions, providing space for groups that cannot normally be accommodated in other facilities. Such halls are generally designed to host a wide range of social and business functions and do not establish a particular concept.

Figure 2–3   *Catering hall. (Courtesy of Ridgewell's Caterers, Bethesda, MD.)*

Facilities

The flexibility, and often the originality, of function spaces are important to the success of a catering hall. Customers will travel considerable distances to social functions held in facilities that offer a unique setting or experience. Wedding receptions are often planned in locations over an hour away from the site of the ceremony because the bride and groom want a specific setting for their party. Annual social functions are constantly looking for new and different themes to draw attendees. Popular catering halls provide such variety. Catering hall concepts can range from futuristic to country western, offering menu and entertainment packages to match.

Customer Profile

The customer base for a catering hall depends on the pricing structure of the menus and package plans. The kind of functions that a catering hall promotes also affects the customer profile.

Off-Premise Catering

Catering halls have a great deal of flexibility in the type of business that they solicit. The amount of off-premise catering that can be handled is limited only by the ability to service it. Location, transportation routes, and population density play a major role in determining this segment of the business. The ability to transport food and equipment and provide service and production staff are other limiting factors.

Independent Caterers

Independent caterers are private businesses offering catering services to the general public. These businesses combine a catering hall facility with off-premise catering services or operate without a formal function facility. Those caterers who provide only on-site catering must arrange for a space for storage and kitchen production. Kitchens can be leased from schools or churches to provide the caterer with commercial refrigeration and production space. Others, such as Ridgewell's Caterers in Washington, D.C., have production facilities and warehouse space to handle large volumes of business. Figure 2–4 shows Ridgewell's Caterers, the largest caterer in the Washington area, at work.

Many independent caterers focus on off-premise catering, maintaining only a small catering hall with limited facilities to house their production and storage facilities. They concentrate on both business and social functions within a wide geographical area.

Figure 2–4 *Ridgewell's Caterers. (Courtesy of Ridgewell's Caterers, Bethesda, MD.)*

An excellent example of this concept is Jack Francis Catering in Conshohocken, Pennsylvania. The catering hall is located on the side street of a small working class town directly adjacent to the city of Philadelphia. The building is small and offers only one function space. Off-premise catering represents the major portion of this company's business; it services prominent business and social functions in a wide variety of settings in the Philadelphia area. On a busy Saturday, Jack Francis Caterers can handle as many as 25 different functions in as many different locations.

In order to successfully cater this many functions, the operation has to be extremely well-organized. Although equipment needs, staffing, and transportation are major concerns, the primary product, food, is the most important issue.

Menu Duplication

The key to successful catering service in this example is to duplicate as many of the menu items as possible by limiting kitchen production to a minimum number of menu items. All surrounding items, salads, and desserts should be standardized. The main course selection should be flexible, although only three or four main course items should be available for any particular day. The items should be chosen for their ability to be precooked for completion in another location. They should have excellent holding properties and retain heat. An example of a menu selection is shown in Figure 2–5.

This menu offers one appetizer and salad and two choices of dessert. Dessert #2 is a chocolate dessert shell filled with frozen yogurt. These can be preassembled, frozen, and transported to function locations within reasonable proximity to the main production kitchen. The gâteau chocolate, as well as the breads, can be contracted from an outside baking source. Whipped cream is served with the cake using a high-quality product from aerosol containers.

Selection for Saturday March 9, 1991

Appetizer
Fresh Fruit Melon Boat

———

Salad
Mixed Seasonal Greens

———

Breads
Fresh Baked Assorted Rolls

———

Main Course Item Selection
Filet of Beef
Lamb Chops
Breast of Capon
Rolled Filet of Fish

———

Vegetables and Starches
1. Vichy Carrots
Roasted Red Potatoes
2. Whole Green Beans
Wild Rice Pilaff

———

Dessert
1. Gâteau Chocolate
2. Frozen Dessert Shell

Figure 2–5   *Menu item duplication.*

The main course offers a choice of two meats, one poultry, and one fish. All four of these items fulfill the requirements for preproduction and holding properties. Two vegetable selections are offered, one appropriate for the meat dishes and one better-suited for the poultry and fish but acceptable for any of the main course selections. Standardization procedures such as these, which minimize the problems of serving multiple parties in off-premise settings, ensure that the food presentation is of the best possible quality.

Private Clubs

Private clubs offer a self-contained facility that operates both full service dining rooms and private function space, very much like a full service restaurant. Private clubs, however, are totally dependent on their membership for both dining room and catering business. Functioning as nonprofit organizations they are prohibited by law from accepting or soliciting business from nonmembers. Private clubs may, however, cater functions that are sponsored by members and attended by nonmembers, allowing them to service both social and business activities.

Some of the factors that influence the success of restaurant and hotel catering services also affect private clubs. These factors are:

1. Location
2. Facilities

Location

Clubs are broken down into two general classifications: private clubs and country clubs. Private clubs are generally situated in the downtown areas of large towns and cities. The club is used primarily as a location for meetings, private dining, and social and business functions. Country clubs require a suburban location and usually promote a combination of golf, tennis, and/or boating as their primary recreational facilities. Private dining and catering facilities are based in the clubhouse.

Acceptability of location is due primarily to general location and accessibility to major transportation routes. Downtown city locations can cause problems regarding parking and security for people traveling into the city.

Facilities

Club facilities can greatly influence the volume of catering business. Clubs offering spectacular settings, access to garden areas for outdoor functions, or well-designed interiors will easily attract social business (see Figure 2–6).

Figure 2–6 *Club function room photograph.*

Off-Premise Catering

The ability to accept off-premise catering functions is controlled by the same laws regarding the solicitation of nonmember business for in-house functions. Beyond that restriction the same considerations for restaurants and hotels concerning transportation, staffing, production, and service also apply to clubs.

Contract Feeding

Contract feeding companies provide institutions such as hospitals and schools, as well as businesses, with in-house meal programs designed to meet specific foodservice needs. Food production and service is contracted for over a stipulated period of time within designated budget restrictions.

The growth of the contract feeding business in the late 1980s and early 1990s has been significant. As food costs have increased and available labor has decreased, institutions and businesses have turned to outside resources to operate their foodservice programs.

Large corporate businesses have found it profitable to offer employees subsidized foodservice as a benefit. Productivity increases when employees remain in the office complex for meal periods and breaks, reducing the amount of time lost in going out for food.

The major factors that can influence the success of catering services within a contract feeding location are:

1. Facilities
2. Customer profile

Figure 2–7 *Prudential eastern headquarters, function space. (Courtesy of Prudential Life Insurance.)*

Facilities

Contract feeding can be offered in a wide variety of dining room and catering facilities. The type and number of facilities that can be used as function space within a business or institutional setting will determine the volume of in-house catering. Catering functions in these settings are usually business-related, but open area space can be used by private groups for social functions.

A good example of this are the facilities offered at the eastern regional office of Prudential Life Insurance. Foodservice for this facility is handled by ARA, the largest contract feeder in the United States. The building offers a wide variety of facilities, ranging from a cafeteria seating 1,200 people to private dining rooms seating 20. A major meeting room and foyer that can seat 250 people opens out onto a landscaped courtyard that serves as a reception area when weather permits (see Figure 2–7). This space is decorated in soft, business-related tones with colorful and interesting art work. Additional facilities throughout the building provide private dining room space.

Customer Profile

Identifying the customer profile for a large and diverse group of people in a business situation is initially done by job classification level. Private dining room service and business meeting menu selections should be chosen to meet the expectations of the different job levels of the people who attend these functions.

The type of food products that will be popular in the cafeteria area depends on the makeup of the population group. The proximity of the business to a city, the general education level of the customer group, and local and regional food preferences determine the types of food products offered.

Off-Premise Catering

Contract feeding companies working for a business or institution do not involve themselves in off-premise catering unless requested to do so as part of their contract. The contract feeder may, however, promote take-home foodservice.

In addition, supplemental foodservice can be offered throughout the building, providing meals, special party trays, cakes, desserts, and coffee services as requested by employees of the company, who pay for these services independently.

Charcuteries and Delicatessens

Charcuteries are food stores that offer takeout foodservice along with gourmet food products. Many of these products are used as ingredients in the prepared food line. This type of food store usually specializes in a regional or national cuisine. Menu items can range from salads and sandwiches to fully prepared meals. The success of a charcuterie depends on two major factors, location and customer profile.

Location

A charcuterie of this nature should be located in an area where customer interest will support it. Pricing in this type of retail food store is generally higher than delicatessens and supermarkets, requiring a customer base willing to pay the price for gourmet food products. Smaller independent caterers often operate out of a retail outlet, using it as a production and storage location and as a means of advertising.

Delicatessens are food stores that provide everyday food products and offer takeout food services. The location should be in reasonably close proximity to the targeted customer base. Menu item offerings range from sandwiches, salads, and pizza to pre-prepared meals to go. Takeout foodservice of pre-prepared foods is a major segment of the business for this type of foodservice operation.

Off-Premise Catering

The factors affecting the success of off-premise catering for both charcuteries and delicatessens are the same as those discussed for independent caterers.

Summary

The opportunities for foodservice operations to offer catering services are many and varied. Catering management in the 1990s will continue to expand in both volume and diversity as the demand for ready-to-serve pre-prepared foods increases.

The ability of a foodservice operation to successfully offer catering services will be affected by a variety of factors. Location, customer profile, facilities, menu offerings, and style or concept are some of the factors that must be considered before deciding which catering services to offer.

Off-premise catering can be very successful for independent caterers and difficult for full service restaurants. Equipment and resources are the factors that will often determine how well an operation can conduct off-premise catering.

The availability of catering services is limited only by the ability of food-service operations to provide them. Whether in the executive dining room of a large corporation or at a garden wedding, it is possible for foodservice operators from hotels to delicatessens to provide quality food and service.

3

_Catering Food
Service Development_

The successful development of any business rests on a foundation of information characterizing the market for the products or services offered for sale. The population group that represents the customer is known as the target market. Information regarding the target market is gathered through market survey research conducted in the community. The market survey identifies four major segments of the market and investigates them in relation to the type of business being developed. These segments are:

1. Customer
2. Competition
3. Community
4. Labor pool

Each of these four market segments contributes to the success of a food-service operation. It is important to analyze each of these segments in terms of the type of product/service that is being offered. In order for a business to be successful it must be determined that:

1. A target market that needs the product/service exists within the community
2. The target market (customer) can afford to purchase the product/service and perceives a value for that product/service equal to the selling price
3. The business can be competitive with others identified as currently offering a similar product/service in the target market
4. Skilled foodservice production and service personnel are available within the community in numbers great enough to satisfy the requirements of the business

Market Survey

An effective market survey will include the following information:

A. Customer
    1. Population breakdown by age: marital status
                  18–25   _____%M_____%S
                  25–35   _____%M_____%S
                  35–40   _____%M_____%S
                  40–50   _____%M_____%S
                  50–65   _____%M_____%S
                  65–70   _____%M_____%S
    2. Percent population growth in next five years: _____
       Percent population growth in next ten years: _____
    3. Number of households: _____
       Number of two-income households: _____
    4. Average family income for 35- to
       60-year-old population group*   _____

*35- to 60-year-old population group is target market for expendable income/two-income-family profile.

      5. Average family size for 35- to
         60-year-old population   ____
      6. Average education level for 35- to
         60-year-old population group   ____

B. Competition
    1. Number of foodservice operations offering
       catering services: ____
    2. Number of independent catering businesses: ____
    3. Number of competitive catering businesses: ____

C. Community
    1. Number of overall businesses: ____
    2. Percent growth in past five years: ____
    3. Percent growth in past ten years: ____
    4. Percent of retail food and beverage sales
       to total retail sales: ____
    5. Anticipated growth of the community
       for the next ten-year period: ____
    6. Community organization:

    7. Community businesses:

    8. Percent growth of group meeting and conference
       business in last five years: ____
    9. Percent growth of travel tourism business in
       last five years: ____

D. Labor*
    1. Availability of trained foodservice
       production personnel: ____
    2. Availability of trained restaurant
       service personnel: ____
    3. Projected increase/decrease in overall
       labor pool in next five years: ____
    4. Availability of vocational and/or
       community college foodservice programs: ____
    5. Community unemployment rate: ____

*These statistics can be found at the local department of labor or unemployment office.

The market survey results must be analyzed according to the needs of the prospective business. The information from the market survey that will be the most valuable to foodservice businesses offering catering services will be that which indicates:

1. *The availability of expendable income to pay for "extra" food services*

   UNIT OF ANALYSIS: average family income for 35- to 60-year-old population group (Customer, item #4)

   Due to its work patterns, social and business obligations, and family patterns, the 35- to 60-year-old population group constitutes the segment of the population that is most likely to use catering services. Family income should range upward of $35,000 per year to be eligible for target market designation.

2. A *shortage of time for food preparation*

   UNIT OF ANALYSIS: number of two-income households (Customer, item #3)

   The number of two-income-family households indicates the possibility of a shortage of time for food preparation and a need for pre-prepared food products.

3. A *population growth within the age groups whose activities require catering services*

   UNIT OF ANALYSIS: percent population growth over five- and ten-year periods (Customer, item #2)

   Catering services are required by each population group outlined. The 18- to 25-year-old group will hold primarily graduation parties, proms, and weddings; the 25- to 35-year-old group, weddings and social functions; and the 35- to 70-year-old group, social, business, and family-related functions. An anticipated growth in this range of ages will indicate a healthy demand for catering services over a ten-year period.

4. *Business development indicating the availability of funds for community development and marketing efforts*

   UNIT OF ANALYSIS: percent growth of businesses and community (Community, items #2, 3, and 5)

   Growth in the business community indicates both the possible availability of funds for community development, charitable as well as industry-oriented, and increased marketing efforts. Both of these factors are favorable signs of increased demand for catering services for private business and social functions.

5. *Strong presence of charitable organizations*

   UNIT OF ANALYSIS: community organizations (Community, item #6)

   A survey of community organizations that sponsor fundraising functions for charitable programs allows prospective caterers to assess the need for catering services for private parties.

6. *Strong interest from outside sources to hold meetings and conferences within the community*

UNIT OF ANALYSIS: Community businesses (Community, item #8)

A survey of hotels, conference and convention centers, and the chamber of commerce identifies the level of group meeting and conference business. Meetings lasting two days or longer often need outside sources for entertainment and function planning. A growth in this business segment indicates an increased demand for catering services.

Market survey information outlines a profile of the target market and begins to identify characteristics and trends that are important to the success of a business. Using these percentages and statistics as a foundation, management can form a complete picture of the customer, competition, and community by doing further research and looking at the history of local business as a forecast for the future.

Customer

Determining a customer profile for catering services is difficult due to the range of ages that participate in catered functions. Teenagers attend proms and banquets held in a variety of locations, from school gymnasiums to hotel ballrooms. Weddings are popular in the 20- to 25-year-old group. The 25- to 30-year-old plans both business functions and weddings. The 35- to 70-year-old bracket uses catering services in a variety of settings, from tennis tournaments to hospital picnics. Social and business occasions are increasingly serviced by caterers. Even at-home get-togethers and parties incorporate more and more frequently some type of catering service, ranging from party trays to full-course dinners. The lack of time to prepare food causes many singles and two-income families to turn to catering services.

Given the information from the market survey and additional observations, the following customer profile emerges:

1. Age: 35 to 50
2. Average income: $50,000 annual
3. Occupation: Professional
4. Family profile: 4 members, two incomes

This information can now be used to direct marketing efforts toward the customer group that matches this profile.

Competition

Competition can often provide valuable information to new and developing businesses. Catering services that have recently been added to existing foodservice operations or that have opened as independent businesses indicate customer and community needs. Current trends in takeout meals and home delivery also reflect the need and receptiveness of local customers to catering services. The ongoing use of restaurant, charcuterie, and delicatessen take-home meal services shows a perceived value of the time required for food preparation on the part of the customers. Such customers are likely to take advantage of catering services.

A complete analysis of the competition requires a comparison of the variety of catering services, the menu items offered, and especially the pricing structure. Catering services are often priced in a package format, which can include meal and beverage services as well as entertainment or theme programs. It is important to identify the number and type of services contained in the package of each catering business in order to accurately compare prices.

The competition survey in Figure 3–1 outlines the information that is needed for each catering service and foodservice facility offering catering services.

A comparison of competitive catering services reveals trends in private party formats, cuisine menus, and theme and entertainment concepts. The introduction of new theme and menu ideas into the catering market can create new customer interest. Customers who use catering services on an ongoing basis are constantly looking for new and different ideas to highlight both business and social functions. The window of opportunity for new and ongoing catering businesses exists in the identification of unique cuisine, entertainment, and theme concepts that result in quality food and service at a reasonable price.

Prospective new caterers can use the information on the competition survey form to both identify the direct competition and determine how their catering services can compete in the established marketplace. An understanding of why customers choose a certain caterer and facility is important in identifying what services and/or facilities are needed by both customers and the community. Price carries the heaviest weight in customer decisions. However, when the pricing structure for similar services is reasonably close customers will be swayed by four major factors:

1. Availability
2. Location
3. Facilities
4. Service

Availability

Customers usually have a specific date in mind when they begin to plan a private party. Although they have taken the precaution of choosing two or three alternate dates, one of them is clearly preferable.

Location

Most guests drive to private parties, so access to major transportation routes, security, and parking influence the selection of the final location.

Indicate type of foodservice facility:
Full service restaurant   _____
Hotel food and beverage facility   _____
Catering hall   _____
Independent caterer   _____
Country club   _____
Contract feeder   _____
Charcuterie   _____
Delicatessen   _____

Location _____
  1. Access to major roads: _____
  2. Available parking: _____
  3. Difficulties in locating: _____

Services:
  1. Catering services in-house: _____
  2. Outside caterer allowed: _____
  3. Meal service available: breakfast: _____ lunch: _____
     dinner: _____ coffee service: _____ other: _____
  4. Full liquor license or limited: _____
  5. Table service style: _____
  6. Entertainment: _____
  7. Business meeting services: _____
  8. Conference and convention services: _____
    _____
  9. Concept and theme party services: _____
    _____
10. Food service cuisine orientation: _____

Facilities:
  1. Number of function rooms: _____
  2. Total available seating: _____
  3. Breakdown of seating by function room: _____
    _____
    _____
    _____
    _____
  4. Decorative theme: _____
  5. Condition of exterior facilities: _____
  6. Condition of interior facilties: _____
  7. Dance floors: portable: _____ built-in: _____
  8. Bars: portable: _____ built-in: _____
  9. Floor plans available: _____

Figure 3–1 *Competition survey.*

Availability
  Heavily booked: _____ Some dates available: _____
  Many dates available: _____

Service Reputation
1. Food service: good: _____ average: _____ poor: _____
2. Party-planning service: good: _____ average: _____
                              poor: _____
3. Entertainment: good: _____ average: _____
                    poor: _____
4. Meeting services: good: _____ average: _____
                       poor: _____
5. Overall follow-through: good: _____   average: _____
                             poor: _____
6. Invoicing and billing: good: _____   average: _____
                            poor: _____
7. Pricing: competitive: _____ high: _____ low: _____

Completed By: _____
Date: _____

Figure 3-1 *(continued)*

Facilities

The specific needs of a private party can be the determining factor in the final selection of a facility. Social functions often need reception areas for cocktail parties. Dance floors, seating space, outdoor facilities, and audiovisual equipment availability are just some of the facility demands that customers may consider necessary to the success of their function.

Service

The reputation of a catering service for providing a quality product, timely delivery, special attention, and creative abilities also influences the final decision to use a specific catering business.

Customers consider all of these combined factors when making their decision. When Catering Service A does not have the preferable date available but can provide service and facilities to match customer needs, then it will be the final choice. When the facilities of Catering Service B are not exactly what has been planned for but can be adjusted to the function, the location is excellent, and the preferable date is available, then it will be the final choice.

Community

Economic health is the single most important factor regarding the community that can affect the success of catering services. Although fast food and casual family restaurants are considered necessary expenses by many people, full ser-vice restaurants and catering services are generally supported by expendable income that, in times of economic hardship or uncertainty, becomes un-available. Not only individuals but also communities adjust their dining and social activities according to their economic situation. For example, in the early 1990s many state and local governments were experiencing budgetary problems, forcing them to make significant cutbacks in both services and em-ployees. It would have been ill-advised for these governments to support such activities as awards dinners, employee picnics, or business-related functions at a time when the job stability of many of their employees was questionable. Yet, economic difficulties also create a need for alternate funding for many community services that constitutes a potential market for catering services with creative and unique fundraising ideas.

Labor

The availability of a labor force that is both skilled and able to work flexible hours is essential to a successful catering business. Restaurants have their own large full-time staff on call to work at catered functions. Independent catering businesses, however, exist with a skeleton crew of full-time employees supplemented by part-time help as needed. This practice reduces the cost of employees significantly, but catering businesses must be sure of a source of employees. The two major classifications of labor that fulfill catering service needs are kitchen personnel and wait staff.

Kitchen Personnel

Production staff are medium- and high-skilled personnel who have been trained for various levels of food production. These job titles range from line cook to sous-chef to executive chef. A catering service that offers fine quality desserts and baked products will sometimes employ a trained pastry chef.

Preparation staff are low-skill personnel responsible for the preparation of food products before they are put into production. Vegetable, fruit, and salad preparation as well as some simple desserts are those areas that use this classification of personnel.

Cleanup staff are low-skill personnel responsible for dishwashing and kitchen cleanup. Maintaining sanitary facilities is a primary goal for this area of the kitchen.

Wait Staff

The *maitre d'hotel*, often abbreviated to *maitre d'*, manages, along with the executive chef, the execution of catering functions. Assisted by captains for large functions, maitre d's are required to have a knowledge of the management and service functions for catering services.

Service staff are required according to the number of people to be served. The average banquet server is expected to handle 24 guests, 4 tables of 6, 3 tables of 8, or 2 tables of 10. Skill level requirements are directly proportional to the type of service called for by the function. For example, buffet service requires minimal skills, whereas Russian service requires specific table service training.

Cleanup staff or housemen take down tables and chairs and provide general cleaning services. Skill level requirements are minimal.

Labor is one of the most critical supply areas in the foodservice industry in the 1990s. Trained waitstaff is difficult both to find and maintain. Labor turnover is often high, depending on the type of foodservice operation and the average age of the servers. Every age group, though, finds value in the benefits of flexible hours and guaranteed earnings offered by catering work. Employees who are hired on a continual part-time basis know in advance when functions will be held. They can accept or reject work according to their own personal schedules, working around families, college, and other jobs. Wages paid for catering service are based on federally mandated guidelines. Gratuities are charged as a percentage of the price of the food and beverages being served and are divided equally among the servers.

Applying Market Survey Information

Market survey information can be applied to catering menu management in a number of areas of a menu program and is particularly helpful in menu pricing. Competitive catering menu pricing requires a thorough analysis of the menu price segment of the competition survey. In order to develop a successful pricing structure management must establish the following for each menu in a program:

1. What is the competition charging for a similar catering menu? Are portion sizes and quality of food items similar to the competition?
2. How important is this menu to the total menu program? Will a lower selling price and resulting higher food cost create an imbalance in the overall food cost? Will volume sales of this menu create the desired profit at the lower price?
3. Will the average catering customer accept this price as meeting their perceived value of all of the menu items included in the menu?
4. Will this menu price blend into the pricing range for the total menu program?

The responses to these questions will determine how the menu is finally priced. If this price is equal to or less than that of the competition, then it is probably an accurate price. If the original price calculation is higher than that of the competition, management must carefully weigh the benefits and draw-backs of offering a lower price. Unless the average catering customer accepts the price as valid the menu will not be selected. Management often deter-mines price acceptability by using their competitors' efforts as an indication of the probable success of promoting the item for volume sales. The final menu price must blend with other prices in the menu program to create a range from which customers can choose. Large disparities or too many similarities in the range of menu prices can frustrate customers.

Summary

Market survey research is essential to the success of every catering service. The four major segments that a market survey must investigate are customer, competition, community, and available labor pool.

Statistics and data from the market survey provide information that can be used to assemble a profile of the average customer. The customer profile becomes a major means of identifying the target market on which to focus the marketing efforts for the sales of the product service provided by the business.

Customers base the decision on which catering service to use for a private function on four major factors: availability, location, facilities, and service. A thorough survey of the competition regarding these factors identifies those restaurants and catering services that are directly competing for the same target market.

The availability of trained foodservice personnel is a critical concern of every catering business. Catering service does, however, offer to prospective employees the benefits of flexible hours and guaranteed income. Both of these factors have a significant perceived value within the part-time labor pool. Caterers who can create a core of reliable part-time employees, both production and service, will be secure in their ability to service customers.

The application of market survey information throughout the menu program can increase sales as well as customer volume. Menu pricing is one area in which this information can have a significant effect. By thoroughly analyzing the menu prices of those catering businesses that have been identified as direct competition, a pricing structure can be developed to reflect current acceptable menu prices and customer needs.

4

Catering Menu Program

The catering menu program contains a number of menus that represent complete menu formats for the variety of meal services offered for private functions. The basic menus included in a catering program are:

1. Breakfast, lunch, and dinner menus
2. Hors d'oeuvre menu
3. Reception menu
4. Special occasion menus
5. Beverage menus (wine, liquor, cordial, and specialty)

Each menu in the program represents a grouping of menu items into the sequence of the menu format required for a specific meal service. These menu item groupings are based on 6 major factors regarding the catering operation:

1. Style of service
2. Price range
3. Menu item selection
4. Cuisine
5. Food production capabilities
6. Awareness of customer needs

The style of service will determine equipment, staffing, and food production needs. The price range will determine both the forecasted catering sales volumes on a month-by-month basis and the anticipated annual profit. The selection of menu items is based on the skill levels of the personnel and management's goals and objectives for the overall catering operation. Cuisine orientation helps determine the pricing structure of the menu program. Food production capabilities identify menu items within the cuisine that can be successfully produced for catering service based on the available equipment and the skill level of the production personnel. Management's awareness of customer needs is reflected in its knowledge of current trends in dining and eating patterns. If the menu program is to be creative and flexible, catering specifications for every item in the catering menu file must be developed. These specifications will provide a basis for prepricing individual portions of each catering menu item, allowing management to adjust the menu according to customer needs. Creativity and flexibility also involve the ability of the entire operation to react to new and unique concepts and ideas in catering menu development and theme entertainment packaging. This ability will set a catering service apart from the competition within the market segment in which it has established itself.

Menu Formats

The basic menu formats used for catering menu development are based on the classical French menu formats for dinner, luncheon, and breakfast. These are used either whole or in part to present a series of menu items for a preplanned meal program in both institutional and commercial settings. These formats are based on the culinary dictums laid down by Auguste Escoffier in the early 1900s.

APPETIZER	*Wine No. 1*
SOUP	
FISH ENTRÉE	*Wine No. 2*
SORBET	
POULTRY OR BEEF ENTRÉE	*Wine No. 3*
VEGETABLE	
SALAD	
DESSERT	*Wine No. 4*
CHEESE	*Wine No. 5*

Figure 4–1   *Classical dinner menu format. (Courtesy of Johnson and Wales University, Providence, RI.)*

The classical dinner format for catering service offers six or seven courses as shown in Figure 4–1. Including both a fish and meat course, it places the salad course after the main meat course. A sorbet (frozen ice) is offered between the fish and meat course as a palate cleanser. The use of this menu format in its entirety is usually reserved for formal occasions such as that in Figure 4–2. The accompanying beverage program for this menu format offers appropriate optional wines with the appetizer, fish, meat, dessert, and

La Reception
Les Hors D'Oeuvres Varies

Le Diner

Prologue
Le Pave de Saumon aux Caviar et Concombres

Ouverture
Le Consomme Double aux Palmiers

Divertissement
La Ris de Veau Paloise

Interlude
Le Sorbet au Melon

Piece de Resistance
Le Filet de Boeuf Fleuriste

Les Pommes Chateau   Les Tomates Jardini

Pastorale
Le Salade de Saison

Pas de Cing
Les Fromages de Provinces

Finale
Les Oeufs Chocolat aux Nids de Sucre

Epilogue
Les Mignardises
La Demi-Tasse

Figure 4–2   *Commercial classical dinner menu. (Courtesy of Bay Tower Restaurant.)*

cheese courses. After-dinner cordials are offered at the completion of the entire menu service. Russian service is the most appropriate table service style for this format.

The commercial adaptation of the classical menu format most commonly used by catering services is shown in Figure 4–3. The first course is either a soup or appetizer selection. Only one main course selection is offered and the salad course precedes the entrée selection. Cheeses are eliminated from the menu. A sample commercial catering menu using this format is provided in Figure 4–4.

The catering luncheon menu format is governed by the type of function. Business luncheons need to be brief to accommodate either speaker programs or afternoon meeting schedules. Menus for social luncheons are designed around the theme of the occasion. The classical format from which all luncheon menus are adapted is given in Figure 4–5.

An example of a menu following this format is seen in Figure 4–6. This menu offers juice, appetizer, salad, entrée, and dessert as a luncheon menu for a charity fashion show function.

Breakfast was not a formal part of the tradition of French cuisine. Most cultures treat the morning meal as part of their needs for sustenance and daily pattern of life. The English do have a formal breakfast format that includes fish and/or meat, breads, jams, and butter, and often begins with a hot porridge. The nineteenth-century American breakfast was built around the need for a full meal prior to a day involving agricultural work. This assortment of breakfast dishes comes from *365 Breakfast Dishes*, a cookery collection published in 1901 by George W. Jacobs & Co. in Philadelphia.

Main Course Breakfast Dishes

Lobster Cutlets	Dropped Codfish Balls
Beef Heart Saute	Broiled Oysters
Fried Smelt	Veal Soufflé
Fricasse of Rabbit	Tripe à la Lyonnaise
Minced Veal Moulded	Broiled Pig's Feet
Scrambled Mutton	Deviled Clams
Lamb Chops & Hominy Hearts	Stewed Squabs
Spaghetti & Ham Timbales	Minced Calf's Liver

This grouping of hearty dishes would be more appropriate for the main course item on catering luncheon and dinner menus in the 1990. This is

APPETIZER/SOUP

SALAD

MAIN COURSE ENTREE

VEGETABLE

DESSERT

Figure 4–3 *Adapted classical dinner menu format.*

BON DINER

WEDGE OF RIPE SEASONAL MELON
with a
Fresh Lime

~ ~ ~

ROAST BREAST OF CAPON NANCY
Apple and Almond Stuffing
Sauce Grand Marnier

Fluffy Rice au Champignon

A Seasonal Variety of Vegetables

~ ~ ~

FRESHLY TOSSED SALAD GREENS
Penfield Dressing

~ ~ ~

BOMBE GLACE MELBA
A Ring of French Vanilla Ice Cream
Georgia Peaches
Melba Sauce

~ ~ ~
After Dinner Mints
~ ~ ~
Coffee

May we suggest a glass of Clement Colombet Chablis with your dinner.

Figure 4–4 *Catering dinner menu. (Courtesy of Rye Town Hilton Inn, Rye, NY.)*

indicative of the changes that have occurred in diet and eating patterns since the late nineteenth century.

The catering breakfast menu in the 1990s reflects both current trends in meal planning and healthy dining concerns. The general catering breakfast menu outline is given in Figure 4–7. An example of a commercial interpretation is seen in Figure 4–8.

APPETIZER

SALAD

EGGS

ENTRÉE

VEGETABLE

DESSERT

Figure 4–5 *Classical luncheon format. (Courtesy of Rye Town Hilton Inn, Rye, NY.)*

MID-DAY MENU SUGGESTION

APRICOT TULIP

๛ ๛ ๛

BIRD OF PARADISE
Half Hawaiian Pineapple Stuffed with

San Francisco Bay Prawns

or Chicken Salad and
Fresh Pineapple Chunks

Assorted Bread Sticks and Butter

๛ ๛ ๛

ORANGE CHIFFON PIE

๛ ๛ ๛

Coffee

Figure 4–6 *Catering luncheon menu. (Courtesy of Rye Town Hilton Inn, Rye, NY.)*

Style of Service

It is necessary to establish the level and type of table service that a catering service will offer as a daily standard of operation. The selection of a service style is influenced by the skill level of available waitstaff, the cuisine being served, the equipment available, the menu price range, and the customer profile. The styles of table service that are adaptable for banquet service are:

1. French service
2. Russian service
3. American service
4. Buffet service

JUICE

FRUIT

CEREAL/GRAIN

EGGS

MEAT

VEGETABLES

BREADS

BEVERAGES

Figure 4–7 *Catering breakfast format.*

GOOD MORNING!

CHILLED RIPE SEASONAL MELON
Wedge of Lime

FRESHLY MADE SCRAMBLED EGGS
Link Sausages
Or
Rashers of Hickory Smoked Bacon

ASSORTED BREAKFAST ROLLS
Butter and Fruit Preserves

Coffee

FRESHLY SQUEEZED ORANGE JUICE

SMOKED NOVA SCOTIA LOX
with
Fluffy Scrambled Eggs

BREAKFAST ROLLS AND BAGELS
Fruit Preserves = Butter

Coffee

Figure 4–8 *Catering breakfast menu. (Courtesy of Rye Town Hilton, Rye, NY.)*

French Service

French service in American foodservice operations is often combined with various aspects of Russian service. Classical French service requires a *brigade de service*, or six-member dining room staff, and is inappropriate for catering service due to high labor intensity. However, aspects of tableside preparation, such as salad preparation, slicing a whole filet of beef to order tableside, and completing a flambé dessert, are incorporated into formal catering functions. These preparations require that table captains be trained in the correct food preparation techniques so that these menu items will match the quality of the balance of the menu as it comes from the kitchen. An extra per person charge is added to the bill for each additional table service.

Russian Service

The most appropriate and popular style of table service used for the upper level of catering services is Russian service. This service style is ideally adapted to table seatings of 6 to 12 guests. All food items are fully prepared in the kitchen and arranged on platters and serving dishes. Servers portion and serve the food directly to the guests at the table as seen in Figure 4–9. Aspects of French service such as previously discussed are often incorporated with Russian service techniques. Labor requirements for this type of service can be high. Servers must have these table service skills or be trained by management. The number of waitstaff required to successfully accomplish this service style is higher than for other styles due to the amount of time that servers need to spend with each guest.

American Service

American service is the style of table service most commonly used in catering. All food is prepared and served onto plates in the kitchen. The main course item and surrounding vegetables and starches are served on one plate. A plate cover fits tightly over the main plate, keeping the meal warm and allowing plates to be stacked by servers on large banquet trays. Once in the dining rooms the waitstaff can serve large numbers of guests very quickly. This style of table service employs a minimum number of servers and requires basic table service skills.

Buffet Service

Buffet service is a popular style of table service for private functions and is often combined with American service. Appetizer, beverage and dessert may be served to the table with salads, vegetables, and main course items featured on

Figure 4–9 *Russian table service. (Courtesy of Johnson and Wales University, Providence, RI.)*

the buffet. This service style does, however, require more time for the overall meal. Guests must wait until they are directed by table to approach the buffet. To expedite buffet service sections of the buffet are often set up on separate displays around the room as pictured in Figure 4–10. Iced shellfish displays, salad bar presentations, and dessert tables compliment a main course buffet that includes vegetables, starches, entrée items, and often a carving station with a chef slicing meat to order. Buffet service requires the least amount of labor, both kitchen and service. A busy catering operation can increase its flexibility by applying this style of table service to one large function while simultaneously catering another party with American service. Having all of the food items on the buffet table releases kitchen staff to plate up the other party's main course items and allows servers to concentrate on the second party as needed.

Price Range

The pricing structure established by management to meet customer needs and profit goals controls the level of cuisine, the type of menu items selected, and the quality of food product to be used in the menu program.

The selection of menus offered to the customer for any given meal service or function must represent a range of prices deemed acceptable to the average customer for the menu items included. If the menu program is to be successful, the customer's perceived value of the total menu must match the price. This pricing theory applies to all of the catering menus, including beverage services. The pricing method for the overall menu program is covered in detail in Chapter Five.

Figure 4–10 *Buffet service set-up. (Courtesy of Ridgewell's Caterers, Bethesda, MD.)*

Menu Item Selection

The basic objective in selecting the catering menu content is to serve a group of people the same menu items within a given time period in a private function setting for an established price per person. Menu items are chosen according to the way in which they fulfill 3 basic needs:

1. Provide a quality food product in large volumes
2. Are available for purchase through normal distribution channels on a year-round basis
3. Are available for purchase at a price that when combined with other menu items, results in an overall food cost that yields an established food cost percentage.

Cuisine

Catering services can offer a wide range of cuisines in a price range that corresponds to the target market. Ethnic and regional menu item specialties accommodate customers who want to incorporate the overall entertainment theme or concept of their business or social function into the menu. The per person menu price determines the quality of the menu items offered.

The menu in Figure 4–11 comes from Taste Bud in New York City. This operation caters to a corporate clientele that responds well to menus offering versatile fare appropriate for business breakfasts and lunches.

The German menu shown in Figure 4–12 was specifically developed to answer the need for a seven-course German cuisine dinner with an established per person price to be served to a men's organization.

Corporate "Power" Breakfast

10 or more people, includes:
urn of our fresh brewed coffee (2 cups per person)
tray of homemade muffins, danish, pastries,
biscuits, jam
cream, sugar, sweet & low
all paper supplies $3.95 per person

Corporate "Serious Working" Lunch

10 or more people, includes:
cold cut or sandwich platter
assorted fresh breads
health salad or cole slaw
potato salad or macaroni salad
pickles, mustard, mayonnaise, russian dressing
assorted cookie tray
all paper supplies $8.95 per person
(other salads may be substituted
at a slightly higher price)

For Your More Extensive Catering Needs, Please Call Our Direct Catering Line: 447-0555

taste bud

889-4929

585 3rd Avenue (38-39 St.)
Monday-Friday 6:30 AM-4:00 PM

Figure 4–11   *Taste Bud catering menu. (Courtesy of Taste Bud, New York, NY.)*

THE GERMAN HERITAGE SOCIETY

Menu Selection   Speise Karte

Austern Kaiser Wilhelm
(Broiled Oysters in Herb Sauce)

Benrkasteller Kurfurstlay Kayser

Pilza Suppe
(Mushroom Soup)

Bohen Salat
(Green Bean Salad)

Liebfraumilch Rhiensone Kayes

Poschiertes Seezunge
(Poached Filet of Sole)

Weiswein und Weintrauben Sose
(White Wine and Grape Sauce)

Sorbet Weis
(Champagne Sherbet)

Rouladen Krautnusse
(Rolled Beef with Brussels Sprouts and Nuts)

Rotkohl
(Red Cabbage)

Deutsches Kartoffelsalat
(German Potato Salad)

Michelob Bier

Schwartbrot
(Black Bread)

Schwartzwalder Kirsch Torte
(Black Forest Cake)

Kaffee
(Coffee)

Pfeffermintz Schnappes
(Peppermint Schnappes)

Figure 4–12   *German society menu. (Courtesy of the German Heritage Society.)*

The menu in Figure 4–13 is generally used for weddings where an emphasis on Italian menu items has been requested. This standard catering menu from King's Caterers is priced to meet the demands of middle-income families. It is served in a large catering hall with American-style table service.

The Italian cuisine theme menu from the Rye Town Hilton in Figure 4–14 offers a higher level of Italian cuisine and is appropriate for a wide range of social and business functions. The main course item can be changed according to customer budget and requirements. The content of this menu selection causes its price to be higher than the menu in Figure 4–13.

Food Production Capabilities

The capability of a foodservice operation to carry out the preparation and service of a menu is based on the production capacities of both labor and equipment.

Wedding Dinner Menu

* * * * * * * * * * * * * * * *

Antipasta

* * *

Baked Ziti, Parmesan Cheese

* * *

Filet Mignon, (10 oz)

Whole Baked Potato, Sour Cream Sauce

Escarolle with Garlic

* * *

Sweet Table to Serve

Deluxe Italian Pastries

Fruit Bowl Filled with Fresh Fruit

Strawberry Short Cake

Italian Cookies

* * *

Wedding Cake

Figure 4–13 *Italian wedding menu. (Courtesy of King's Caterers, Langhorne, PA.)*

FESTIVALO D'ITALIA

🌿 ANTIPASTI 🌿

CARCIOFI SOTT'OLIO
(Artichoke Hearts)

CROSTINI DI OCCIUGHE   UOVA SODE CON SPINACI
(Anchovies on Toast)   (Spinach Stuffed Eggs)

FUNGHI MARINATI
(Mushrooms in Marinade)

SPUMA DE TONNO   PROSCIUTTO DE PARMA
(Tuna Mousse)   (Parma Style Ham)

🌿 PASTA 🌿

TAGLIATELLE ALLA FORO ROMANO
(Noodles served with a Roman Meat Sauce)

🌿 PIATTI PRINCIPALE 🌿

PETTI DI 'POLLO ALLA ASPARAGI
(Sauteed Chicken Breasts with Asparagus)

PISELLI AL PROSCIUTTO   RISOTTO ALLA ARANCIA
(Roman Green Peas with Ham)   (Fluffy Rice with
                                 Orange Segments)

🌿 DOLCI 🌿

TORTA DI PESCHE   FRUTTA E FROMAGGI
(Peach Gateau)   (Assorted Whole Fresh Fruits
                              AND Imported Cheese)

per person   CAFE IMPERIALE
plus 16% gratuity and 5% state tax

Figure 4–14   *Italian menu. (Courtesy of Rye Town Hilton Inn, Rye, NY.)*

The ability of kitchen staff to produce the menu items selected in the volumes required for a catering menu is a major management concern. Before offering a menu item for customer selection, catering management must consult with the executive chef to be sure that enough skilled staff is available to produce the menu item to meet an established standard of quality in the volumes required to serve the customers' needs.

Certain foods cannot be produced consistently in large volumes and maintain the standard of presentation or taste that the customer expects. An example of this type of menu item is Eggs Benedict. A major ingredient for this item, hollandaise sauce, requires very specific temperature and time controls in order to be served properly. The hollandaise sauce will separate if cooked too long or held above certain temperatures. Once the sauce has been poured over the egg dish it must be served immediately or it will thicken and form a tough outer skin. Attempting to serve Eggs Benedict American-style for 250 guests at the same time poses major production and equipment problems. Stainless steel plate covers stacked one on top of another form condensation on the inside of the cover that, in turn, drips down onto the sauce, breaking through the outer skin and causing the sauce to separate. Timing must be extremely well coordinated between the maitre d' and the kitchen in order to plate up the menu item and get it to the guest as quickly as possible, while it is still hot.

Equipment becomes a major concern in the production of large-volume catering functions. Table service equipment is often supplemented by rental equipment for large parties. Kitchen production equipment, on the other hand, cannot be easily adapted or added to; expensive rentals pose the problems of finding space and an energy supply. A catering service must make an accurate assessment of the ability of existing equipment to produce the menu before committing to a customer.

The German menu in Figure 4–12 was planned to serve 1,000 guests. The food production methods used to prepare each menu item and the ability of existing equipment to hold courses at the desired temperature levels before serving were paramount in the selection of each item. Figure 4–15 outlines each menu item in the order in which it was served, identifying preparation and holding locations and timing for service.

Awareness of Customer Needs

Understanding the impact of current trends in both dining customs and eating patterns in today's society is an important skill for every catering manager to develop. The catering service market is highly competitive and requires an ability to respond to customer needs, often before they are indicated.

Major trends in today's society center around healthy dining. Catering services need to recognize this by offering menus that are both interesting and healthy. Fried foods, heavy sauces, high levels of salt, and rich desserts are discouraged by healthy dining programs. Menus that concentrate on broiled or grilled foods, salads, fruits, and low-fat food items respond to current customer demands. Figure 4–16 features a healthy catering menu.

The flexibility of the menu program determines management's ability to respond to customer needs and change overall menu pricing. Each item is reviewed by both catering management and the kitchen for content, quality, and ability to be used interchangably with other menu items. The portion size, garniture, and cost for each item are listed on a printed format called a banquet specification. Banquet specifications outline each menu item on an individual basis so that the selection of menu items on any given menu can be changed in order to adjust the price up or down. The use of banquet specifications assures management that the food cost for the total menu will

PRODUCTION SCHEDULE: GERMAN HERITAGE SOCIETY   OCTOBER 26

Menu Item	Number of Portions	Preparation Station	Holding Area	Preparation Time
Oysters, Herb butter	1000	Line: broiler	Banquet box	At service
Mushroom soup	1000	Range top	Banquet kitchen	Day before or frozen, reheat proir to service
Green bean salad	1000	Prep kitchen	Walk-in box	Salad: day before Set-up: afternoon
Filet of sole	1000	Banquet oven	Banquet box	At service
Champagne sherbet	1000	Prep kitchen	Pantry freezer	Two days before
Rolled beef	1000	Banquet kitchen	Walk-in box/ banquet oven	Day before, reheat for service
Red cabbage	1000	Canned/ banquet kitchen	Banquet range	At service
German potato salad	1000	Banquet kitchen	Walk-in box/ front line ovens	Two days before, reheat for service
Black bread	1000	Vendor/ pantry area	Pantry area	Day of delivery
Black forest cake	1000	Vendor/ pantry area	Tray racks Portion sliced	Day of delivery Tray up: afternoon

Figure 4–15 *Production requirements—German menu.*

reflect the desired food cost and produce a quality product for the guest. Item pricing and the application of the specifications to price alteration is discussed in Chapter Five.

Creativity and flexibility are attitudes and skills that encourage caterers to adapt to new and unique ideas for functions presented by customers. Responding to these ideas requires a thorough knowledge of the capabilities of the entire catering operation, from facilities to production. Catering menu specifications, flexible kitchen formats, creative menu planning, and an ability to communicate can provide a catering service with an edge in today's highly competitive market.

HEALTHY CATERING MENU

CONSUMME EN TASSE

***

BELGIAN ENDIVE & MACHE SALAD
Tomatoes & Orange Yogurt Dressing

****

BROILED FILET OF ATLANTIC SOLE
Lemon Sauce

***

Rice   Pilaff
Whole Baby Carrots

***

Whole Wheat & Rye Breads

***

MEDLEY OF FRESH SEASONAL FRUITS & BERRIES

***

DECAFFINATED COFFEE, TEA & HERBAL TEAS

Figure 4–16   *Healthy catering menu.*

Summary

The catering menu program contains a series of menus to be offered for a variety of catering services and meals. The factors that influence the success of the menu program are table service style, price range, cuisine orientation, food production capabilities, customer awareness, and creativity and flexibility.

Basic menu formats for dinner, luncheon, and breakfast outline the course presentation of menu items for catering service. Each format is adaptable to the needs of each individual customer. The actual number of menu items to be offered in a menu format will depend on the style and service of the catering operation.

The style of table service selected by a catering service reflects the abilities of the entire staff and the level of cuisine being served. The styles of table service most appropriate for catered functions are Russian service and American service. Buffet service combines aspects of different methods of table service, food production, and presentation.

Menu item selection is based on the need to provide quality food products in a large volume. These items must be available for purchase on a year-round basis at a price that will allow the caterer to meet the desired overall food cost percentage for the menu.

The ability to offer a variety of cuisines allows caterers the capability to respond to customer needs. Ethnic and regional items, as well as diet and health-related foods, can be incorporated into menus representing a wide price range.

The ability of both service and kitchen personnel to produce required menu items is basic to the success of the menu program. It is important that management accurately assess the production capabilities of both labor and equipment when selecting menu items.

A successful menu program must be flexible and open to new and unique ideas in menu development. The competition for catering service business in the 1990s requires that operators be able to adjust their pricing structure and production capabilities to meet the demands of both business and social clientele.

5

Catering Menu
Pricing and Controls

Criteria for Menu Pricing

The importance of catering services to an organization often determines the way in which catering menus are priced and controlled.

Independent Caterers

Independent catering businesses rely totally on the revenues generated from catering functions, so they cannot depend on volume sales alone to allow for profit. Instead, menus must be priced to realize a profit on the sale of every menu item, whether one portion or 100.

Full Service Restaurant Catering

Full service restaurants offering catering services can approach catering menu pricing from two directions:

CASE 1. Extra revenue from catering sales helps to augment downturns in restaurant sales or increased costs. If the revenue is not critical to the ongoing success of the operation, menu prices can run a higher food cost, providing service value to the customer.

CASE 2. Revenue from catering services helps to keep restaurant prices down by absorbing overhead and labor costs. Profit realized from catering services is important to the continued success of the operation. Food cost percentages for catering menu prices should be equal to or lower than restaurant menu prices in order to realize the full potential for increased profits.

Hotel Catering

Hotel catering menu revenues can be an important part of the overall hotel cash flow system. Local business and social catering sales are independent of conference and convention sales. Often catering business is high when room sales are low, as during holiday periods and summer weekends. Catering menu sales provide much-needed revenues for the operation during these slow periods.

The percentage of total food and beverage sales represented by catering sales amplifies the importance of catering menu pricing. Hotel full service restaurants generally have a higher food cost percentage than local free-standing restaurants. Hotel dining rooms have many hours of low business because they are often not the focus of local business, and therefore run higher costs due to overproduction and labor costs. Food cost percentages for catering menus should be kept significantly lower than hotel restaurant percentages to balance the overall food cost percentage. For example, a hotel dining room runs a 40 percent food cost with total revenue of $25,000 for the month. Catering runs a 30 percent food cost with total revenue of $75,000 for the month. An analysis of food purchases and inventories for the month shows that the total average food cost for the month is 32 percent.

Country Club Catering

Country Club menu prices can be competitive with other local catering services. Because private clubs must be nonprofit, catering menu prices do not have to be set to realize a designated profit. Yet, as in the case of hotels, catering services generate a cash flow for country clubs. Club managers use the excess profit margin gained from catering menus to help balance higher costs in the restaurant area. The result is a more even cash flow for the entire club and a lower overall food cost percentage for combined food operations.

Contract Feeding Catering

Contract feeders, like country clubs, use catering functions to offset higher food costs in other areas of their operations. Menu prices are developed to be below the local competition in order to satisfy the contract customer, but high enough to generate extra revenue.

Charcuterie and Delicatessen Catering

Charcuteries and delicatessens must be careful that their catering menu prices include all of the costs incurred in providing catering services, as well as sufficient profit. Because both of these types of businesses operate as retail food stores rather than as foodservice operations, the danger of underpricing catering menus is very real. Management should use the competition survey to accurately determine pricing. Of the pricing methods discussed in this chapter, actual cost pricing is the most effective for this type of operation.

Menu Pricing Formats

Catering menu pricing is based on two pricing formats. *Table d'hôte*, or the fixed-price format, is the menu pricing format that has been traditionally applied to catering menus. Individual item pricing, or *à la carte*, has been increasingly incorporated into catering menu pricing.

À la Carte Pricing

The à la carte format is used when items are added or substituted to a preestablished menu. For example, asparagus may be priced at an additional $2.50 per person, shrimp cocktail at $7.50 per person, and baked alaska at $5.00 per person. These individual item prices are added to the total menu price. Under pressure from increasing food costs and customer demands for a wider choice of menu items many catering businesses are offering à la carte prices on items in every category of the menu, as shown in Figure 5–1. Such menus can be easily reorganized according to customer needs.

Package Pricing

The surrounding catering menus such as hors d'oeuvre, beverage, dessert, and special function menus must be approached in a similar way.

The pricing structure of the surrounding menus is often controlled by the package prices developed for the menu program. Package prices include a number of catering services for a total per person price. These services can include cocktail reception (hors d'oeuvres and beverages), dinner, flowers, entertainment, after-dinner bar, and gratuities and taxes. Any number of services to be included in the per person price; the costs for flowers and entertainment are broken down on a per person basis and added into the total package price. This marketing approach often creates the impression for the customer that the overall price for the function is less expensive than if flowers and entertainment were charged separately at a flat fee.

Price Range

Catering menus should be offered within a pricing range of no more than $12.00 to $15.00. A range with a high of $45.00 per person and a low of $18.00 per person, for example, is too wide. Customers do not like to have to make a value judgment that results in the choice of an expensive menu when an acceptable one is available at a much lower price. Customers want to feel comfortable about their decision, believing that they made the best selection given the range of prices available to them.

~LUNCHEON~

Appetizer Salads

Spinach Salad, Croutons, Chopped Egg, Roquefort Dressing - $5.50
Red Leaf, Bibb Lettuce Salad, Mustard & Red Wine Vinaigrette - $5.00
Caesar Salad - $5.00
Boston Lettuce, Radicchio Salad, Walnut Dressing - $5.00
Romaine Salad, Four Seasons Dressing - $4.00
Boston Lettuce, Watercress, Endive, Shallot Dressing - $5.50
Sliced Tomato Salad with Roasted Red Pepper & Buffalo Mozzarella - $6.50
Zucchini Spaghetti with Tomato & Goat Cheese - $6.50
Artichoke Hearts, Wild Mushrooms, Vinaigrette Dressing - $6.00

Salad Entrees

Marinated Chicken with Sesame Oil & Zucchini Salad - $16.00
Fruit Plate in Season with choice of Sorbet,
Cottage Cheese or Yogurt - $13.50
Cold Lobster with Celery Root - $24.50
Assorted Cold Country Platter of Beef, Ham, Turkey, Brie Cheese,
Potato & Vegetable Salad - $16.25
Jumbo Shrimp with Lump Crabmeat Salad - $21.00
Nicoise Salad with Tuna Fish - $15.00
Seafood Pasta Salad - $16.50
Angel Hair Pasta with Roasted Duck, Snow Peas,
Quail Eggs & Vinaigrette Dressing - $16.00
Roasted Swordfish with Red Bliss Potato Salad,
String Beans & Red Pepper - $18.50
Oriental Chicken Salad with Crisped Vermicelli & Coriander - $15.00

18% GRATUITY & 6% SALES TAX WILL BE ADDED TO ALL CHARGES
2/90

Figure 5–1 À la carte catering menu. (Courtesy of Four Seasons Hotel, Philadelphia, PA.)

~LUNCHEON~

Meat Entrees
Sauteed Medallion of Veal Rib Eye, Tomato, Lemon & Capers - $27.00
Sauteed Lamb Steak, Port & Green Peppercorn Sauce - $21.00
Sauteed Breast of Chicken, Roasted Red Pepper Cream Sauce - $20.00
Grilled Beef Rib Eye, Watercress & Mustard Sauce - $25.00
Grilled Tenderloin of Beef, Bordelaise Sauce with Fried Shallots - $26.00
Sauteed Chicken Breast, Sesame Ginger Sauce - $20.00
Roast Cornish Hen, Lime Sauce - $19.00
Mixed Grill with Medallions of Beef, Veal & Lamb, Mustard Seed Sauce - $28.00
Sauteed Lamb Chop, Shallot Sauce - $25.00
Veal Stew with Roasted Tomato & Mushroom Ravioli - $19.00
Sauteed Chicken Breast, Lemon & Herb Jus - $20.00
Canneloni filled with Veal & Spinach, Prosciutto Cream Sauce, Garlic Toast - $18.00

Fish Entrees
Braised Boston Sole with Salmon Mousse, Lemon Butter Sauce - $24.00
Sauteed Salmon Fillet, Basil Cream or Leek & Vermouth Sauce - $24.00
Grilled Swordfish, Coriander Sauce - $25.00
Sauteed Florida Grouper, Julienne of Leek & Champagne Sauce - $23.00
Grilled Tuna with Ginger - $23.00
Dover Sole with Basil & Tomato - $32.00 (One Week Notice)
Sauteed Red Snapper Fillet, Basil Sauce - $25.00
Sauteed Trout Fillet, Sweet Corn & Chives - $23.00

Desserts
White Chocolate Mousse Cake - $5.00
Raspberry, Dark or White Chocolate Mousse - $4.00
Creme Caramel, Grand Marnier Sauce - $4.25
Chocolate or Vanilla Cheesecake, Raspberry Sauce - $5.00
Dark Chocolate Mousse Cake - $4.50
English Sherry Trifle with Custard Sauce - $4.00
Fresh Fruit Salad in Season, Oat Bran Cookie - $4.50
Mixed Fruit Tart - $5.00
English Lemon Meringue Tart - $4.00
Select Sorbets of Pear Almond, Raspberry, Lemon or Mango - $4.00
Apple Pie - $4.50
Bread Pudding with Vanilla Sauce or Raspberry Coulis - $4.25
Linzer Torte with Vanilla Cream or Ice Cream - $5.00
Hot Chocolate Souffle Pudding with Vanilla Cream Sauce - $6.50
Pavlova Meringue with Fresh Fruit Cake - $4.75

18% GRATUITY & 6% SALES TAX WILL BE ADDED TO ALL CHARGES
2/90

Figure 5–1   (continued)

Catering Menu Pricing Methods

Catering menu pricing requires a knowledge of the total overall costs of an operation, an understanding of management's goals and objectives regarding costs and profit, and a realistic analysis of the position of catering services within the entire operation.

Catering menu prices must reflect all of the costs of the operation as well as the desired profit. Four components of pricing must be considered to achieve catering menu prices that will generate enough revenue to cover costs as well as profit: overhead cost, labor cost, food cost, and profit. The selling price is equal to the sum of these four price components. Methods of menu pricing and pricing formulas are used to determine the selling price depending on which factors and costs are already known and which need to be calculated.

Only a few of the methods used by the foodservice industry to calculate food costs and menu prices are applicable to catering due to its limited menu pricing formats.

These methods are:

1. Actual cost method
2. Food cost percentage method
3. Factor pricing

Actual Cost Method

The actual cost method is applied in situations where the selling price has already been established but the amount of money available for the cost of food needs to be calculated. Once the cost of food has been determined management can turn to the Catering Specification Form in Figure 5–2 to find appropriate menu items that can be combined to match the available food cost.

The actual cost method determines the percentage of the selling price represented by each of the four price components, based on costs currently paid by the foodservice business and a preestablished profit percentage goal.

Cost	Percent of Selling Price
Total	100%
Overhead	−25%
Labor	−30%
Profit	−10%
Available for food cost	35%

CATERING SPECIFICATIONS

APPETIZERS

MENU ITEM	PORTION SIZE	COST PER PORTION
FRUIT CUP	6 oz Mixed Fresh and Canned Fruit	.86
MELON	1/2 Fresh Seasonal Melon	.98
MARINATED SHRIMP	6 oz Baby Shrimp, Papaya Slice	1.05
CONSOMME EN TASSE	6 oz consomme 2 Cheese Straws	.47
CLAM CHOWDER	6 oz New England / Manhattan	.35

SALAD

CAESAR SALAD	6 oz Greens with Dressing	.55
MARSEILLES SALAD	6 oz Mixed Greens with Dressing	.68
MARINATED VEGETABLE	7 oz Mixed Vegetable	.85

ENTREES

STUFFED BREAST OF CHICKEN / BOURSIN	8 oz Stuffed	3.50
FILET OF ATLANTIC SOLE	6 oz Fresh	2.90
LONDON BROIL WITH MUSHROOMS	7 oz Top Sirloin Mushroom Sauce	3.10
ROAST SIRLOIN OF BEEF, SLICED	8 oz Sirloin Marchand du Vin Sauce	3.75

DESSERT

CHOCOLATE MOUSSE	3 oz Chocolate Mousse Whipped Cream	
KEY LIME PIE	1/6 Slice of Pie	.75
BOMBE MARIE LOUISE	Frozen Bombe Chocolate Sauce	.65

Figure 5–2 *Catering menu specification form.*

In this example the customer has expressed a need for a menu priced at $20.00 per person. The amount of money available for food cost is calculated as follows:

Cost	Percent of Selling Price	Selling Price
Total		$20.00
Overhead	25%	− 5.00
Labor	30%	− 6.00
Profit	10%	− 2.00
Available for food cost	35%	$ 7.00

From the Catering Menu Specification Form in Figure 5–2, management now selects appropriate menu items to total a selling price of $20.00.

Menu Item	Cost	Selling Price
		$20.00
Fresh fruit	$ .98	
Salad	.55	
Entrée (chicken)	3.50	
Vegetable	.40	
Starch	.25	
Roll & butter	.20	
Dessert	.75	
Beverage	.30	
Total food costs	$6.93	
Selling price	$20.00	
Actual food cost percentage	35%	

Food Cost Percentage Method

The food cost percentage method of menu pricing is the method used most frequently in restaurant operations to price individual menu items. Its application as a method of pricing catering menus is to determine what the selling price should be, based on a known food cost percentage. This method also allows management to determine how much money is available for food cost once the food cost percentage has been established.

Two out of the following three factors must be known in order to apply food cost percentage to menu pricing.

1. Food cost percentage
2. Cost of food
3. Selling price

The food cost percentage method consists of three pricing formulas, one for determining each factor. The formulas and their abbreviations are:

1. Food Cost ÷ Food Cost % = Selling Price

$$FC \div FC\% = SP$$

2. Food Cost ÷ Selling Price = Food Cost %

$$FC \div SP = FC\%$$

3. Selling Price × Food Cost % = Food Cost

$$SP \times FC\% = FC$$

The formulas can be applied to catering menu pricing as follows:

1. Management is conducting a periodic review of the catering menus in order to evaluate the cost of food and current selling prices. If food costs have increased it will be necessary to increase selling prices. Management would like to maintain a 30 percent food cost percentage for this selection of menus. By dividing the food cost by the food cost percentage the new selling price can be calculated.

$$(FC) \$9.75 \div (FC\%)\ 30\% = (SP)\ \$32.50$$

2. Management wants to maintain the current selling price for a catering menu. The current food cost is known. If the current food cost percentage based on these two factors is not acceptable then the food cost will have to be decreased. By dividing the food cost by the selling price the food cost percentage can be calculated.

$$(FC) \$3.85 \div (SP)\ \$12.00 = (FC\%)\ 32\%$$

3. The customer has asked for a catering menu priced at \$20 per person. Management knows that the selling price must result in a 35 percent food

cost. In order to develop a menu it is necessary to know the amount of money available for the cost of food. By multiplying the selling price by the food cost percentage the food cost can be calculated.*

$$(SP) \$20.00 \times (FC\%) \; 35\% = (FC) \; \$7.00$$

*This formula was used to calculate the food cost in the actual cost method.

Factor Pricing

The factor pricing method establishes a factor that represents the food cost percentage. The factor is based on the number of times that the percentage can be divided into 100:

$$100\% \div 40 \; (\text{percentage}) = 2.5 \; (\text{factor})$$

The factor is multiplied by the food cost to calculate the selling price:

$$3.35 \; (\text{food cost}) \times 2.5 \; (\text{factor}) = \$8.37$$

Management can apply the factors for the food cost percentages that are most commonly used in their operation to quickly calculate selling prices. The chart in Figure 5–3 identifies the factors for a range of food cost percentages.

Food Cost%	Factor	Food Cost%	Factor	Food Cost%	Factor
20	5.00	30	3.33	40	2.50
21	4.76	31	3.23	41	2.43
22	4.55	32	3.13	42	2.38
23	4.35	33	3.00	43	2.32
24	4.17	34	2.94	44	2.27
25	4.00	35	2.85	45	2.22
26	3.85	36	2.78	46	2.17
27	3.70	37	2.70	47	2.12
28	3.57	38	2.63	48	2.08
29	3.45	39	2.56	49	2.04
				50	2.00

Note: Decide what percentage food cost you wish and then multiply actual food cost by the desired percentage factor to arrive at the desired selling cost. Example: If an item has a food cost of 25¢ and you want a food cost of 28%, look up the factor opposite 28 (3.57) and multiply this by 25¢ (25¢ × 3.57 = 89.3¢). The selling price would probably be 90¢.

Figure 5–3 *Food cost percentage factor chart. (Source:* Lendal H. Kotchevar, *Management by Menu, 1975, p. 134.)*

Maintaining Food Cost Percentages

The foodservice industry in the 1990s is experiencing financial pressures from every side. Customer counts and revenues are decreasing while operating and food costs are increasing. Competition intensifies daily for a customer group that is shrinking in size. The result is shrinking profit margins requiring managers to be constantly aware of the percentage that cost is representing of the selling price. When the percentage of cost is above that necessary to maintain a desired profit, either the selling price or the cost must be adjusted. Because customers usually respond to increased prices by turning to the competition, management should raise prices only when necessary and at specific predetermined times in their planning schedules.

Developing selling prices for catering menus that accurately meet the needs of both the caterer and the customer requires a thorough analysis of both the business and the customer profile. As discussed in chapter four, management must set a level and a range of prices that meet its established goals and objectives regarding catering revenue and profit. It is important to maintain this level and range as menu prices and menu items change. By increasing prices on an individual menu basis, management can lose track of the range of menu prices. Suddenly the original $12 to $15 spread can suddenly slip to $20 to $22, resulting in customer confusion as to which end of the range they should choose.

Management recognition of the value perceived by customers is crucial to the maintenance of successful menu pricing. A menu price of $28.00 per person for a 12-ounce strip sirloin steak may yield an acceptable food cost percentage for management but meet with resistance from customers. If customers do not perceive that the price represents the true value of the menu item then they will hesitate to select it. In some cases, prices may need to be lowered in order to increase sales. Management should review the entire menu to determine which surrounding items can be replaced to reduce the overall food cost of the menu.

Food Cost Review

In order to maintain successful menu prices, caterers must not only listen to customer reactions to menu item content and menu prices, but also periodically evaluate the competition's menu prices for similar items and content and monitor food costs daily, weekly, and monthly to maintain desired food cost percentages and profit margins.

Daily and weekly reviews of purchasing prices helps management to identify price increases on food products that significantly affect the overall food cost. Items that are sold in large volume should be watched diligently for price increases. For example, prime rib of beef is a popular catering menu entree.

If 40 percent to 50 percent of the catering menus for the week require prime rib and the cost of beef has risen, the food cost percentage on this item could increase, thus reducing overall profits. A daily price review keeps management aware of possible problems. The food cost on the menu can be lowered by changing surrounding items on the menu, such as vegetables, or adjusting the portion size of the prime rib serving. Catering menus that specify 'chef's vegetable choice' can be flexible.

Weekly reviews compare total food purchases and inventory requisitions against sales for the week.

Weekly Review for 6-day Period

Inventory Requisitions	$3450.00
Food purchases	900.00
Total costs	$4350.00
Total sales	$15,000.00

(FC) $4350.00 ÷ (SP) $15,000 = (FC%) 29%

This information can also be posted daily or be reviewed on a weekly and monthly basis as in Figure 5–4.

Sales Mix and Contribution to Profit

The sales mix is a means of ranking menu items according to their contribution to the overall volume of sales. Actively used in restaurant management as a means of tracking the popularity of individual menu items, the sales mix has limited use in a catering menu program. It is important, however, to periodically evaluate the sales to identify those menu items that are creating the highest volume sales.

It is also necessary to assess the contribution each menu item makes to overall profit in order to ensure that the menu price is actually generating the desired profit margin. For example; a catering menu for prime rib of beef that has been priced below cost for competitive reasons may result in an increased volume of sales but at the same time be draining the overall profit margin. In order to restore the profit margin, management may need to change some of the surrounding menu items or identify another entree item to promote.

Pricing Analysis of a Sample Menu Program

Contribution to profit is the analysis of the menu price and the food cost of a menu item to determine how profitably the menu item is priced. The

DAILY FOOD & BEVERAGE COST CONTROL

DATE:
PERIOD: From: _____   *To:* _____
Overall Food Cost: _____   *Food Cost %:* _____
Overall Beverage Cost: _____   *Beverage Cost %:* _____
Average Daily Food Cost: _____   *Food Cost %:* _____
Weekly Food Cost: _____   *Food Cost %:* _____

Food Cost Month To Date: _____
Food Cost % Month To Date: _____

Actual Food Cost Month To Date: _____   *Forecasted Month To Date:* _____
Actual Food Cost Year To Date: _____   *Forecasted Year To Date:* _____

Actual Beverage Cost Month To Date: _____   *Forecasted Month To Date:* _____
Actual Beverage Cost Year To Date: _____   *Forecasted Year To Date:* _____

DAY:	SUN.	MON.	TUES.	WED.	THURS.	FRI.	SAT.
SALES:							
BANQUET FOOD:							
BANQUET BEVERAGE:							
REST. 1 FOOD							
REST. 1 BEVERAGE							
REST. 2 FOOD							
REST. 2 BEVERAGE							
TOTAL F&B:							

TOTAL WEEKLY SALES: FOOD: _____   *BEVERAGE:* _____
AVERAGE DAILY SALES: _____

Figure 5–4 *Daily food cost report.*

differential between the menu price of an item and its food cost is called the contribution to gross profit. Gross profit refers to all monies left after the food cost is deducted from the selling price. Remaining costs must then be deducted in order to calculate the *net profit*. In order to answer customer needs, a well-balanced menu includes items that represent high, medium, and low contributions to profit. An item may have a low contribution to profit and a low volume of sales, but its appearance satisfies a certain percentage of customers. The profit from menu items with a high contribution of profit and high volume sales balances the loss of profit on other items.

In Figure 5–5 the food cost, food cost percentage, and menu price of four menus are reviewed. The optimum catering food cost percentage in these examples is 30 percent. The following discussion evaluates the alternatives and considerations in the pricing of the menus.

The total catering menu for a 10-ounce portion of prime rib of beef costs $7.60, with a 40 percent food cost when sold for $19.00. The contribution to gross profit is $11.40. If the food cost percentage is dropped to meet the 30 percent optimum, then the menu price increases to $25.00 and the contribution to profit becomes $17.40. An alternative to raising the menu price is adjusting the portion size and/or the surrounding menu items.

The total catering menu for an 8-ounce stuffed filet of flounder costs $6.55, with a 30 percent food cost when sold at $21.50. The contribution to profit is $14.95. The management may wish to increase the sales volume of this menu. However, lowering the selling price to $18.50 raises the food cost percentage to 35 percent and reduces the contribution to profit to $8.40. Thus, management must carefully review the position of this menu in both the overall price range and the sales mix. If the menu price is toward the top of the range and sales are low, then the menu price should be dropped to $18.50.

The total catering menu for grilled pork tenderloin costs $6.90, with a 30 percent food cost when sold at $22.75. The contribution to profit is $15.85.

Menu Item	Total menu Food cost	Food cost percentage	Menu price	Contribution to profit (CP)
10 oz. Prime rib	$7.60	40%	$19.00	$11.40
		30%	$25.00	$17.40
8 oz. Flounder	6.55	30%	21.50	14.95
		35%	18.50	8.40
Pork tenderloin	6.90	30%	22.75	15.85
Seafood brochette	9.25	33%	28.00	18.75
	8.90	36%	24.50	15.60

Figure 5–5 *Contribution to profit.*

This item has been incorporated into the menu program to give variety to the entrée selection and the pricing range. Sales are low but the item is purchased in preportioned cuts, minimizing waste and labor. Management should give this item a positive evaluation and consider ways in which it could be promoted in specialty menus.

The total catering menu for seafood brochette costs $9.25, with a 33 percent food cost when sold at $28.00. The contribution to profit is $18.75. Customer interest for this item is high, so the low volume of sales indicates it is overpriced. In addition, current production labor requirements for this item restrict the size of the group for which this item can be prepared. Purchasing has identified a high-quality pre-prepared raw shellfish brochette that could be substituted to lower labor costs and minimize waste. The use of the pre-prepared brochette would also allow this menu to be sold to large parties. By using the pre-prepared product the food cost drops to $8.90. A selling price of $24.50 yields a 36 percent food cost with a contribution to profit of $15.60, whereas a selling price of $25.95 yields a 34 percent food cost and a contribution to profit of $17.05. Management must decide which of these two prices will receive the most customer response. If the difference in anticipated sales is minimal then the higher menu price would be used. If, however, greater sales are forecasted with the lower $24.50 menu price then it should be used.

This review concludes with the following observations:

1. As the volume sales leader, prime rib has the highest potential for contribution to profit (CP). The sale of 500 prime rib dinners per week results in a CP of $5,700 compared with the sales of 200 flounder for a CP of $2,990. To help offset high food costs, management can take advantage of volume purchasing discounts on prime rib. Another alternative is to increase the prime rib menu price to $21.50 for a 35 percent food cost and a CP of $14.00. Although the food cost percentage will still be above the optimum, the price increase of $2.50 will be more acceptable to customers than the $6.00 increase needed to reach the 30 percent figure.

2. The balanced range of prices for these four items is: $18.50, $21.50, $22.75, and $25.95:

   - Flounder is dropped to $18.50 because fish is perceived by the customer to have a lower value than prime rib.
   - Prime rib is increased to $21.50 to lower its food cost percentage.
   - Pork remains the same.
   - Seafood uses the new pre-prepared product and takes on the higher menu price due to the value perceived by the customer and the need for a cap over $25.00 to the prime rib price range.

Control systems that monitor production, purchasing, and costing on a daily, weekly, and monthly basis are instrumental in achieving the revenue and profit goals.

Summary

Menu pricing is important to the ongoing success of every catering operation and service. Established food cost percentages that accurately reflect the needs of the operation yield profits.

Catering menu prices are calculated based on the amount of revenue needed to cover the four price components: overhead cost, labor cost, food cost, and profit. The three menu pricing methods most adaptable to catering menus are the actual cost method, the food cost percentage method, and the factor pricing method.

Maintaining successful pricing requires daily and weekly monitoring of food costs to ensure desired food cost percentages and profit margins. Control systems such as food cost reviews, the sales mix, and contribution to profit analysis are used to achieve successful menu prices.

A successful menu program must meet management goals and objectives for revenues and profits. Properly applied menu pricing techniques and the application of control systems are necessary for any catering operation to be profitable.

6

Catering Beverage Management

Beverage services, when offered, constitute a major element in catering operations. Beverages fall into two major classifications, nonalcoholic and alcoholic.

Any beverage that does not include alcohol as an ingredient is classified as a nonalcoholic beverage. The service of nonalcoholic beverages at social and business functions is becoming increasingly popular. Even foodservice operations that serve alcohol are promoting nonalcoholic versions of traditionally alcohol-based drinks with a high level of success.

Alcoholic beverages are categorized as wine, beer, or distilled spirits such as scotch, gin, bourbon, and rum. Alcohol in spirits results from the fermentation of ingredients such as fruit, grains, and sugar. Proof indicates the quantity of alcohol in a distilled spirit. In the United States proof is defined as twice the percent of alcohol by volume. For example, bourbon containing 45 percent alcohol by volume is 90 proof. Wine and beer have much lower proof designations than spirits.

Well-managed beverage sales can be a profitable extension of a catering operation. The relationship of food sales to beverage sales is called the food and beverage mix. Whereas a maximum of 60 percent of the revenue from menu item sales is retained as gross profit, as much as 80 percent of beverage sales may go to profit, depending on the markup management chooses to take. Catering beverage services and package pricing can be designed to incorporate the theme or concept of the function or convention according to customer needs. In order to be complete, however, the issues of server relations and liquor liability for a beverage program must be reviewed.

Nonalcoholic Beverages

A heightened awareness of the negative effects of alcohol consumption, stronger drunk driving laws, and increased liability on the part of anyone dispensing alcohol have combined to decrease the overall consumption of alcohol in the United States. The resulting increase in prices has triggered further consumption declines. Thus the 1991 Beverage Alcohol Forecast by the Bureau of Foodservice Research indicates that increases in beverage prices have led to only minimal growth in alcoholic beverage revenues.

Nonalcoholic versions of traditionally alcohol-based drinks mixed with creative substitutions of fruits and flavorings, can be successfully promoted. *Mr. Boston Bartender's Guide,* a standard beverage recipe book for the foodservice industry since 1935, lists a number of nonalcoholic drinks. For example:

1. Orange Smile: replaces grenadine syrup with raspberry syrup, mixed with orange juice and egg
2. Pineapple cooler: adds powdered sugar and carbonated water to pineapple juice
3. Lady Love Fizz: combines egg whites, sweet cream, and lemon juice

Drinks such as these, along with a variety of fruit-based daiquiris and margaritas, can prove to be profitable additions to catering beverage menus.

The catering department of the Chicago Hilton Hotel in Chicago, Illinois, offers as a standard option for their beverage services nonalcoholic bars serving fruit-based drinks, sodas, and bottled waters. A comparison of beverage costs shows the following potential for increased profit:

Catering Beverage	Price	Beverage Cost%	CGP
Vodka martini	$4.50	18%	$3.69
Strawberry daiquiri	4.50	10%	4.00

In this example the cost of the nonalcoholic beverage is 8 percent lower than the alcoholic beverage. For every dollar in sales the strawberry daiquiri will contribute 90 cents to gross profit, whereas the vodka martini will contribute 89 cents. Although alcohol is often the highest cost factor in a beverage, customers perceive an equally high value for a nonalcoholic fruit-based beverage.

Food and Beverage Mix

The ratio of food sales and beverage sales to total sales is called the food and beverage mix. This measure of the result of sales is often referred to in terms of a ratio of 60/40 (60 percent from food, 40 percent from beverages) or 70/30 (70 percent from food, 30 percent from beverages). Because beverage sales often generate higher profit margins than food sales, this relationship is important to overall profits.

Dramatic downturns in the consumption of alcoholic beverages has affected the food and beverage mix for many operations. Between 1980 and 1990 the typical mix for combined foodservice operations changed as follows:

Item	Percentage 1980	Percentage 1990
Food	64.7%	77%
Beverage	35.3%	23%

Source: *Restaurant Hospitality*, 64:3 (March 1980): p. 55. National Restaurant Association, *Restaurant Industry Operations Report*, 1990.

Alcoholic beverage consumption dropped 14.3 percent over a 10-year period, indicating a significant change in customer beverage preferences.

Catering Beverage Pricing

Beverages for catering services are sold by the drink, by the bottle, and by time period. Customers may choose to buy beverages for catering functions by the bottle to be served by bartenders from stationary bars. At the end of the function customers are billed for every bottle consumed, even opened bottles only partially finished. For functions where consumption will not justify setting up a full bar at bottle prices, customers are charged according to a record of each drink consumed. As shown in the beverage menu in Figure 6–1, hosted drinks range in price according to name brand content. Package beverage prices offer a flat fee over a given time period and are discussed later in this chapter.

Another option is a cash bar, where guests must pay for their own beverages. Pricing on cash bars reflects current individual drink prices for restaurants and lounges. In other cases, wine is purchased by the bottle to be served by the waitstaff during the meal. The catering wine and beverage menu in Figure 6–1 lists a variety of beverage options.

Conditions on beverage services, such as those listed at the bottom of Figure 6–1, are common to all catering operations. Bartender fees are subject to local union wage scales but are often reduced or eliminated if total beverage sales exceed established limits. In this example the $50 bartender charge for a cash bar and $40 charge for a host bar is cancelled if bar receipts reach $350 and $300 respectively in a 2-hour period.

Beverage Pricing Method

The method used to price beverages for catering functions is similar to that used by restaurants. Prices for each type of grain alcohol or spirit range according to the type and quality of alcohol. Both bottle and per drink prices are based on the amount of profit management wants to make from the total sales on a bottle of alcohol. For example, if $15.00 is the purchase price paid for a fifth (⅕ gallon) of scotch and the desired beverage cost percentage is 50 percent then catering beverage sales must total $30.00 for the contents of the bottle whether sold by the drink or by the bottle. If 2 ounces of scotch are poured for a single drink, this 25-ounce bottle will yield 12 drinks. If drinks are sold at $2.50 each, total revenue for the bottle will be $30.00.

$$\text{Beverage cost} \div \text{Beverage cost \%} = \textit{Selling price per bottle}$$
$$\$15.00 \div .50 = \$30.00$$

$$\text{Bottle size} \div \text{Drink portion size} = \textit{Yield}$$

$$\text{Selling price per bottle} \div \text{Yield} = \textit{Selling price per drink}$$
$$\$30.00 \div 12 = \$2.50$$

This pricing formula assumes that each drink will be portioned correctly and that there will be no loss or waste from the bottle.

WINE AND BEVERAGE LIST

LIQUORS BY THE DRINK

HOSTED BAR

Premium Brands	$3.75
Deluxe Brands	4.00
Cordials and Brandy	4.25
Wine by the Glass	3.00
Beer, Domestic*	3.00
Beer, Imported*	3.75
Bartles & Jaymes	3.00
Soft Drinks	1.50

Please add 17% service charge to all above prices and *local sales tax to beer and soft drinks only

CASH BAR

Premium Brands	$4.25
Cordials and Brandy	4.75
Wine by the Glass	3.25
Beer, Domestic*	3.25
Beer, Imported*	4.25
Bartles & Jaymes	3.25
Soft Drinks	1.75

BANQUET WINE LIST

Bin No	Item	Full Bottle
	AMERICAN RED	
238	Cabernet Sauvignon, Sterling	$32.50
269	Cabernet Sauvignon, Concannon Signature	22.00
266	Cabernet Sauvignon, Beaulieu Beautour	23.00
239	Zinfandel, Sutter Home	19.50
250	Merlot, Firestone	28.50
	AMERICAN WHITE	
310	Chardonnay, Concannon Signature	21.50
308	Chardonnay, Monterey Classic	20.50
312	Sauvignon Blanc, Concannon Signature	20.75
305	Sauvignon Blanc, Charles Krug	21.00
2409	Chenin Blanc, Fetzer	18.50
284	Johannisberg Reisling, Chateau Ste. Michelle	18.75
	BLUSH WINE	
466	White Zinfandel, Beringer	19.50
307	White Zinfandel, Sutter Home	17.50
	SPARKLING WINE	
322	Domaine Chandon Brut	39.50
321	Korbel Brut	24.50
398	Sperone Asti Spumante	19.00
1392	Piper Sonoma Brut	26.00
2410	Domaine Ste. Michelle Champagne Brut	16.50

HOUSE WINES
Concannon Vintage
Red — White — White Zinfandel
(750 ml) $15.00   (1.5 liter) $26.50

BEVERAGE

The Opryland Hotel, as a licensee, is responsible for the administration of the sale and service of alcoholic beverages in accordance with the Tennessee Alcohol Beverage Commission's regulations. It is a policy, therefore, that all liquor and wine must be supplied by the hotel.
All cash bars are subject to a $50.00 labor charge if a minimum sale of $350.00 is not achieved over a 2-hour period.
All hosted bars are subject to a $40.00 labor charge if a minimum sale of $300.00 is not achieved over a 2-hour period.

All prices in this proposal are subject to change without notice
until confirmation of a menu.

Figure 6–1 *Catering beverage menu I. (Courtesy of The Opryland Hotel, Nashville, TN.)*

In order to make beverage pricing consistent it is advisable to standardize the per drink cost. To maintain an approximate 50 percent beverage cost management sets a standard drink price of $2.75 per drink based on the following averaging of beverage cost as seen in the example in Figure 6–2.

Total Beverage Cost	Total Beverage Revenue	Total Per Drink Yield
$15.00	$30.00	12
12.50	28.00	16
18.50	36.00	12
$46.00	$94.00	40

Total sales ÷ Total drink yield = *Drink price**

$94.00 ÷ 40 = $2.35

Menu price × Drink yield = *Total sales*

$2.75 × 40 = $110.00

Beverage cost ÷ Total sales = *Beverage cost %*

$46.00 ÷ $110.00 = 42%

*Drink price is rounded up to create a marketable price.

The selling price of $2.35 per drink is raised to a menu marketing price of $2.75 per drink, which will actually yield a $110.00 beverage revenue and a 42 percent overall beverage cost.

Where the market will bear higher beverage prices, such as in large cities and metropolitan areas, beverage costs can be set as low as 18 percent. In Figure 6–3 the same pricing methods used in Figure 6–2 are applied to a case where the predetermined beverage cost percentage is 18 percent and the drink size for scotch and bourbon is 1 oz. All beverage prices are calculated accordingly and adjusted to a marketable menu price.

The calculations in this figure have been carried out to include the contribution to gross profit (CGP) in order to show the profit potential in catering beverage pricing.

Beverage	Bottle Size	Drink Size	Bottle Cost	Beverage Cost	Drink Price	Bottle Price
Scotch	25 oz.	2 oz.	$15.00	50%	$2.50	$30.00
Gin	25 oz.	1.5 oz.	12.50	45%	1.75	28.00
Bourbon	25 oz.	2 oz.	18.50	51%	3.00	36.00

Figure 6–2 *Catering beverage pricing I.*

Beverage	Bottle	Drink Size	Bottle Cost	Beverage Cost	Drink Price	Menu Price	Bottle Price	CGP
Scotch	25 oz.	1 oz.	$15.00	18%	$3.36*	$3.50	$84.00	$69.00
Gin	25 oz.	1.5 oz.	12.50	18%	$4.25*	$4.25	$68.00	$55.50
Bourbon	25 oz.	1 oz.	18.50	18%	$4.08*	$4.25	$102.00	$83.50

*Prices are rounded up to create marketable beverage prices

Figure 6–3   *Catering menu pricing II.*

Spirit and wine sales by the bottle are commonly priced for a minimum of a 100 percent markup or a 50 percent beverage cost. The wine selection in Figure 6–1 is priced by the bottle with an average markup of 150 percent per bottle. The beverage list in Figure 6–4 offers both bottle and per drink prices for spirits. The average markup on the bottle prices is 175 percent.

Package Pricing

Catering beverage services are often combined with food and other services into pricing packages for a variety of business and social functions. In situations where the customer would like a fixed price for beverages, prices are calculated based on the use of either house brands or name brands, on an hourly scale. The following guidelines are generally followed:

One hour open bar at reception, per person

House brands	$4.75
Premium brands	$5.75

Two hour open bar after dinner, per person

House brands	$6.50
Premium brands	$8.00

Hourly prices are based on an average of the probable consumption of alcoholic beverages in a one-hour time period. Women consume an average of 0.5 to 1 drink during the first hour and men 1.5 to 2. By basing the price per person for the first hour of a function on the current per drink price, management can be reasonably sure of accurately estimating consumption. In this example the following calculation was applied:

1 drink (women) + 1.5 drinks (men) = 2.5 *drinks* ÷ 2
= 1.25 *drinks per person*
Housebrands: $3.75 + $5.63 = $9.38 ÷ 2
= $4.69 (4.75)*
Premium brands: $4.50 + $6.75 = $11.25 ÷ 2
= $5.63 (5.75)

* adjusted menu price

The Banquet Staff
OF THE HOTEL DU PONT

BEVERAGE PRICE LIST

BANQUET DEPT.

SCOTCH	Liter	1½ oz. Drink
Johnnie Walker "Red"	$45.00	$4.50
Dewars (White Label)	45.00	4.50
J & B	45.00	4.50
Haig & Haig Pinch	45.00	4.50
Cutty Sark	45.00	4.50
Johnnie Walker "Black"	60.00	5.00
Chivas Regal	60.00	5.00

AMERICAN WHISKEY		
Seagram 7 Crown	$38.00	$4.50

CANADIAN WHISKEY		
Canadian Club	$42.00	4.50
Seafram VO	42.00	4.50
Seagram Crown Royal	60.00	5.00

IRISH WHISKEY		
Jameson	$42.00	$4.50

BOURBON		
Old Grand Dad (86)	$42.00	$4.50
Jack Daniels (90)	42.00	4.50
"Black"	42.00	4.50
Wild Turkey (100)		

GIN		
Tangueray	$45.00	4.50
Beefeater's	45.00	4.50
Gordon's	38.00	4.25

VODKA		
Smirnoff	$40.00	$4.25
Stolichnaya	45.00	4.50
Absolut	45.00	4.50

RUM	Liter	Fifth	1½ oz Drink
Bacardi (light or dark)		$42.00	$4.25

SHERRIES APERITIFS			
Harvey's Bristol Cream	$28.00		$3.50
Dry Sack	28.00		3.50
Tio Pepe		28.00	3.50
Dubonnet (Blonde or Red)		28.00	3.50
Lillet (Blonde or Red)		28.00	3.50
Campari		42.00	3.50
Sandemans Port "Founders"	30.00		4.25
Vermouth	28.00		3.50

SODAS	Liter	Splits
7-Up, Gingerale, Tonic	$ 3.00	$ 1.50
Coca Cola		1.50
Diet Tab, Fresca, Coca Cola		1.50
Perrier		1.50
Bitter Lemon		1.50

BEERS		
St. Pauli Girl, Heineken		$ 4.00
Bud, Miller, Miller Lite, Michelob		3.50

CORDIALS	Liter	Snifter/ Rocks 2½ o
Cordial - Group A	$65.00	$ 5.50
Cordial - Group B	45.00	5.50
Cognacs	60.00	5.50
Martell "Cordon Bleu"	90.00	8.00

PUNCHES	(Per Gallon)
Egg Nog	$40.00
Champagne	45.00
Whiskey	45.00
Bloody Mary	45.00
Sautern	35.00
Fruit	25.00

Prices Subject to 17% Service Charge or Bar Service Charge

1/91

Figure 6–4 *Catering beverage menu II. (Courtesy of Hotel DuPont, Wilmington, DE.)*

However, it is important to evaluate the type of function and the attendees before quoting a per person drink price. The consumption level of some groups can be considerably higher than others.

The pricing structure for additional periods of time is also based on an averaging of consumption levels and the format of the reception or meal. If guests are consuming a full meal, alcohol consumption after the meal will be less than if the party is a reception that continues for three to four hours. Most women will consume a small amount of alcohol after a meal. An average of 1 to 1.5 drinks over a 2.5-hour period is considered normal. Men will consume an average of approximately one drink per hour. For example, the beverage price for a 2-hour period after the meal would be calculated as follows:

$$1.5 \text{ drinks (women)} + 2 \text{ drinks (men)} = 3.5 \text{ } drinks \div 2$$
$$= 1.75 \text{ } drinks \text{ } per \text{ } person$$
$$\text{House brands: } \$5.63 + \$7.50 = \$13.13 \div 2$$
$$= \$6.56 \text{ } (6.50)^*$$
$$\text{Premium brands: } \$6.75 + \$9.00 = \$15.75 \div 2$$
$$= \$7,87 \text{ } (8.00)^*$$

* These figures are rounded off to create marketable beverage menu prices

Wine to be served with the meal is calculated by dividing the per bottle price by 6 (the average number of glasses yielded from a bottle). In prepriced packages management can select a house wine on which to base the price. Wine prices can be set in terms of either 1 glass or 2, with the latter based on a consumption level of 1.5 glasses per person:

Wine	Bottle Price	Yield	Per person	
House	$15.00	6 glasses	$2.50 (1 glass)	$5.00 (2 glasses)
Premium	$24.00	6 glasses	$4.00 (1 glass)	$8.00 (2 glasses)

A complete beverage package incorporating the examples in this section would be:

	House Brand	Premium Brand
Reception	$ 4.75	$ 5.75
Wine	5.00	8.00
2-hour bar	6.50	8.00
Total per person	$16.25	$21.75

These prices are then added to the total of the food package, gratuities and taxes, and other catering services. Examples of beverage package price lists are seen in Figure 6–5.

Bar Service

Open Bars are priced as follows:

First Hour $5.50/person
Second Hour $2.50/person
Third Hour $2.00/person
Fourth Hour $2.00/person

- We stock only premium brands of liquor, wine and beer.
- A limited wine, beer & soda bar charged on consumption, is available.
- A Cash Bar is available upon request.
- Any bar for under 30 people, or a Cash Bar, is subject to a **$25.00** charge for the Bartender.
- You may set the hours of operation of your bar, but bar hours are limited to a total of 4 hours.
- Special wines are available upon request.
- Perfect for Showers and Brunches:

Mimosa .... $2.25 per glass
Champagne .... $2.50 per glass
Asti Spumanti .... $2.75 per glass
Virgin Mary .... $1.50 per glass
Wine .... $2.00 per glass
Spiked Punch .... $2.00 per glass

Bloody Mary .... $2.50 per glass
Cape Codder .... $2.50 per glass
Screwdriver .... $2.50 per glass

Fruit Punch .... $1.50 per glass

Figure 6–5 *Beverage package price lists. (Courtesy of The Inn at Nichols Village, Clarks Summit, PA.)*

```
                    COCKTAIL RECEPTION AND PARTIES


                         HOSTED RECEPTION


     Beverage Service Per Drink - Using 1 1/4 Ounce Measure

Call Brand Liquors      $3.50   Premium Host Liquors      $3.75
     House Wines        $3.25           Host Wines        $3.25
     Domestic Beer      $2.75           Domestic Beer     $2.75
     Imported Beer      $3.00           Imported Beer     $3.00


ABOVE PRICES DO NOT INCLUDE 16% SERVICE CHARGE OR 10% STATE TAX


*********************************************

                       CASH BAR RECEPTION

          Premium Brand Cocktails      $4.00
          Call Brands Cocktails        $3.75
          Cordials                     $3.75 - $4.25
          Premium Wines                $3.50
          Domestic Beer                $3.00
          Imported Beer                $3.25
          Soft Drinks or Fruit Juices  $2.00

           BARTENDER CHARGE PER BAR $30.00
       WILL BE WAIVED WITH SALES OF $175.00 PER BAR



GUARANTEES OF ATTENDANCE ARE REQUIRED 72 HOURS IN ADVANCE
```

Figure 6–5   *(continued) (Courtesy of the Portland Maine Marriott, Portland, ME.)*

Catering Beverage Menu Planning

Profitable catering services develop specialty menus to include appropriate wines and cordials. Depending on the formality of the meal up to seven wines and cordials can be matched with menu items in each category of the menu format. Figure 6–6 lists a sauvignon blanc with the appetizer course, a beringer chardonnay following the soup course, a Los Carneros reserve chardonnay with the fish course, a pinot noir with the beef course, and a dessert wine, brachetto d'acqui, with the fruit dessert.

APPETIZER

Simi Sauvignon Blanc

SOUP

Beringer Chardonnay

FISH

Beaulieu Vineyards Los Carneros Reserve Chardonnay

BEEF

Beaulieu Vineyards Los Carneros Pinot Noir

DESSERT

Brachetto D'Acqui

Figure 6–6 *Five-wine dinner menu. (Courtesy of Johnson and Wales University, Providence, RI.)*

```
┌─────────────────────────────────────────────────┐
│                     MENU                          │
│                                                   │
│                                                   │
│          Archestratios - Epicurios Cuisine        │
│                                                   │
│                                                   │
│                  Stuffed Cabbage                  │
│   Cabbage stuffed with fresh Nova Scotia salmon   │
│   and seafood mousse and served with tomato       │
│       vinaigrette and horseradish sauce.          │
│                                                   │
│                                                   │
│                  Tomato Bisque                    │
│                                                   │
│                                                   │
│                 Nest of Fettuccine                │
│  Combination of lobster and black pasta served    │
│  with lobster sauce and garnished with caviar     │
│                   American.                       │
│                                                   │
│                                                   │
│                  Beggars Bundle                   │
│   Assorted fresh New England seafood wrapped in   │
│   phyllo and served with yellow and red pepper    │
│                    sauce.                         │
│                                                   │
│                                                   │
│                    Sorbet                         │
│                                                   │
│                                                   │
│                   Braised Veal                    │
│  Served with pearl onions, mushrooms and baby     │
│                 vegetables.                       │
│                                                   │
│                                                   │
│                  Spring Salad                     │
│   A colorful bouquet of fresh julienned           │
│      vegetables on a bed of fresh greens.         │
│                                                   │
│                                                   │
│          Fresh Fruits in Meringue Shells          │
│           Served With Red Current Sauce           │
└─────────────────────────────────────────────────┘
```

Figure 6–6   *(continued)*

Each of the red or white wines shown on the seven course dinner menu in Figure 6–7 will complement the food item with which it is being served. This blending of food with wine is often referred to as "marrying" foods and wines. When menus of this caliber are being planned, it is important that caterers work with beverage and wine experts to choose a variety of wines for the entire menu and yet achieve the marriage of food and wine. Developing elaborate menus such as this can be expensive; however, distributors are excellent resources for finding the best wine available within the desired price range.

The menu in Figure 6–7 is a formal seven-course meal that incorporates seven wines and cordials.

An excellent guide to the effective marriage of food and wines is the table in Figure 6–8 from *The New Larousse Gastronomique*. This type of reference guide is invaluable to menu planners who may have selections of various wines but lack the knowledge to match them to the appropriate foods.

MENU

Archestratios-Epicurios Cuisine

Mommessin Cuvee St. Pierre White

Oysters Alexia
Oysters with seafood stuffing, cooked
in their own juices and baked
slowly to blend in the flavors.

Canteval

Seafood Symphony
A medley of the ocean's harvest,
topped with puff pastry.

Maitre D'Estournel '84 White Bourdeaux

Baked Stuffed Filet of Sole
Stuffed with seafood mousse and
served with spinach sauce.

Principessa Gavi, 1983

Baked Stuffed Shrimp
This delicacy of the sea is served fresh
and stuffed with lobster and crab meat.

Lime Sherbet

Croissants

Mommessin Macon Village

Chicken à la Grecque
Fresh boneless breast of chicken
cooked with lemon and oregano.

Rodney Strong Cabernet Sauvignon

Roast Tenderloin of Beef
Garnished with stuffed new potato
and broccoli flowerets.

Salad Katerina
Created for this special occasion and
served with House of Socrates Dressing.

Brachetto D'Acqui

Pears Anna
Poached to perfection and
served with raspberry sauce.

Coffee or Tea

Figure 6–7   *Seven-course dinner menu. (Courtesy of Johnson and Wales University, Providence, RI.)*

TABLE RELATING WINES TO FOOD

Food	White wines	Red wines	Rosé wines	Food	White wines	Red wines	Rosé wines
HORS-D'ŒUVRE COLD MEATS	*Dry & light* Bourgogne aligoté Petit chablis Mâcon blanc Sancerre Pouilly-fumé Montlouis Crépy Edelzwicker Sylvaner	*Light* Bordeaux supérieur Passe-tousgrains Givry Mâcon rouge Beaujolais Chinon, bourgueil Gris meunier	Bordeaux clairet Bourgogne rosé Anjou, touraine Côtes de Provence Saint-pourçain Rosé de Béarn	FISH, CRUSTACEANS, IN SAUCES	*Dry* (full-bodied for highly seasoned sauces) Graves Chablis Meursault Cortoncharlemagne Les montrachet Pouilly-fuissé Hermitage blanc Condrieu Riesling Arbois blancvin jaune *Mellow wines* (for sweet sauces) Sauternes Monbazillac Vouvray Coteaux du Layon Gewurztraminer		
FOIE GRAS	*Fine wines* Graves Meursault Montrachet Champagne Coulée de serrant Riesling Hermitage blanc Château-grillet *Fine sweet wines* Sauternes Barsac Quart-de-chaume Bonnezeaux Gewurztraminer Frontignan Samos	*Grands crus* Médoc, graves Saint-émilion Pomerol Musigny Romanée-conti Beaune, volnay Hermitage Banyuls grand cru Porto		GRILLED WHITE MEATS		*Light-bodied* Médoc, graves Beaune Savigny Volnay Beaujolais Chinon, bourgueil Saumurchampigny	
ENTRÉES	*Dry or mellow* Graves, cérons Meursault Chassagnemontrachet Beaune blanc Champagne Vouvray Saumur Anjou Riesling	*Supple* Margaux Saint-julien Beaune Savigny Mercurey Beaujolais Chinon Bourgueil	*Fruity* Sancerre rosé Rosés d'Anjou ou de Touraine Pinot rosé d'Alsace	WHITE MEATS WITH WHITE WINE SAUCES	Graves Sauternes Montrachet Meursault Riesling Vouvray Anjou Champagne		
OYSTERS AND SHELLFISH	*Dry* Graves Entre-deuxmers Chablis Pouilly-fuissé Chassagnemontrachet Chevaliermontrachet Champagne Champagne nature Riesling Sancerre Pouilly-fumé Quincy Savennières Roche-auxmoines Muscadet Gros-plant Cassis, bandol Arbois blanc			WHITE MEATS WITH RED WINE SAUCES		Saint-émilion Chambertin Beaujolais Chinon Bourgueil	
FISH, CRUSTACEANS, GRILLED OR POACHED	*Dry* See above		*Dry* Cassis, bandol Côtes de Provence Tavel, lirac Rosé de Béarn	GRILLED OR ROAST RED MEAT		*Well-matured* Médoc, graves Saint-émilion Pomerol Côtes de Nuits Côtes de Beaune Morgon Fleurie Moulin-à-vent Hermitage Cornas Côte-rôtie Châteauneuf-du-pape	
				RAGOÛTS, HAM, PORK STEWS		Bordeaux supérieur Côtes de Fronsac Cahors Madiran Santenay Mercurey Beaujolais Sancerre rouge Touraineamboise Côtes du Rhône	

Figure 6–8 *Wine and food table. (Source:* Montangé, *The New Larousse Gastronomique,* 1984, pp. 991–92.)

TABLE RELATING WINES TO FOOD

Food	White wines	Red wines	Rosé wines
FEATHERED GAME	Champagne Arbois- vin jaune	Margaux Saint-julien Graves Musigny Beaune Volnay Beaujolais de crus Arbois rouge Hermitage	
OTHER GAME	Château- chalon	Pauillac Saint-estèphe Saint-émilion Pomerol Tous les grands crus de la Côte de Nuits Corton Pommard Côte-rôtie Châteauneuf- du-pape	
COAGULATED CHEESES		Médoc, graves Saint-émilion Pomerol Vins de la Côte de Beaune Beaujolais Chinon Bourgueil	
FERMENTED CHEESES		Pomerol Canon-fronsac Vins de la Côte de Nuits Corton Morgon Hermitage Côte-rôtie Châteauneuf- du-pape	
VEINED CHEESES	Sauternes Meursault Arbois- vin jaune Gewurz- traminer Champagne	Vins de la Côte de Nuits Hermitage Châteauneuf- du-pape	
GOATS' MILK CHEESES	Sancerre Pouilly-fumé Mâcon blanc Arbois blanc	Mercurey Givry Beaujolais Chinon Bourgueil	Bordeaux clairet Bourgogne rosé Sancerre rosé
DESSERTS	Champagne Vins mousseux de méthode champenoise Sauternes Barsac Monbazillac Vouvray moelleux Coteaux du Layon Muscat d'Alsace Gewurz- traminer Muscat de: Rivesaltes, Frontignan, Lunel, Beaumes-de- Venise, Samos	Maury Rivesaltes Grand roussillon Banyuls Porto Madère Malaga	

Wine suitable for accompanying soups and egg dishes are not included here; ordinary carafe wines do very well.

Figure 6–8 *(continued)*

Alcohol Service and Liability

A growing awareness fostered by citizens groups concerned about the number of automobile accidents that cause deaths and severe disabilities has resulted in stricter drunk driving laws and increased liability for operators who serve alcoholic beverages. State liquor laws prohibit the sale of alcohol to a minor throughout the United States. Other laws regarding the sale of alcohol vary from state to state and are open to court interpretation.

According to John Sherry in *Legal Aspects of Foodservice Management*, many states have statutes called *dramshop acts,* that hold operators liable for deaths of or injuries to third parties resulting from illegal sales of alcohol to customers. Although foodservice operators are becoming increasingly susceptible to the legal ramifications of any alcohol-related accident that occurs after a patron has left their establishment, this susceptibility is greatest in cases involving third party liability because these have few defenses. An injured third party who sues under the dramshop acts is usually required to prove that a licensed seller sold alcohol illegally, thereby causing or contributing to the intoxication of the customer whose actions resulted in the victim's injury.

In addition to the dramshop acts, injured third parties may charge foodservice operators with common law negligence either for noncompliance with statutes prohibiting the sale of alcohol in certain situations of for failure to anticipate the effects of poor supervision of the premises. In some states the common law rule is expanded to hold servers responsible for expecting that any sale to an obviously intoxicated patron with a known intent to drive a motor vehicle poses a reasonably foreseeable threat to other drivers or pedestrians.[1]

Foodservice operators who offer catering beverage services face the same tasks of identifying minors and intoxicated patrons as do lounges and restaurants. The atmosphere of a private party does not absolve caterers from the legal responsibilities regarding the service of alcohol, even in situations where the host purchases all of the alcohol from the operator, who merely dispenses it to guests. The liquor license of the business governs the service of all alcohol within the establishment. Therefore bartenders and servers are responsible for identifying minors and exercising prudent judgment in the service of alcohol to individuals who exhibit signs of intoxication. In particular, they will be held accountable for the knowledge that an intoxicated individual represents a danger on the roads because in a private party situation they can assume that all guests intend to drive a motor vehicle.

This pressure of liability increases the need for foodservice operators to initiate training programs and policies in their establishments that will help them to protect themselves from lawsuits and liquor law violations. The use of training programs that are nationally recognized by insurance companies and the courts can act both to decrease premiums for liquor liability insurance and to provide evidence of intent and concern on the part of management for responsible alcohol service.

In the past few years a number of training programs for alcohol service have been developed. Of these, TIPS (Training for Intervention Procedures) and SERVSAFE–Responsible Alcohol Service are the most widely recognized.

The TIPS program concentrates on providing servers with keys to identify customers who are on the verge of becoming intoxicated. Some of these signs are:

1. Drinking too fast
2. Becoming loud, mean, argumentative, and obnoxious
3. Complaining about drink strength or preparation
4. Slurring words
5. Lighting more than one cigarette
6. Becoming clumsy and changing walk

The following quote from the TIPS brochure explains the benefits of the program.

The first step in dealing with the effects of intoxication is understanding what causes it. TIPS training helps participants understand how what's going on inside the body influences what's going on outside. Alcohol serving professionals develop a "sixth sense" about customers who are on the verge of becoming intoxicated. TIPS training shows them how to use intuition as a spring board to action, teaching strategies that can stop an overdrinking problem before it has a chance to start. TIPS demonstrates how the total environment of a bar or restaurant can help customers drink more responsibly. TIPS training can be especially valuable, teaching participants how to prevent a customer from becoming intoxicated with firmness, concern, and respect. No student in the program is certified without effectively participating in role playing to test their judgment and help them apply what they've studied. A written examination is also required for certification, which must be renewed every three years. TIPS training saves lives, keeps families intact, eases the financial burden on local communities, and helps keep insurance rates down. It's one solution to the problem of drunk driving.[2]

This program is made available through certified instructors who hold training programs locally.

The SERVSAFE–Responsible Alcohol Service Program is offered by the Educational Foundation of the National Restaurant Association, and its logo, which is often featured on table tents or beverage menus, and manuals are pictured in Figure 6–9.

This program concentrates on training managers in either formal training sessions or correspondence programs. Written materials and videos help managers to train servers in their own establishments, incorporating the individual needs of their businesses. Managers and servers must pass a written exam before receiving a certificate of completion.

The SERVSAFE program covers many of the same issues as the TIPS program. In addition, the program helps managers to assess the level of liability

RESPONSIBLE ALCOHOL SERVICE PROGRAM

Figure 6–9 *SERVSAFE—Responsible Alcohol Service Program logo and manuals. (Courtesy of the National Restaurant Association.)*

risk for their individual business and provides servers with training to increase food and beverage profitability by promoting the sale of premium brands and food accompaniments to drinks.

To effectively develop policies and training programs management should research state and local liquor laws and discuss the level of risk that their operation carries in terms of third party liability. Insurance companies that specialize in alcohol liability insurance are an excellent resource.

Summary

Well-managed beverage sales can be a profitable extension of every catering operation. Both alcoholic and nonalcoholic beverages can contribute to the success of a beverage program.

Catering beverage sales contribute to overall profitability if properly evaluated and priced. Because catering beverages are sold by the bottle, drink, and time period a variety of opportunities are available to create highly profitable beverage prices. Catering menus for special occasions can serve wine either by the bottle or glass to increase beverage sales.

Catering foodservice operators must be aware of liquor liability laws and the need for server training programs. TIPS and SERVSAFE–Responsible Alcohol Service are two nationally recognized training programs for alcohol service.

Endnotes

1. John E. H. Sherry, *Legal Aspects of Foodservice Management* (New York: John Wiley & Sons, 1984), p. 53.
2. *Life Saving Training for Alcohol Serving Professionals* (New York: Insurance Information Institute, April 1988).

7

Catering Menu Design

The physical design of catering menus combines different sales and marketing techniques to achieve the goal of selling catering packages. The presentation of menus influences which catering service or hotel customers choose. In many instances catering menus are reviewed by customers in their homes or offices without the assistance of a sales representative who can guide their selections. By the time catering management reaches the customer, initial decisions have often already been made.

The presentation of catering menus in an effective marketing format can lead customers to purchase the most profitable menus and services. The presentation format includes a number of design elements:

1. Package covers
2. Design format
3. Layout
4. Typeface
5. Paper and color
6. Illustration and graphic design
7. Copy

Unlike restaurant menus, in which the selection of menu items is an impulse purchase, the choice of catering menus is given considerable thought and often conducted by a committee. Because catering functions involve anywhere from 10 to 10,000 guests and represent important business and social occasions, as well as sizable financial investments, at least two people are usually involved in the menu selection process. A catering menu that effectively incorporates marketing techniques into its overall presentation and design will be more persuasive to group decision-makers.

Package Covers

The design format of catering menus and services is shaped by the package cover presentation. The catering package cover is an optional design piece used as a folder in which to present contracts, correspondence, menus, and other information regarding both functions and the foodservice or hotel operation.

The design format of the package cover determines the shape and size of the insert pages. The most common format is a two-panel 9-by-12-inch cover such as that in Figure 7–1. This size fits easily into business mailing envelopes and is standard in the printing industry. The pocket flaps on the inside of the cover hold material in place. Figure 7–2 shows an alternative format using one inside pocket for materials and leaving the other panel available for merchandising information about the company. Figure 7–3 pictures a vertical-fold envelope with a pocket. The size of this piece is $8\frac{1}{2}$ by 10 inches with insert pages cut in staggered sizes.

Finally, the package cover design in Figure 7–4 incorporates a book format with an inside pocket on the back cover panel. Book pages offer merchandising information on a variety of facilities and services. The pocket holds the menu selections.

FOUR SEASONS HOTEL - PHILADELPHIA

~ CATERING INFORMATION ~

Menus

Enclosed for your consideration are Four Seasons Hotel banquet menus. Please note that the prices quoted are current and do not include the 6% Pennsylvania Sales Tax, nor the 18% gratuity charge which is applicable to food and beverage costs. These prices are subject to change, but may be confirmed three months prior to your event.

Cocktails

Cocktails for your function are purchased on a per drink basis. Should you request a hosted bar, a labor charge of $60.00 per bartender is applicable. Cash bars require a cashier at $25.00 each.

For smaller groups of 15 or less, butlered cocktails are available.

A copy of our wine list is enclosed. A more elaborate wine list is available on request. All prices quoted for liquor and wines are exclusive of gratuity and are subject to change.

Payment Policy

A deposit is required for all social functions. Upon cancellation, 50% is immediately refunded and the balance returned once the space is resold with a comparable event.

Guarantees

The final attendance for all food functions must be specified 48 working hours (two business days) in advance, before 12:00 Noon. Once received by the Catering Office, the number will be considered a guarantee and not subject to reduction. Guarantees for food functions of 10 persons or less will be assessed an additional charge:

> Breakfast - $35.00
> Lunch - $50.00
> Dinner - $50.00

Linen

The hotel linen is white, sized to cover our 72" round tables, three-quarters of the way to the floor

---

~ REFRESHMENTS ~

I
Coffee, Tea & Decaffeinated Coffee
Fresh Fruit Basket
Raw Vegetables
$5.00 Per Person

II
Coffee, Tea & Decaffeinated Coffee
Fresh Sliced Fruit Presentation
Raw Vegetables
Assorted Cookies
$7.50 Per Person

Freshly Pressed Juices of Apple, Orange, Grapefruit,
Apricot, Vegetable, Peach & Grape - $3.25 Each

Granola Bars - $1.00 Each

Assorted Fruit Tartelettes, Pastries,
Brownies & Cookies
$3.50 Per Person

Assorted Soft Drinks - $2.00 Each

Perrier - $2.50 Each

Figure 7–1 Two-pocket package cover. (Courtesy of Four Seasons Hotel, Philadelphia, PA.)

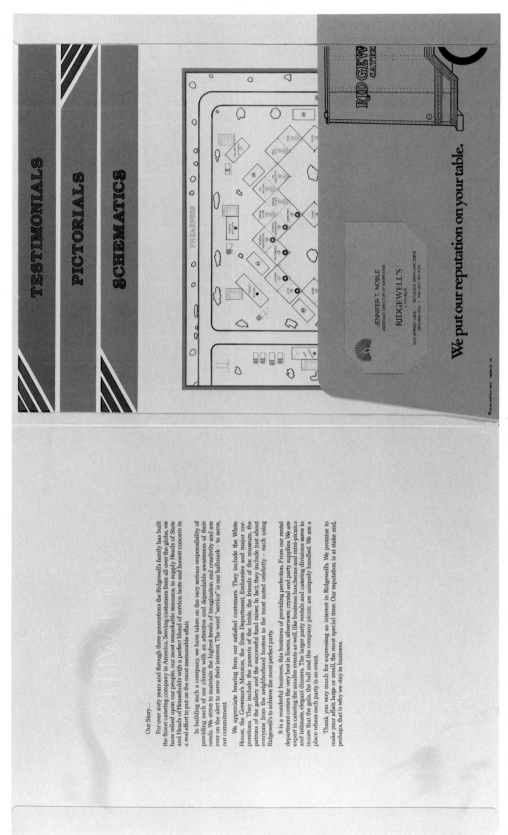

Figure 7-2 One-pocket package cover. (Courtesy of Ridgwell's Caterers, Bethesda, MD.)

Figure 7–3   *Vertical-fold package cover. (Courtesy of Opryland Hotel, Nashville, TN.)*

Figure 7–4   *Book format package cover. (Courtesy of King's Caterers, Langhorne, PA.)*

Package cover sizes and shapes that use die cuts in their design are generally limited to conference and convention centers and hotels. Individual catering businesses rarely invest in the design and printing expense required for these presentations. The simpler cover formats in Figures 7–1 and 7–2 are effective sales presentations that fit within stricter budget requirements.

Design Format

A wide range of design formats are available to present catering menus. The most basic and traditional banquet menu format consists of a single-panel page. The single panel may incorporate a number of different menus, as in Figure 7–5, or only one menu, as in Figure 7–6. A variation on the single panel is a deck of single sheets cut in staggered sizes to fit into a package cover. The design in Figure 7–7 uses a vertical layout, whereas the design in Figure 7–8 uses a horizontal layout. Figure 7–7 includes a full range of banquet menus including beverage lists and meeting breaks. The overall presentation is much more consolidated than in Figure 7–8. A book format pictured in Figure 7–9 offers a concise reference guide to menu selections. With an interior page graphic, these menus are dramatic and appealing.

Other design formats are outlined in Figure 7–10.

Layout

Layout refers to the placement of typeface and illustrations on the design format. On a catering menu outlining a complete meal, items are listed in the order in which they are served, as in Figure 7–11. Often illustrations are used to add interest to the page presentation.

Special design work can create dramatic and appealing layouts such as in Figure 7–9. When the cover of the menu is closed, the die-cut ridge in the upper-right-hand corner reveals the title of the menu package and the illustration of a Mardi Gras mask. As the menu cover is opened the balance of printed material is laid out horizontally across the lower two-thirds of the menu.

Many catering services use the word processing capabilities of electronic typewriters or personal computers to generate menus. In theory this provides them with the capability to create specialty menus for customers, change menu items and prices quickly, and print small quantities of menus at reduced costs. The results however, are not always satisfactory. The menu in Figure 7–12 has a crowded layout that is difficult to read and makes selection of menu items almost impossible.

Ideally, the buffet menu selection offered in this menu should be separated into two completely different menus each highlighting a selection of menu items in each category. Customers become confused when too many choices are presented on one menu, especially when group decisions are involved.

~ BREAKFAST MENUS ~

I
Fresh Juices
Scrambled Eggs with Bacon, Sausage & Ham
Country Fried Potatoes
Bakery Basket
Butter & Preserves
Coffee, Tea & Decaffeinated Coffee
Milk
$13.00 Per Person

II
Fresh Juices
Omelette with Cheddar Cheese
& Fine Herbs
Bacon, Sausage & Ham
Bakery Basket
Butter, Preserves or Honey
Coffee, Tea & Decaffeinated Coffee
Milk
$14.50 Per Person
(30 Person Maximum)

III
Fresh Juices
Traditional Eggs Benedict
Country Fried Potatoes
Broiled Tomato
Bakery Basket
Butter & Preserves
Coffee, Tea & Decaffeinated Coffee
Milk
$16.00 Per Person
(50 Person Maximum)

IV
Fresh Juices
Sliced Fresh Fruit
French Toast with Challah Bread
Powdered Sugar, Cinnamon & Maple Syrup
Bacon, Ham & Sausage
Bakery Basket
Butter & Preserves
Coffee, Tea & Decaffeinated Coffee
$13.50 Per Person

V
Fresh Juices
Sliced Fresh Fruit
Breakfast Steak with Scrambled Eggs
Country Fried Potatoes
or
Buttered Grits
Bakery Basket
Butter & Preserves
Coffee, Tea & Decaffeinated Coffee
$18.00 Per Person

LOW CHOLESTEROL EGGS MAY BE SUBSTITUTED FOR ALL EGG ENTREES

18% GRATUITY & 6% SALES TAX WILL BE ADDED TO ALL CHARGES
2/90

Figure 7–5   *Multiple-menu format. (Courtesy of Four Seasons Hotel, Philadelphia, PA.)*

BANQUETSTAFF
OF THE HOTEL DU PONT

BUFFET

DINNER SUGGESTIONS
$39.50

CAESAR SALAD
SLICED FRENCH BREAD - MELBA TOAST
* * * * *

ROAST SLICED TENDERLOIN OF BEEF, BEARNAISE
(Carved by Chef at Buffet)

SAUTEED SHRIMP SCAMPI, PROVENCALE

CHICKEN AND VEGETABLE STIR-FRY

CROQUETTE POTATO, WILLIAM

BAKED RICE PILAF

STIR-FRY VEGETABLE

STUFFED PORK LOIN WITH DRIED FRUIT

SEAFOOD TERRINE, DILL SAUCE

BREAST OF ROAST LONG ISLAND DUCKLING

TORTELINI PASTA SALAD

CRABMEAT SALAD

MUSHROOM SALAD
* * * * *

ASSORTED FRENCH PASTRIES
ICE CREAM - SHERBET
PETITS FOURS - MACAROONS
* * * * *

COFFEE - BREWED DECAFFEINAED - TEA
* * * * *

Menu price subject to change $45.00/person for less than 25 Guests
Chef Labor (if requested) $30.00/hr. - 2 hr. minimum
Service Charge 17% Additional

Figure 7–6   *Single-menu format. (Courtesy of Hotel DuPont, Wilmington, DE.)*

Opryland Hotel Price List
Hors d' Oeuvres
Gourmet Dinners
Dinner
Luncheon
Breakfast
General Information and Catering Policies

To facilitate your selection of foods, meals, party and banquet services, special decorations and entertainment, we proudly present to you the following information:

Repertoire
of
Opryland Hotel Catering
with suggestions for your guidance

Our unsurpassed resources in food and beverage stewardships, culinary and service skills afford you complete assurance that all commitments will be carried out, absolutely on schedule, and to your complete satisfaction.

The menus feature a selection of our most popular items. These are, of course, merely suggestions and we would be delighted to arrange banquet menus to suit your particular requirements. We are also able to prepare and serve all well-known regional and national dishes of this and many foreign countries. The different theme parties can be accompanied with the appropriate decorations, entertainment and costumes for the service personnel.

In order to assure you and your guests of a well-organized function, we must also adhere to the following catering policies:

I. Payments and Deposits
Billing arrangements for all events must be made in accordance with hotel policies. All requests for direct billing must be authorized by our credit department. A determination of a deposit or payment in advance is predicated on information received from our credit department. If a deposit is required, it becomes non-refundable ninety days prior to the event.

Figure 7–7 *Menu deck, vertical layout. (Courtesy of Opryland Hotel, Nashville, TN.)*

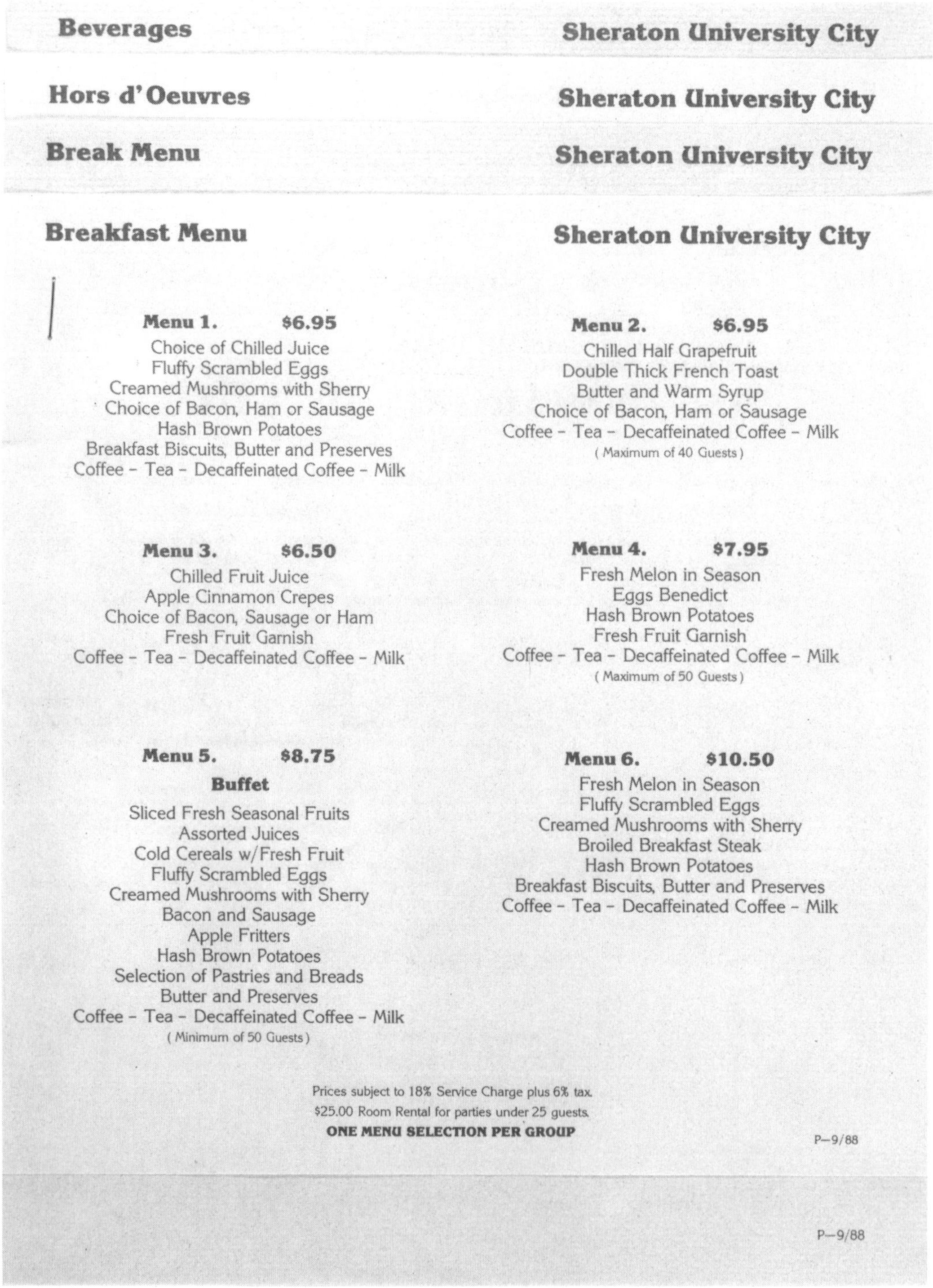

Beverages   **Sheraton University City**

Hors d'Oeuvres   **Sheraton University City**

Break Menu   **Sheraton University City**

Breakfast Menu   **Sheraton University City**

Menu 1. $6.95
Choice of Chilled Juice
Fluffy Scrambled Eggs
Creamed Mushrooms with Sherry
Choice of Bacon, Ham or Sausage
Hash Brown Potatoes
Breakfast Biscuits, Butter and Preserves
Coffee – Tea – Decaffeinated Coffee – Milk

Menu 2. $6.95
Chilled Half Grapefruit
Double Thick French Toast
Butter and Warm Syrup
Choice of Bacon, Ham or Sausage
Coffee – Tea – Decaffeinated Coffee – Milk
(Maximum of 40 Guests)

Menu 3. $6.50
Chilled Fruit Juice
Apple Cinnamon Crepes
Choice of Bacon, Sausage or Ham
Fresh Fruit Garnish
Coffee – Tea – Decaffeinated Coffee – Milk

Menu 4. $7.95
Fresh Melon in Season
Eggs Benedict
Hash Brown Potatoes
Fresh Fruit Garnish
Coffee – Tea – Decaffeinated Coffee – Milk
(Maximum of 50 Guests)

Menu 5. $8.75
Buffet
Sliced Fresh Seasonal Fruits
Assorted Juices
Cold Cereals w/Fresh Fruit
Fluffy Scrambled Eggs
Creamed Mushrooms with Sherry
Bacon and Sausage
Apple Fritters
Hash Brown Potatoes
Selection of Pastries and Breads
Butter and Preserves
Coffee – Tea – Decaffeinated Coffee – Milk
(Minimum of 50 Guests)

Menu 6. $10.50
Fresh Melon in Season
Fluffy Scrambled Eggs
Creamed Mushrooms with Sherry
Broiled Breakfast Steak
Hash Brown Potatoes
Breakfast Biscuits, Butter and Preserves
Coffee – Tea – Decaffeinated Coffee – Milk

Prices subject to 18% Service Charge plus 6% tax.
$25.00 Room Rental for parties under 25 guests.
ONE MENU SELECTION PER GROUP

P—9/88

P—9/88

Figure 7–8 *Menu deck, horizontal layout. (Courtesy of Sheraton University City, Philadelphia, PA.)*

Figure 7–9 *Book format. (Courtesy of New Orleans Hilton, New Orleans, LA.)*

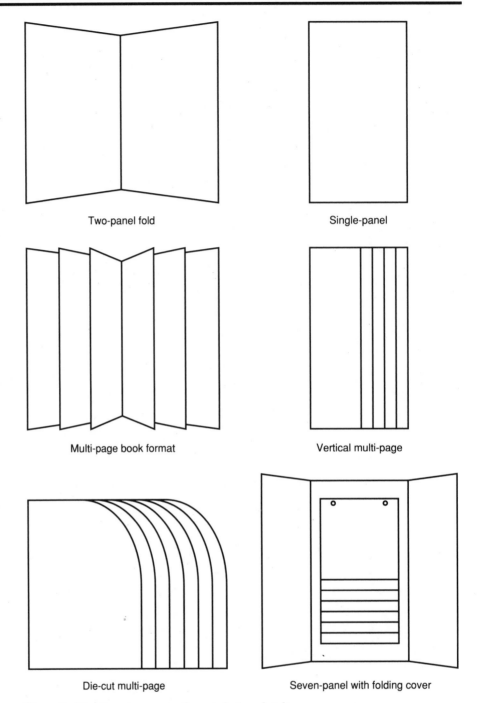

Two-panel fold

Single-panel

Multi-page book format

Vertical multi-page

Die-cut multi-page

Seven-panel with folding cover

Figure 7–10   *Catering menu format design sketches.*

**GENERAL OGLETHORPE'S
SUNDAY DINNER**

MOCK TURTLE SOUP

★　　★

TURBOT A LA CREME
Parslied Potatoes
Bell Peppers and Tomatoes

★　　★

FRESH GARDEN GREENS
Vinaigrette Dressing

★　　★

Rice Croquettes

★　　★

MARIE LOUIS ICE CREAM

★　　★

Coffee and Iced Tea

Figure 7–11 *Illustrated catering menu. (Courtesy of DeSoto Hilton, Savannah, GA.)*

Salad:
Tossed Garden Greens
Caesar Salad

Entrees (select 2):
carved: Prime Ribs of Beef
Roasted Turkey Breast
Fillet of Fish en Croute
Roast Tenderloin of Beef
Roast Rack of Lamb

grilled: Medallions of Swordfish - herb butter
Medallions of Salmon - lime butter
Medallions of Tuna - soy-ginger butter
Shrimp with Garlic & Herbs

Vegetable (select 1):
Steamed Green Beans with Almonds
Brandied Carrots
Snow Peas with Julienne Carrots
Mixed Fresh Seasonal Vegetables

Starch (select 1):
Baked Stuffed Potatoes
Oven Roasted New Potatoes with Butter & Parsley
Rice Pilaf

Pasta (select 1):
Pasta Primavera
Fettucini Alfredo
Tortellini with Light Cheese Sauce

Included:
Waldorf Salad
Dinner Rolls
Assorted Breads

Dessert (select 1):
Light & Dark Chocolate Mousse
Chocolate Marquis Cake
Fruit Tart
Cheesecake
Apple Strudel

Figure 7–12   *Banquet buffet menu from word processor. (Courtesy of Seamen's Inn, Mystic, CT.)*

However, if the menu is left intact, the format should be developed into three distinct areas—entree items, side items and surrounding items—as seen in Figure 7–13.

Typeface

The selection of a typeface for a menu layout is important to the overall success of the menu. The style and size of a typeface can influence a customer's decision to buy selected menu items. Menus that are difficult to read will either be passed over completely by customers or quickly skimmed and then discarded.

To create interest, establish a mood or character, and increase readability, a variety of the hundreds of different typeface styles and sizes should be incorporated into the overall design of the menu. Careful selection of UPPERCASE (capital) and lowercase letters is one method of providing useful contrasts. Another is varying the thickness, or typeweight, of the typeface. Depending on the message that is to be conveyed some bold typefaces are more effective than thin ones. To analyze the uses of typefaces, the menu layout can be divided into four separate areas:

1. *Course headings* separate the menu into sections such as appetizer, entrée or dessert. The primary use of typeface for this section is to create interest and unify the overall design. Readability is not a major concern.
2. *Menu item names* must stand out on the menu page. The primary function of typeface in this section is to highlight menu items in a style that is easy to read and comfortable to the eye.
3. *Descriptive copy* identifies menu item ingredients and provides other information of interest to customers. Typeface should be easy to read and be presented in a different style or weight than the menu item typeface.
4. *Merchandising copy* provides catering service and special interest information. Merchandising copy is usually placed at the bottom of the menu or on separate panels or pages. Type style can be decorative to highlight the overall menu design.

A variety of typeface styles that are commonly used in menu design are featured in Figure 7–14. Many of these typefaces are available in computer software programs for word processing and desktop publishing.

Typeface selection for each area of the menu should provide spacing, contrast, and design emphasis. A contrast in typeface size makes menu item selection easier for the customer. Descriptive copy should always be in a lower case than the menu item to create a contrast. Course headings should provide design emphasis and spacing between the menu sections.

The menu in Figure 7–15 is an example of a menu that has been generated on a word processor using standard business letter typeface. By varying the typeface selections and the case size and by using a laser printer this menu takes on a whole new look in Figure 7–16.

CARVED ENTREES (select one)

Prime Ribs of Beef   Roasted Turkey Breast

Fillet of Fish en Croute   Roast Tenderloin of Beef

Roast Rack of Lamb

GRILLED ENTREES (select one)

Medallions of Swordfish   Medallions of Salmon

Medallions of Tuna   Shrimp with Garlic & Herbs

VEGETABLES (select one)

Steamed Green Beans with Almonds   Brandied Carrots

Snow Peas with Julienne Carrots   Mixed Fresh Seasonal Vegetables

STARCH (select one)

Baked Stuffed Potatoes   Oven Roasted New Potatoes

Rice Pilaf

PASTA (select one)

Pasta Primavera   Fettucini Alfredo

Tortellini with Light Cheese Sauce

INCLUDED IN THE BUFFET

Waldorf Salad   Tossed Garden Greens

Caesar Salad

DESSERT (select one)

Light & Dark

Chocolate Mousse   Chocolate Marquis Cake

Fruit Tart   Cheesecake

Apple Strudel

Figure 7–13 *Revised banquet buffet menu.*

Crab Meat Canapé

Fried Spring Turkey

Candied Sweet Potatoes   Cauliflower, Tomato Meringue Pudding

French Salad

Strawberry Baked Alaska

Gooseberry Tarts Crust

*Pennsylvania Dutch Stuffed
Shoulder of Pork*

❦ Broiled Lobster in Clam Shells   ❦ Crabmeat Cocktail

❦ Shrimp Rounds

CRAB-MEAT CANAPÉ   CANDIED SWEET POTATOES

CAULIFLOWER, TOMATO MÉRINGUE PUDDING

FRIED SPRING TURKEY

Veal and Oyster Pie.   Quenelles of Veal.   Veal Kidney Pie.

Stewed Apples with Rice.   Gooseberry-and-Cream Tarts.

Figure 7–14 *Typeface style selections.*

Sautéed Steaks Stuffed with Oysters

Beef with Almonds and Olives
Carne Machada à la Anduluza

Fried Meatballs
Keftedes Tiganites

Steak with Onions
Côte de Boeuf à la Marseillaise

Poached Salmon with Hollandaise Sauce

Chicken Cacciatore

Chocolate Bavarian Cream

Jambalaya

LENTIL SOUP
A wonderfully hearty, whole-meal soup.

BAKED RED SNAPPER
WITH SOUR-CREAM STUFFING

COLD CUCUMBER SOUP

RED SNAPPER FLORIDIAN

CRAB AND TOMATO BISQUE
Serve this creamy pink treat in patty shells for a lovely luncheon.

SHERIFF HOUSE TROUT
(Sheriff House, Stockbridge, England)

LOBSTER AND AVOCADO SALAD

TROUT GRENOBLOISE

Schaschlik Spiess
(GERMAN STYLE KEBABS)

RATATOUILLE

Bratwurst in Bier, Berliner Art
(PORK SAUSAGE LINKS IN BEER, BERLIN STYLE)

MAINE CHICKEN PIE

PETITS FOURS GLAZE

HOLLANDAISE SAUCE

Steak with Caper Sauce

Figure 7–14   *(continued)*

<u>Appetizer</u>

Fruit Cup
Clam Chowder
French Onion Soup
Chef's Soup of the Season
Prosciutto & Melon

<u>Salad</u>

Tossed Garden Greens

Rolls & Butter

<u>Entree</u>

Stuffed Breast of Chicken
apple-bread stuffing
($21.95, $27.00 w/ tax & gratuity)

Chicken Medallions Francaise
white wine & lemon butter
($21.95, $27.00 w/ tax & gratuity)

Roast Turkey
apple-bread stuffing
($21.95, $27.00 w/ tax & gratuity)

Rock Cornish Game Hen
wild rice stuffing, supreme sauce
($23.58, $29.00 w/ tax & gratuity)

Stuffed Filet of Sole
seafood stuffing
($26.02, $32.00 w/ tax & gratuity)

Sole Almondine
($23.58, $29.00 w/ tax & gratuity)

Baked New England Scrod - lemon butter
($21.95, $27.00 w/ tax & gratuity)

Sliced Tenderloin of Beef
burgundy or bearnaise sauce
($26.02, $32.00 w/ tax & gratuity)

Figure 7–15 *Banquet dinner menu with standard typeface. (Courtesy of Seaman's Inn, Mystic, CT.)*

Baked Stuffed Shrimp
seafood stuffing
($26.02, $32.00 w/ tax & gratuity)

Roast Prime Rib of Beef
($27.64, $34.00 w/ tax & gratuity)

Grilled Filet Mignon
sauce bearnaise
($27.64, $34.00 w/ tax & gratuity)

Filet Mignon & Shrimp
petite filet & baked stuffed shrimp
($29.27, $36.00 w/ tax & gratuity)

all entrees include selected starch and fresh vegetable

<u>Dessert</u>

Old Fashioned Apple Strudel
Ice Cream
Fruit Tart
Carrot Cake
Chocolate Mousse
Cheesecake - ($1.00 extra charge)
Chocolate Marquis Cake - ($2.00 extra charge)

Coffee, Tea, and Decaffeinated Coffee

Prices in effect through December, 31, 1991.
Prices shown include Appetizer, Salad, Selected Entrees, Dessert,
Coffee or Tea.

Extra charge prices are per person and do not include tax and gratuity.

Please choose one appetizer and dessert for your entire party, and please
limit your entree selection(s) to no more than two choices.

The minimum number of orders for Prime Rib is 20.
The minimum number of orders for Sliced Tenderloin is 10.

Figure 7–15 *(continued)*

Appetizer

FRUIT CUP
CLAM CHOWDER
FRENCH ONION SOUP
CHEF'S SOUP OF THE SEASON
PROSCIUTTO & MELON

Tossed Garden Greens

Rolls & Butter

Entree

STUFFED BREAST OF CHICKEN
apple-bread stuffing   ($21.95)

STUFFED FILET OF SOLE
seafood stuffing   ($26.00)

SLICED TENDERLOIN OF BEEF
burgundy or bearnaise sauce   ($26.00)

BAKED STUFFED SHRIMP
seafood stuffing   ($26.00)

GRILLED FILET MIGNON
sauce bearnaise   ($27.75)

all entrees include selected starch and fresh vegetable

Dessert

OLD FASHIONED APPLE STRUDEL
ICE CREAM
FRUIT TART

Figure 7–16   *Banquet dinner menu with revised typeface.*

Paper and Color

Although budget considerations are a factor in selecting package designs and paper stock, management should define the image that they would like the menu package to convey to customers before they select paper stock and colors. Inexpensive throwaway menus printed on light paper stock in black ink on white will convey a very different image than menus presented on a textured 24-weight bond paper in pastel colors with a contrasting print color.

Color is an important part of every menu's design presentation. Color can be used in catering menus to elicit specific physical and emotional reactions from the reader. Bright reds and purples excite, soft pinks soothe, and light blues create a feeling of confidence. Shades of brown convey mediocrity, hues of green create unrest, and yellow tones indicate cheerfulness.

Regional and international cuisine themes can also be accented through creative use of color. Bright reds, blues, and yellows reinforce a menu with a Mexican theme. Green, yellow, and orange symbolize freshness and natural flavors in healthy dining menus. Fine dining menus often use gold inks to contrast with a second print color on cream parchment stock to establish a rich, formal tone.

An example of the skillful use of paper and color is provided by Ridgewell's Caterers in Bethesda, Maryland, which has created a variety of menu presentations and information sheets to respond to its wide customer base. From the White House to private at-home functions, Ridgewell's serves corporate and social customers of every caliber. Its logo is a rich purple with the company name in raised gold letters. Paper stock selections include a heavily laminated package cover, glossy four-color information sheets, two-color medium-weight menu listings, and one-color lightweight mail stuffers. The use of purple throughout their printed material reinforces the feeling of richness and quality that the company projects onto all of its catering functions. Photographs are used on the more expensive pieces, as are graphic sketches and illustrations where appropriate.

Illustration and Graphic Design

As is the case with catering menus in general, only a few of the examples in this chapter incorporate graphic designs and illustrations into their overall format. Those catering menus that do make this attempt are highly successful. The marketing goals of creating interest, reinforcing the theme, and directing customer attention goals can all be achieved with illustration and graphic design. The menu in Figure 7–17 uses illustration to highlight the theme of the menu.

Many food and beverage illustrations can be obtained from printers as well as clip-art design books. These illustrations can be pasted onto menu layouts to reinforce regional cuisine, party themes, or historical locations, and provide entertainment and humor.

Copy

Copy consists of the written words used on a menu to identify menu items and describe item contents for the customer. Menu copy is broken down into three categories: accent copy, descriptive item copy, and merchandising copy.

Accent copy is used in course headings and menu item names to create customer interest. In catering menus, accent copy, particularly foreign language terms, can help to establish themes and reinforce cuisine orientation. Historical reference and humor are other tools of accent copy.

Descriptive copy informs the customer about the contents of menu items. It is important, especially in catering menus, to keep this description as brief as possible. Ingredients that are highlighted by descriptive copy should encourage the selection of the menu item by creating interest or emphasizing the quality of preparation. Detailed sentences that overdescribe menu items are inappropriate for catering menus. Words such as crisp, fluffy, light, creamy, smooth, rich, blended, and fresh evoke a positive association with a customer's previous experience with a food item. Superlatives such as "best ever" and "to perfection" should be avoided because they create customer expectations that may not be met by this menu item.

Merchandising copy provides information about catering services and/or the catering operation. Information about catering services should state policies and prices as clearly as possible to avoid misunderstandings that can result in customer relations problems during and after functions.

Well-written copy in all sections of the menu can have a positive impact on the total menu program. Customers who find information to be stated in a clear and interesting manner will be more comfortable in their decisions and willing to consider additional services that can increase the caterer's overall revenues and profits.

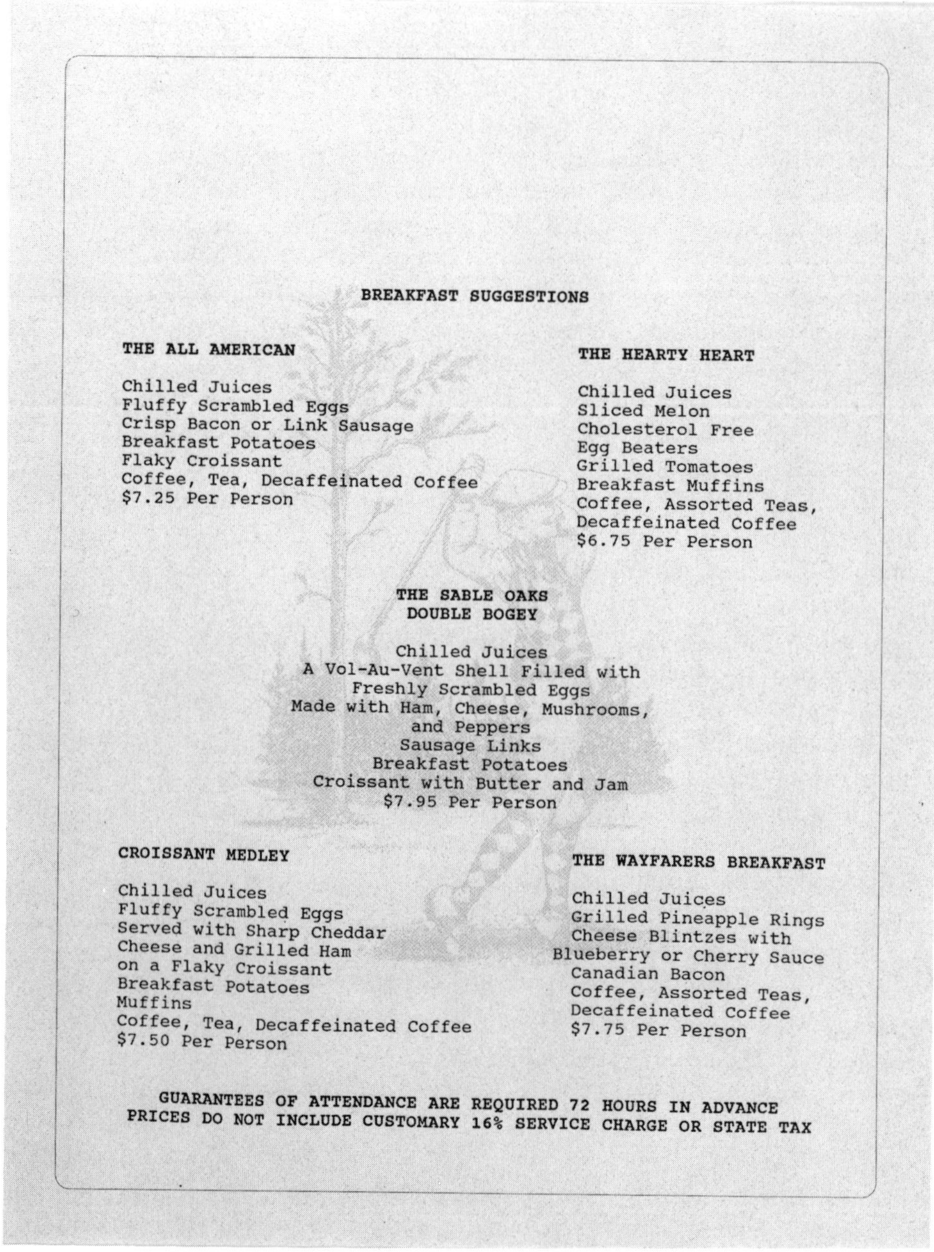

BREAKFAST SUGGESTIONS

THE ALL AMERICAN

Chilled Juices
Fluffy Scrambled Eggs
Crisp Bacon or Link Sausage
Breakfast Potatoes
Flaky Croissant
Coffee, Tea, Decaffeinated Coffee
$7.25 Per Person

THE HEARTY HEART

Chilled Juices
Sliced Melon
Cholesterol Free
Egg Beaters
Grilled Tomatoes
Breakfast Muffins
Coffee, Assorted Teas,
Decaffeinated Coffee
$6.75 Per Person

**THE SABLE OAKS
DOUBLE BOGEY**

Chilled Juices
A Vol-Au-Vent Shell Filled with
Freshly Scrambled Eggs
Made with Ham, Cheese, Mushrooms,
and Peppers
Sausage Links
Breakfast Potatoes
Croissant with Butter and Jam
$7.95 Per Person

CROISSANT MEDLEY

Chilled Juices
Fluffy Scrambled Eggs
Served with Sharp Cheddar
Cheese and Grilled Ham
on a Flaky Croissant
Breakfast Potatoes
Muffins
Coffee, Tea, Decaffeinated Coffee
$7.50 Per Person

THE WAYFARERS BREAKFAST

Chilled Juices
Grilled Pineapple Rings
Cheese Blintzes with
Blueberry or Cherry Sauce
Canadian Bacon
Coffee, Assorted Teas,
Decaffeinated Coffee
$7.75 Per Person

GUARANTEES OF ATTENDANCE ARE REQUIRED 72 HOURS IN ADVANCE
PRICES DO NOT INCLUDE CUSTOMARY 16% SERVICE CHARGE OR STATE TAX

Figure 7–17 *Menu with graphic illustration. (Courtesy of the Portland Maine Marriott, Portland, ME.)*

Summary

The presentation of catering menus directly reflects the style of the catering service. Package covers combine menus with other catering services and information to present a complete overview of the business to the customer. Many catering services use the word processing capabilities of their computer system combined with a laser printer to create menus with a professional image. The design elements of layout, typeface, paper stock, color, and illustration can be utilized to create interest and develop sales. Menus that present items in entertaining and easy-to-read formats will be given more consideration by customers, ultimately increasing sales.

8

Food and Beverage Operational Controls

The success of an ongoing catering operation is dependent on the operational controls that management establishes in order to monitor the daily productivity and profitability of the business. Operational controls are functions carried out within a foodservice operation to ensure food and beverage products that meet established standards of quality as efficiently as possible. Operational controls cover the following areas:

1. Costing
2. Pricing
3. Purchasing
4. Production
5. Presentation
6. Service

Costing and pricing were discussed in chapters five and six, and service will be discussed in chapter ten. The areas of purchasing, production, and presentation are the focus of this chapter. Quality control is the term used for the processes employed to meet the standards set for purchasing, production, and presentation. The objective is to produce food and beverage products following standardized recipes using ingredients purchased at prices that meet established food cost guidelines.

Purchasing controls define the criteria for quality by which food items are selected. These criteria, combined with established food cost goals, determine which products are purchased. Professional purchasing requires a knowledge of a wide range of food products and their expected yields. An awareness of waste-reducing and labor-saving products and their applications can enhance the profitability of a catering service operation.

Production controls ensure consistency in the amount of each ingredient used, the set of directions followed, the number of portions yielded, and the taste and texture obtained each time a food product is prepared. To accomplish this goal a standard recipe for a predetermined portion size and yield must be developed for every item in the menu file.

Presentation controls establish guidelines for the size and type of dish or glass to be used, the portion size of the food or beverage product, and the sauce and/or garniture. Often called plate architecture, plate presentation is important for maintaining customer satisfaction as well as standardizing costs.

Purchasing Controls

Purchasing controls, usually called purchasing specifications, outline the exact requirements for the quality and quantity of a food product as well as the purpose for which the food product is to be used. Specifications should include the following information:

1. Product name with preferred brand names if available
2. Quantity to be purchased, designated by purchasing unit, such as case, pound, or bunch

3. Indication of federal grade, such as U.S. Grade A
4. Unit by which prices are quoted, such as dozen, #16's, or gallon
5. Identification of the intended use of the product and any factors that can further describe the item to be purchased.

The bid form in Table 8–1 lists the simplified purchasing specifications for four poultry items. The unit price and total amount are completed by the purchasing agent once the price has been received from the vendor bidding on this purchasing order.

The purchase of quantity food products that consistently yield a specified number of portions helps to control food costs not only for individual items, but also for the overall menu. In order for a menu price to generate a consistent food cost percentage, menu item costs must remain constant. Table 8–2 outlines purchase quantities for fish and shellfish.

In this example a 1-pound fillet of fish will yield 2 to 3 portions between 3.4 ounces and 5.1 ounces in size. A yield of 100 portions requires between $19\frac{3}{4}$ pounds and $29\frac{1}{2}$ pounds of fish fillets. The exact amount of fish fillet to be

Table 8–1 *Purchasing specifications.*

Item	Supplies	Quantity	Unit	Unit Price	Amount
1.	Chicken, fresh chilled fryer, 2-1/2 - 3 lb, ready-to-cook, U.S. Grade A	500	lb		
2.	To be delivered Chicken, fresh chilled fowl, 3-1/2 - 4 lb, ready-to-cook, U.S. Grade B To be delivered	100	lb		
3.	Turkey, frozen, Young Tom 20 -22 lb, ready-to-cook, U.S. Grade A To be delivered	100	lb		
4.	Ducks, frozen roaster duckling, 5 - 5-1/2 lb, ready-to-cook, U.S. Grade A To be delivered	50	lb		

Vendor _____

(Source: Kotschevar, Quantity Food Processing, 2nd ed., p. 34.)

Table 8–2   *Purchase quantities.*

Item: Fish, fresh or frozen	Unit Weight of Purchase	% Yield as cooked	Number of cooked portions per unit	Size (oz) of Portions per Purchase Unit	Number of Units per 100 Portions
Fillets	1 lb	64	2 to 3	3.4 to 5.1	19¾ to 29½
Steaks	1 lb	58	2 to 3	3.1 to 4.6	21¾ to 32½
Dressed	1 lb	45	2 to 3	2.4 to 3.6	28 to 41¾
Drawn	1 lb	32	2 to 3	1.7 to 2.6	39¼ to 58½
Whole (round)	1 lb	27	2 to 3	1.4 to 2.2	46½ to 69½
Breaded, raw	1 lb	85	3 to 4	3.4 to 4.5	22 to 29¾
Breaded, fried	1 lb	95	3 to 4	3.8 to 5.1	19¾ to 26½
Lobster, in shell	1 lb	25	16 to 20	about one	100 to 125
Lobster meat	1 lb	91	2 to 3	4.9 to 7.3	13¾ to 20¾
Oysters, shucked	1 lb	40	2 to 3	2.1 to 3.2	31¼ to 47
Scallops, shucked	1 lb	63	2 to 3	3.4 to 5.0	20 to 30
Shrimp, cooked	1 lb	100	2 to 3	5.3 to 8.0	12½ to 19
Shrimp, raw	1 lb	50	2 to 3	2.7 to 4.6	25 to 37½
Shrimp, raw	1 lb	62	2 to 3	3.3 to 5.0	20¼ to 30½

(*Source:* Kotschevar, *Quantity Food Processing*, 2nd ed., p. 447.)

ordered depends on the actual production portion size, which is determined in the final production specifications.

Efficiency is an important consideration in purchasing. Advances in food technology have provided innovative food preparation methods for pre-prepared and/or preportioned food products. For catering menu management these methods can provide significant savings in both food product and labor costs. Food products from beef cuts to vegetables cuts are available in single- or multi-portion packs. A variety of sealing and packaging techniques from the cryovac method to quick-chill have made available food products whose quality and safety is assured over a longer period of shelf life than if the products were broken down or butchered at the foodservice location.

Quick-chill combines bulk food preparation methods with refrigeration and freezing to create specified portion packages of food products. This process is applied mainly to soups, sauces, vegetables, and bulk ingredients and is used in large contract feeding situations, multi-chain restaurant food distribution systems, and institutional foodservice operations. In the final cooking process water is drawn off from the product, reducing both the weight and volume. The temperature is rapidly lowered as the product is quickly packaged and sealed. Refrigeration during processing under constant temperatures in an atmosphere relatively free of bacteria that cause food spoilage reduces the risk of food-borne illnesses. Quick-chilled food products can be easily shipped over long distances and stored with extended shelf lives.

Sous vide is a food processing method that is revolutionizing the foodservice industry, with dramatic implications for catering in particular. Raw food products are packaged in individual or multi-portion packs using the cryovac sealing method, in which air inside the package is drawn out and the package closure is heat-sealed. They are then marked for storage under refrigeration for specified periods of time. Sous vide food products are put into production by placing them in hot water for a designated cooking period.

Both the quick-chill and sous vide methods provide catering managers with cost-saving food products that meet quality and quantity purchasing standards.

Production Controls

Standard Recipe

A standard recipe consists of a written set of instructions that act as a guideline for the combination of specified amounts of ingredients to produce a desired product. Recipes are standardized in order to control the consistency of taste, texture, and yield.

The ideal standard recipe includes a list of ingredients, their appropriate weights and/or measures, and specific directions for incorporating them into the product. A card format works the best for most operations although those using a computerized foodservice system employ a variety of recipe formats.

The recipe card divides the recipe into sections that are easy to identify, read, and follow while cooking. For example, the recipe card presented in Figure 8–1 is formatted in two sections, one for the salad recipe and the other for the vinaigrette.

Figure 8–2 offers an alternate format. It is important that a recipe card offer accurate information concerning ingredients, weight and measure, directions, and yield.

Ingredients

Any food item that is included in the preparation of the recipe must be listed regardless of the amount used. In order for a recipe to consistently produce the same taste, texture, and yield the same ingredients and proportions must always be used. Each ingredient should be described accurately with limited preparation directions, such as "peeled, cooked shrimp" or "sliced green onions" (see Figure 8–1).

Weight and Measure

Either the weight or the measure for each ingredient must be included in the recipe. Some cards list both in order to make production more accurate. For example in Figure 8–2 peeled tomatoes are listed in both pounds and quarts, and chicken breasts are listed by both pounds and piece count. Weight for both liquid and dry products is measured on a scale and given in either ounces, as for diced onions, or pounds, as for chicken breasts (see Figure 8–2).

Measure is listed by pieces, cans, slices, bunches, or by indication of standard measure. For instance, in Figure 8–1 lettuce leaves are measured by the piece, lime juice by the cup, and kidney beans by the quart.

SWEET PEPPER & SHRIMP SALAD

Ingredients	Weights	Measures	Directions	Yield: 24 servings
Spicy Lime Vinaigrette	—	—	1. Prepare Spicy Lime Vinaigrette. Reserve.	
Le Rouge Royale® sweet red peppers	3 lbs.	6	2. Rinse peppers. Remove core and seeds. Cut into strips.	
Le Jaune Royale® sweet yellow peppers	3 lbs.	6	3. Toss peppers and vinaigrette with remaining ingredients except avocados and lettuce leaves. Chill until ready to serve.	
Peeled, cooked shrimp	4 lbs.	2 qts.		
Jicama strips	1 lb., 8 oz.	1½ qts.		
Cooked kidney beans	3 lbs., 8 oz.	2½ qts.	4. For individual servings, line plate with 2 lettuce leaves. Slice ¼ avocado and arrange on plate. Spoon 12 oz. (2⅓ cups) pepper salad on plate.	
Cooked corn kernels	2 lbs.	1½ qts.		
Sliced green onions	6 oz.	1½ cups		
Avocados	—	6		
Lettuce leaves	—	48		

SPICY LIME VINAIGRETTE   Yield: Approx. 4½ cups

Vegetable oil	—	3 cups	1. Whisk all ingredients together until thoroughly blended.
Lime juice	—	1½ cups	
Dijon-style mustard	—	2 Tbs.	
Chopped cilantro	—	2 Tbs.	
Grated lime peel	—	1 Tbs.	
Salt	—	1 Tbs.	
Ground cumin	—	2 tsp.	
Chili powder	—	2 tsp.	

Nutrients per serving based on using Le Rouge Royale® peppers only:

								Percentages of USRDA:	
Calories	570	Carbohydrates	40 g	Fat-Total	37 g	Sodium	471 mg	Vitamin A	76%
Protein	26 g	Dietary Fiber	15 g	Cholesterol	147 mg			Vitamin C	395%

SUN ☼ WORLD. Foodservice Department, P.O. Box 1028, Coachella, CA 92236   (619) 347-8693

Figure 8–1 *Sample recipe card I. (Courtesy of Sun World, Coachella, CA.)*

Directions

Directions should be stated as simply and clearly as possible. In many kitchens English is spoken as a second language, so staff members may have difficulty in reading long preparation explanations. The directions in Figure 8–1, for example, are accurate and to the point.

Yield

The yield is the number of portions that a recipe will produce. A portion is the amount of food product that has been allotted for a single serving. Portions are given by weight or measure. For example, the recipes in both Figures 8–1 and 8–2 yield 24 servings. In Figure 8–1 the determined portion per serving is identified as 12 oz. or 2⅓ cups in step four of the directions. The recipe will yield 24 - 12 oz. portions or 56 cups bulk measure.

The recipe in Figure 8–3 yields 24 portions of Poached Chicken Breast Princesse. As an example of a professional cooking recipe, Figure 8–3 provides weight and measure for all ingredients as well as the conversion for U.S. metric measurement. It can be used by cooks and chefs from different backgrounds conveniently.

GARLIC POTATO CAKES WITH CHICKEN AND TOMATO SAUCE
FROM: DAKOTA'S DALLAS, TX **JIM SEVERSON,** CHEF

YIELD: 24 SERVINGS
PORTION: 2-3 PANCAKES, ½ CHICKEN BREAST, ¼ CUP SAUCE

IDAHO POTATOES

Ingredients	Weight	Measure
GARLIC POTATO CAKES: approximately 48 patties		
Idaho® Shredded Potatoes, fresh, frozen or dehydrated (prepared)	4 pounds	
All-purpose flour		¼ cup
Butter, melted		¼ cup
Garlic, minced		2 tablespoons
Salt		1½ tablespoons
Cracked black pepper		1½ tablespoons
Fresh herbs, minced, optional		
Oil, for frying		

Method

1. Mix all ingredients together in bowl. To serve: Form 2-ounce portions (loosely formed into patties). Fry in hot skillet or on flat-top with oil until very crispy, brown exterior and moist, cooked interior. Serve 2 or 3 patties per serving with chicken breast and ¼ cup tomato sauce, accompanied by green vegetables. Fresh herbs may be turned into the potato mixture for added flavor combinations: Tarragon, chives, oregano, thyme, basil.

Ingredients	Weight	Measure
SPICY GRILLED FREE RANGE CHICKEN BREAST: 24 breasts		
Olive oil		½ cup
Garlic, minced		3 tablespoons
Cracked black pepper		3 tablespoons
Red chili pepper flakes		1½ teaspoons
Chicken breasts, wing bone on, skinned	15 pounds	24
Oil, for grilling		

1. Mix olive oil, garlic, pepper and chili flakes to form paste.

2. Rub each 10-ounce breast with paste; cover; refrigerate 1 to 2 hours.
3. Oil grill top. As ordered, grill chicken breast until golden brown and cooked through. Remove from heat. Let stand 5 minutes before slicing breast and serving with tomato sauce underneath.

Ingredients	Weight	Measure
TOMATO-BASIL SAUCE: 1½ quarts sauce		
Olive oil		3 tablespoons
Onion, diced	15 ounces	3 cups
Cracked black pepper		3 tablespoons
Garlic, minced		2 tablespoons
Fennel seeds, crushed		2 tablespoons
Diced, peeled tomatoes (plum or Roma)	3 pounds	1½ quarts
Fresh basil, chopped		¾ cup
Salt		1½ tablespoons

1. In skillet, heat oil. Add onion and sauté until it starts to turn brown.
2. Add pepper, garlic and fennel and sauté 2 minutes.

3. Add tomatoes and cook 2 more minutes. Remove from heat.
4. Stir in basil and salt. Process in food processor until chunky. Serve warm.

FOR MORE INFORMATION OR ADDITIONAL RECIPES, CONTACT **THE IDAHO POTATO COMMISSION,** P.O. BOX 1068, BOISE, ID 83701.

Figure 8–2 *Sample recipe card II. (Courtesy of the Idaho Potato Commission.)*

Accurate and easy to read recipe cards are an important part of quality control. They help to assure a quality quantity food product and are instrumental in maintaining food cost control.

Production Sheet

The final step in reaching the goal of consistency in production is the production sheet. The information on a production sheet regarding the menu and the number of expected guests is taken from catering function sheets that present all of the details for a catering function (see Figure 8–4). For each menu item to be produced during a given meal service the production sheet lists the number of portions to be prepared, the food cost, and the selling price. After the function the actual number served is noted and the value of the waste from overproduction is calculated.

The production sheet also acts as a tool that allows management to organize the production of multiple parties, indicating where a duplication of menu items will make kitchen production more effective. Figure 8–5 shows a catering production sheet.

The menu in Figure 8–4 is posted on the production sheet seen in Figure 8–6 along with the menus for two other catering functions. The total

Recipe 116 ~ Poached Chicken Breast Princesse

| | | Portions: 24 | Portion size: ½ chicken breast
2 oz (60 ml) sauce
plus garnish |

U.S.	Metric	Ingredients	Procedure
24	24	Boneless, skinless half chicken breasts, from twelve 3-lb (1.2 kg) chickens	1. Select a baking pan just large enough to hold the chicken breasts in a single layer. Butter the inside of the pan.
as needed		Butter Salt White pepper	2. Season the chicken breasts with salt and pepper. Place them in the pan, presentation side (that is, the side that had the skin on) up.
¼ cup	60 ml	Lemon juice	
1½ qt approximately	1½ l	Chicken stock, cold	3. Sprinkle with the lemon juice and add enough chicken stock to barely cover the chicken.
			4. Cover the chicken with a buttered piece of parchment or waxed paper.
			5. Bring to a simmer on top of the stove. Finish poaching in a 325°F (165°C) oven or over low heat on the stove. Cooking time will be 5–10 minutes.
			6. Remove the chicken breasts from the liquid. Place them in a hotel pan, cover, and keep them warm.
3 oz	90 g	Beurre manié: Butter, softened	7. Reduce the poaching liquid over high heat to about 2½ pt (1.1 l).
3 oz	90 g	Flour	8. Knead the butter and flour together to make a beurre manié (p. 129).
2½ cups	6 dl	Heavy cream, hot Salt	
			9. With a wire whip, beat the beurre manié into the simmering stock to thicken it. Simmer a minute to cook out any starchy taste.
			10. Add the hot cream to the sauce. Season to taste.
72	72	Asparagus tips, cooked, hot	11. Place each chicken breast, well drained, on a plate and coat with 2 oz (60 ml) sauce. Garnish with 3 asparagus tips. Serve immediately.

Variations

116A. Alternative Method: Poach the chicken as in basic recipe. Plate immediately and coat with preprepared Suprême Sauce. Save poaching liquid for next day's sauce.

116B. Poached Chicken Breast Florentine: Poach the chicken as in basic recipe. Place each portion on a bed of buttered spinach (well drained). Coat with Mornay Sauce. Optional: Sprinkle with parmesan cheese and brown under the broiler.

116C. Other sauces may be used to coat poached chicken breasts, including
    Allemande
    Aurora
    Hungarian
    Ivory
    Mushroom

Figure 8–3 *Example of a professional cooking recipe.*

Listing:			Person in Charge:		
Organization:			Bus. Phone		Res. Phone
Person Calling:			Bill To:		
Address:			Organization:		
City	State	Zip	Address:		
Bus. Phone	Res. Phone		City	State	Zip

DAY & DATE

Function	DINNER	RECEPTION		
Room	LAFAYETTE	LAFAYETTE FOYER		
Time	7:00 P.M.	6:00 P.M.		
Attend.	175	175		
	Guar. 170 Set 180	Guar. Set	Guar. Set	Guar. Set

MENU:

Bibb & Frisee Salad

Filet of Sirloin
  pecan-basil crust
  Madagascar pepper sauce

Green Beans & pimento

Roasted Red Potatoes

Rolls & Butter

Grand Marnier Mousse

Coffee/Tea

NUMBER SERVED _____ CAPT. _____

SPECIAL INSTRUCTIONS:

- □ Auditorium ____
- □ Schoolroom ____
- □ Conference ____
- □ U Shape ____
- □ Rounds ____
- □ Hollow Sq. ____
- □ Lounge ____
- □ Head Table __8__
- □ Exh. Table ____
- □ Reg. Table ____
- □ Blackboard ____
- □ Easel ____
- □ Flip Chart ____
- □ Piano ____
- □ Platform ____
- □ Entert. ____
- □ Dance Floor ____
- □ Linen Color ____
- □ Flowers ____
- □ Incoming Mer. ____
- □ Candelabra ____
- □ Table Nos. ____
- □ Telephone ____
- □ Screen ____
- □ 16 MM ____
- □ 35 MM ____
- □ Overhead ____
- □ Other ____
- □ Projector Table ____
- □ Tape Recorder ____
- ☒ Standing Podium ☒ Mike
- □ Table Podium □ Mike
- □ Standing Mike ____
- □ Neck Mike ____
- □ Table Mike ____

- □ BAR _Cash Bar_
- □ HOUSE ____
- □ PREMIUM _Premium Brands_
- □ BEER ____
- □ BAR ____
- □ BARTENDER ____ 50.00
- □ CASHIER ____

- □ WINE (RECP.) ____
- □ WINE (MEAL) ____
- □ CHAMPAGNE ____
- □ MINERAL WATER ____
- □ SOFT DRINKS ____
- □ CORDIALS ____
- □ OTHER ____

Figure 8–4 *Catering function sheet I. (Courtesy of Hotel DuPont, Wilmington, DE.)*

ITEM	# OF ITEM TO BE SERVED	FOOD COST	TOTAL FOOD COST	ACTUAL # SERVED	ACTUAL FOOD COST	SELLING PRICE	TOTAL REVENUE	F.C. %	OVERAGE	VALUE	WASTE F.C. %
			TOTAL ESTIMATED CUSTOMER COUNT: 375			ACTUAL # SERVED: 381					
			DATE: TIME:			CHEF:					
Bibb Salad	375	$ 1.31	$491.25	380	$ 497.80						
Sirloin/F	175	$ 4.59	$803.20	180	$ 826.20						
Chicken Br	145	$ 2.88	$417.60	148	$ 426.24						
Salmon/F	55	$ 4.65	$255.75	53	$ 246.45						
Green Beans	375										
Red Potato	175										
Rice Pilaf	200										
Cream Puff	145	$ 1.31	$189.95	147	$ 192.57						
Mousse/GM	230	$ .88	$202.40	233	$ 205.04						
					$1568.10						

Figure 8–5 *Catering production sheet. (Source: Scanlon, Marketing by Menu, 2nd ed., 1990, p. 219.)*

ITEM	# OF ITEM TO BE SERVED	FOOD COST	TOTAL FOOD COST	ACTUAL # SERVED	ACTUAL FOOD COST	SELLING PRICE	TOTAL REVENUE	F.C. %	OVERAGE	VALUE	WASTE F.C. %
			TOTAL ESTIMATED CUSTOMER COUNT:			ACTUAL # SERVED:					
			DATE: TIME:			CHEF:					

Figure 8–6 *Prefunction production sheet.*

production count for this meal period is 375. Although three different entrées are being served, the salad and dessert are duplicated on two menus, the vegetables on all three, and the potatoes on two. Kitchen management for these three functions will be greatly simplified by the ability of the chef to review the combined menu requirements on the production sheet.

Both purchasing staff and the kitchen receive menu requirements well in advance of the functions. Two weeks of planning time is needed by most hotels and caterers. This allows last-minute functions, changes, and emergencies to be handled as efficiently and cost effectively as possible by written catering function change memos. Figure 8–7 is an example of a simplified function sheet format detailing the function arrangements that include the second menu on the production sheet in Figure 8–8. Many catering facilities do not provide extensive audio visual equipment. The simplified catering function sheet format provides space to list special requirements and is much less complicated for a wide range of service and production staff to read.

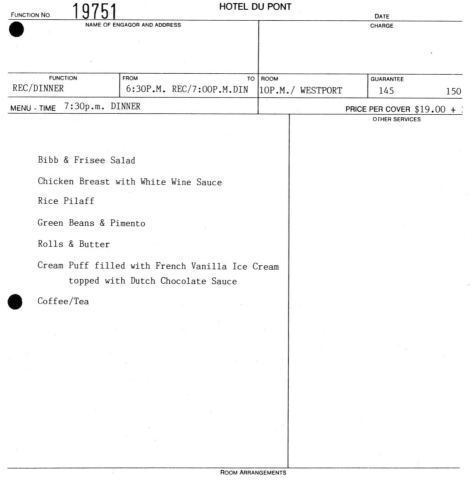

Figure 8–7 *Catering function format II. (Courtesy of Hotel DuPont, Wilmington, DE.)*

TOTAL ESTIMATED CUSTOMER COUNT: 375						ACTUAL # SERVED: 381					
DATE:　　TIME:						CHEF:					
ITEM	# OF ITEM TO BE SERVED	FOOD COST	TOTAL FOOD COST	ACTUAL # SERVED	ACTUAL FOOD COST	SELLING PRICE	TOTAL REVENUE	F.C. %	OVERAGE	VALUE	WASTE F.C. %
Bibb Salad	375	$ 1.31	$491.25	380	$ 497.80	$ 3.75	$ 1425.00	35	5	$ 18.75	
Sirloin/F	175	$ 4.59	$803.20	180	$ 826.20	$ 17.00	$ 3060.00	27	5	$ 85.00	
Chicken Br	145	$ 2.88	$417.60	148	$ 426.24	$11.50	$ 1702.00	25	3	$ 34.50	
Salmon/F	55	$ 4.65	$255.75	53	$ 246.45	$ 17.25	$ 914.25	27			
Green Beans	375										
Red Potato	175										
Rice Pilaf	200										
Cream Puff	145	$ 1.31	$189.95	147	$ 192.57	$ 3.75	$ 551.25	35	2	$ 7.50	
Mousse/GM	230	$ .88	$202.40	233	$ 205.04	$ 2.50	$ 582.50	35	3		
					$1568.10		$5175.00	30			

Figure 8–8　*Completed production sheet.*

Following production the actual number of items served as well as the actual food cost is entered in the appropriate columns. Total food cost and food cost percentage can now be calculated for each function as well as for the meal period by applying the food cost formula presented in Chapter Five.

$$\text{Total food cost} \div \text{Total revenue} = \text{Food cost }\%$$

Fluctuations in individual item costs as well as food cost percentages can be identified for each function. Overage can also be analyzed and its source traced to either a reduction in the number of expected covers or overproduction in the kitchen. Most catering functions have a guarantee policy that requires payment for a predetermined guest count, helping the caterer to absorb food costs when actual guest counts fall short of the expected numbers.

The completed production sheet in Figure 8–8 details the actual food costs, revenues, and food cost percentages for the meal period. For the sirloin filet, 175 portions were prepared with an individual food cost of $4.59 for a total food cost of $803.20. The actual number served was 180, for an actual food cost of $826.20. The selling price was $17.00 with total revenue of $3,060.00. Food cost percentage was calculated to be 27 percent. Production overage was 5 portions with a value of $85.00. The chef was required to locate 5 additional portions of sirloin filet to meet service needs. Total actual number served for the meal period was 381. Total actual food cost was $1,568.10 and total revenue $5,175.00. Overall food cost percentage for all three functions was 30 percent.

Sales Mix Evaluation

The sales mix is an evaluation of the sales pattern of major catering menu items. Item sales are recorded over an established period of time and evaluated on the basis of two major factors: popularity and contribution to sales. In Figure 8–9 the sales of appetizer, entrée, and dessert items for a hotel catering department are recorded. At the end of the period sales for each item are totaled and the percentage of sales that each item represents is calculated. The item is then ranked according to total sales to rate its popularity. The final step in the sales mix process is to calculate the contribution to profit of each item. Decisions are then made as to which items will remain and which will be deleted from the catering menu item list.

Presentation Controls

Presentation standards contain three important elements that contribute to the maintenance of a consistent quality in the appearance of the finished product as it is presented to the guest:

1. Size and type of dish or glass
2. Portion size
3. Garnish

The visual appearance of the portion size of food items must fit the plate size so that kitchen staff do not add to the portion in order to fill up the plate. Consistent portion size is also an important function in maintaining established food costs. Even though it can have a profound effect on both guest satisfaction and profitability, the final garnish is often overlooked in the development and production of menu items.

Plate architecture is the design of the actual placement of food items on the plate. The primary purpose of plate architecture is to establish a standard presentation which, when photographed, accompanies the recipe card as a guide for the final step in the production process. Figure 8–10 is an example of the design sketch of the plate and Figure 8–11 is a photograph of the final plate setup.

Many catered functions, particularly business occasions, are often attended by the same people on a routine basis. Whether as a guest or as a customer these people develop a level of expectation for the quality of food and service of a catering business. Maintaining a consistent presentation is an important part of meeting customer expectations.

Catering Menu Meeting

As an additional operational control, weekly catering menu meetings bring together key management personnel to review upcoming functions. Communication between production and service staff is necessary to successfully carry out a number of catering functions within the same time period.

Catering Menu Sales Mix

Items: appetizer, entree, dessert   *Period:* _____

	Week 1	Week 2	Week 3	Week 4	Week 5
shrimp cocktail					
crabmeat mshrms					
vegetable crudite					
escargot					
soup: French					
soup: lobster bisque					
fruit w/yogurt					
Total Appetizer					
Entree:					
N.Y. sirloin					
chicken veronica					
veal oscar					
filet mignon					
prime rib					
swordfish					
stuffed flounder					
Total Entree:					
Dessert:					
mousse					
chambard cake					
cheesecake					
derby pie					
Total Dessert					

Figure 8–9   *Catering menu sales mix.*

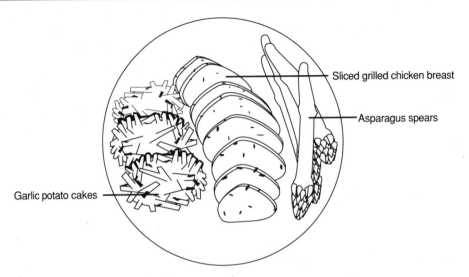

Figure 8–10   *Plate architecture design. (Courtesy of the Idaho Potato Commission.)*

Identifying possible logistical problems for multiple functions, such as shortages in service staff, timing schedules between functions, and availability of table service equipment, linens, tables, and chairs, is an important goal of menu meetings.

Figure 8–11   *Plate architecture photograph. (Courtesy of the Idaho Potato Commission.)*

Purchasing is another area where menu meetings are often highly effective. Function sheets are reviewed with the chef, purchasing agent, maitre d' and sales staff. Current fluctuations in the prices of main menu items such as beef and fish can be recognized and steps taken to restructure menus to account for increased food costs.

Catering menu meetings should be held on a regularly scheduled basis as an ongoing method of operational controls. When key staff understand that they will have a formal means of discussing areas of interest and concern with other staff members they will use this time effectively and reduce haphazard communications.

Beverage Controls

Profitable beverage management requires many of the same controls as are applied to food production.

Standard Recipe

A thorough knowledge of established beverage recipes is important if the desired taste, texture, and yield are to be consistently achieved. It is important for management to issue a standard beverage recipe guide to enable the same beverage to be produced at the same time at a variety of different locations by different bartenders. The beverage recipes in Figure 8–12 are examples of two different types of alcohol-based beverages.

Martini

Measure	Ingredient	Directions
1 ¾ ounces ¾ ounces	Gin Vermouth (dry) Olive or Lemon zest	1. Chill stemmed glass 2. Fill mixing glass half full with ice 3. Pour gin into mixing glass 4. Pour vermouth into mixing glass 5. Using stirer gently mix liquids 6. Using spring strainer pour ingredients into chilled glass 7. Add olive or lemon zest

Whiskey Sour

Measure	Ingredient	Directions
1 ½ ounces 2 ounces	Whiskey Lemon mix Cherry	1. Fill mixing glass half full with ice 2. Pour lemon mix into mixing glass 3. Pour whiskey into mixing glass 4. Using metal cup as cover shake in a quick even movement and turn over 5. Using spring strainer pour ingredients into sour glass 6. Add cherry

Figure 8–12 *Beverage recipes.*

Purchasing

Purchasing alcoholic beverages requires a knowledge of spirits and wines. A purchasing agent must have a thorough knowledge of types of wines, vintages, and the appropriate marriage of wines and foods in order to construct a well-developed wine list. Maintaining an adequate inventory is the most important factor of profitable beverage purchasing. Stock levels must be held as low as possible while still providing sufficient beverages to service functions.

Alcoholic beverage purchasing specifications should include the following information:

1. Product name with preferred brand names listed
2. Quantity to be purchased, such as liter, fifth, gallon
3. Indication of proof, such as 80% proof, 100% proof, or 175% proof
4. Unit by which prices are quoted, such as case, keg, or barrel

The principal advantage to beverage purchasing for catering operations is that beverage requirements can be estimated well in advance of functions. Catering functions generally maintain standard bars, limiting the varieties of drinks and liquors served. A standard catering bar will usually offer drinks made from scotch, gin, vodka, rye, bourbon, and wine. Additions to this selection are made at the discretion of the customer. Liqueurs are offered only at special functions.

Presentation

Beverage presentation is supported by an established selection of glassware that is associated with specific wines and drinks. Often the shape of the bowl of the glass has been developed to enhance the "bouquet," or supply adequate space for ice and liquid. Garniture can add to the customer's perceived value of the drink by creating a pleasing presentation.

Summary

Three sets of controls important to establish in a foodservice operation cover the areas of purchasing, production, and presentation. The goal of these controls is to achieve a consistent quality of food and beverage production and service. Quality controls must be implemented to carry out the steps necessary to achieve and maintain the standards set by the operation.

Successful purchasing requires that specifications be developed for each food item, identifying the desired quality and quantity of the food product. These specifications provide the basis for the bidding process, ensuring that the highest quality product is purchased for the lowest price.

Successful production requires that a standard recipe card be developed for every menu item as a guideline to produce a food product with a consistent taste, texture, and yield. The production sheet outlines each menu item to be prepared prior to production and contains a record of the actual amounts produced and served as well as total costs and sales revenues. The catering sales mix uses the information from the production sheet to evaluate the sales and profitability of each menu item.

Successful presentation requires that the plate size, portion size, and garnish for each menu item be established in order to serve the same product on a consistent basis.

Profitable beverage management employs many of the same operational controls as food production, including beverage specifications, drink recipes, and established presentational styles.

9

Computerized Catering Menu Management

Computer applications in all types of foodservice operations are essential to the overall success of the business. The consistent and thorough application of management principles to restaurant and catering operations is necessary in order to generate the profits required for continued operations. Unfortunately, food service operators often choose to sidestep management principles in an effort to handle the operational controls of the business with manual reporting systems.

Computer systems used by catering operations can range from simple to complex and from inexpensive to expensive. Whereas restaurant operations require front-of-the-house terminals, keyboards, and printers, independent catering operations can limit their investment to a microcomputer and software programs. Caterers with larger volumes of business may decide to purchase laser printers, modems, additional terminals, and keyboards. The type of operation influences whether investment in desktop publishing is worthwhile. Restaurants entering the catering business with computerized foodservice systems already in place can integrate additional compatible software systems to expand their current operations.

The application of computer foodservice management systems to catering menu management offers the opportunity to integrate existing institutional computer business systems into a retail foodservice environment. Institutional/business foodservice operations are involved with a variety of foodservice functions catering to large groups in environments ranging from schools and hospitals to businesses offering their employees cafeterias and dining rooms on the premises. These operations are often required to provide catering services in addition to their established food services. Common to both retail catering operations and institutional/business and industry operations is advance knowledge of menu requirements, volume production needs, and purchasing requirements. The application of software systems specifically designed for volume feeding can greatly enhance the effectiveness of catering menu management. Because many of these software programs are compatible with a variety of hardware systems, the catering department of a large hotel or restaurant can implement them just as effectively as an independent caterer or contract feeder. This chapter gives just a sampling of the forms available to management with a computer system. The forms illustrated in the subsequent figures were provided by CBORD Foodservice Management Systems in Ithaca, NY.

Purchasing

The application of a computer software system to the purchasing program of a catering operation allows a comprehensive analysis of vendor bids and quotations as well as the ability to generate purchase orders based on final vendor selections.

Bid and quote forms are issued to vendors according to the specifications developed for every food product used in the operation. As discussed in Chapter Eight, these specifications must detail the exact requirements for the food product. The bid and quote form in Figure 9–1 is for produce. The specification identifies the grade, purchase unit, the purchase unit weight, the quantity to be ordered and the item file number.

```
REPORT#: 255   * * * CBORD FOODSERVICE MANAGEMENT SYSTEMS * * *        PAGE:   1
OPTION : 7.3.2.3.8.    MENU MANAGEMENT SYSTEM - V4.1.35Z              NOV 05 90
                       THE CBORD GROUP TRAINING CENTER                 1511 HOURS
                             BID AND QUOTE FORM


Vendor      : _____
Purchase Group: 07 WEEKLY PRODUCE BID
...........................................................................................

                    Purchase   Purchase Order   Item Bid Price Exp                     Vendor
Item Name    Grade  Unit       Unit Wgt Quantity Nmbr (Per PU)  Date  Yield  Brand Name Order #
...........................................................................................

APPLES TABLE    A      LB          1      150    405 <_____><_____><____><RED DELICIOUS    ><_____>
2 1/4" MIN DIA FIRM FLESH  BRIGHT SKIN GOOD AROMA
CARTON OF 120'S OR 125'S 47 LBS/CARTON 5 LB TARE


AVOCADO         A    AVOCADO       1      100    408 <_____><_____><____><_____><_____>
3-4" DIA LARGE GREEN FRUIT YIELDING GENTLY WHEN PRESSED
SEED RATTLES 8-12 OZ EACH  16-28/FLAT
16 LBS/FLAT  3 LBS TARE

BANANAS         A      LB          1      200    402 <_____><_____><____><CHIQUITA         ><_____>
RIPE  APPROX 6" LENGTH   CUT HANDS PRACTICALLY FREE FROM
SCARS BRUISES AND UNBROKEN SKIN  3/LB
45 LBS/CARTON  5 LBS TARE

BLUEBERRIES     A     PINT         2       40   3967 <_____><_____><____><_____><_____>
90-130 PER PINT;  RIPE AND DRY, FREE FROM STICKS, LEAVES
AND STEMS


CABBAGE GREEN   A      LB          1      175    388 <_____><_____><____><_____><_____>.
1 1/2 LBS MIN  FIRM SOLID AND HEAVY FOR SIZE  FREE FROM
DISCOLORATION 4 LEAVES WRAPPER


CANTALOUPES     A      LB          1       25    409 <_____><_____><____><_____><_____>
5" MIN DIA UNIFORM SIZE WELL DEVELOPED NETTING COVERING
YELLOWISH SKIN SHOULD BE HEAVY FOR THEIR SIZE  FIRM
CRATE 36'S

CARROTS         A      LB          1      130    393 <_____><_____><____><_____><_____>
4" MIN LENGTH 1 1/2" DIA AT TOP  FIRM SMOOTH UNIFORM AND FAIRLY
WELL COLORED


CARROTS         A      LB          1      175   3907 <_____><_____><____><_____><_____>
4" MIN LENGTH 1 1/2" DIA AT TOP  FIRM SMOOTH UNIFORM AND FAIRLY
WELL COLORED


CELERY          A      LB          1      250    387 <_____><_____><____><_____><_____>
ORIGINAL CRATES EASTERN 4 DOZ
CRISP BRITTLE FREE FROM PITHYNESS AND BLACK HEARTS WELL
DEVELOPED AND WELL FORMED

--------------------------------------------------------------------------------------
```

Figure 9–1   *Bid and quote form I.*

For example, the written notes specify an apple with a minimum diameter of $2\frac{1}{4}$ inches. The apple must be firm to the touch, not spongy or soft, the outer skin must be bright in color, and the fruit must have a good aroma before being cut. This apple should be purchased in cartons containing 120 to 125 pieces with a weight of approximately 47 pounds to the case. Package size for purchase should not weigh less than 5 pounds. The additional identification noted under brand name, Red Delicious, indicates the type of apple to be purchased.

The bid and quote form in Figure 9–1 is sent to each vendor that is invited to bid on a particular "purchase group," which in this example is produce. The vendor completes the form by writing its name at the top and filling in the rest of the information on the form. The form is returned to the purchasing department where the information is entered into the software system. The system will analyze several vendor quotes and print a number of reports, permitting the purchasing department to make decisions based on quality, price, brand, and yield. Once a vendor has been selected for each product, the software system will update the appropriate menu item files with the new purchase price, automatically adjusting recipe costs. Yield on this form refers to the amount of usable product that will be obtained from this purchase. The vendor order number is the number assigned to each vendor by the purchasing department.

When all of the bids have been gathered, a vendor is chosen and entered on the form in Figure 9–1 along with the price and brand name. PG refers to the product group under which the item is listed. 501 is the number assigned to that specification. Item number is the identification number for that particular food item. User item number refers to the designated use of the product.

The final step in the purchasing process is to generate a purchase order for each vendor who has been selected in the bidding process. The purchase order in Figure 9–2 indicates the items that Costa Produce has been designated to provide. The term *NET 10* indicates that the foodservice operation will pay this bill in full in 10 days. The item number, name, brand name, and grade are carried over from the bid and quote form (Figure 9–1). The quantity to be ordered, the purchase unit, and the vendor's order number are also indicated.

Inventory

Tracking and valuing inventory manually is a time-consuming and tedious task that is difficult to accomplish efficiently. However, computerizing the inventory process allows management to be aware of the current inventory status on a daily or even hourly basis. Projected on-hand balances can be compared to actual balances and the value of inventory can be continuously calculated. In addition, management can identify instances when the actual use of a product varies from the projected production requirements.

The inventory item status report in Figure 9–3 identifies each item by product number and name. Storage location codes for freezers, walk-in boxes,

```
REPORT#: 248   * * * CBORD FOODSERVICE MANAGEMENT SYSTEMS * * *        PAGE:   1
OPTION : 7.3.2.4.2.    MENU MANAGEMENT SYSTEM - V4.1.35Z              NOV 05 90
                       THE CBORD GROUP TRAINING CENTER                1506 HOURS
                            PURCHASE ORDER

Vendor : 12 COSTA PRODUCE
Address: 123 STATE STREET                           Terms   : NET 10
                                                    Lead Time:

      ITHACA        NY 14850
..................................................................................
-- Item --          Brand        Grade   Vendor    Order  Purchase   Price ------- Extended -------
Nmbr Name           Name                 Order #   Quantity Unit                  Cost    Weight
..................................................................................

406 ORANGES         SUNKIST         A    F-333____    10    88/CASE   12.50    125.00    270

409 CANTALOUPES                     A    F-4237___    25    LB         1.75     43.75     25

405 APPLES TABLE    RED DELICIOUS   A    F-439____   150    LB         0.68    102.00    150

408 AVOCADO                         A    F-654       100    AVOCADO    1.02    102.00    100

413 GARLIC FRESH                    A    F-890        25    LB         2.00     50.00     25

402 BANANAS         CHIQUITA        A    V-128____   200    LB         0.35     70.00    200

391 PARSLEY                         A    V-129____    15    LB         0.09      1.35     15

384 TOMATOES                        A    V-222____   300    LB         1.76    528.00    300

425 POTATOES WHOLE PEELED           A    V-231       120    30# BAG   12.00   1440.00   3600

386 CUCUMBERS                       A    V-238____   225    LB         0.90    202.50    225

379 LETTUCE ROMAINE                 A    V-337____   250    LB         0.61    152.50    250

380 ONIONS GREEN                    A    V-417        50    LB         0.28     14.00     50

374 LETTUCE ICEBERG                 A    V-447____   150    LB         0.51     76.50    150

 45 POTATOES SWEET                  A    V-539____   125    LB         0.42     52.50    125

387 CELERY                          A    V-542____   250    LB         0.32     80.00    250

385 PEPPERS GREEN                   A    V-555____   100    5 LB       3.50    350.00    500

734 MUSHROOMS WHITE                 A    V-655        50    LB         1.22     61.00     50

393 CARROTS                         A    V-870____   130    LB         0.59     76.70    130

274 TURNIP WHITE                    A    V-901____    25    LB         1.65     41.25     25

378 ENDIVE                          A    V-9993___   150    HEAD       0.58     87.00    150

..................................................................................
TOTAL(S)                                                          3656.05  6590.000
----------------------------------------------------------------------------------
```

Figure 9–2 *Purchase order.*

```
REPORT#: 287   * * * CBORD FOODSERVICE MANAGEMENT SYSTEMS * * *        PAGE:    1
OPTION : 7.5.1.9.1.    MENU MANAGEMENT SYSTEM - V4.1.35Z                SEP 19 9C
                       THE CBORD GROUP TRAINING CENTER                  1644 HOURS
                       INVENTORY ITEM STATUS REPORT
```

Storage Location: 01 FREEZER

Item Nmbr	Item Name	Storage Locations 01-02-03-04-05	Issue Unit	IU/PU	Stk Unit	On Hand	- Committed	=Available	On Order
541	BEANS LIMA FZ	01 _ _ _ _	20# BOX	1.00	P	25.00	5.00	20.00	5.00
469	BEEF CORNED INSIDE RND FZ	01 _ _ _ _	LB	1.00	_	35.00	6.00	29.00	15.00
3909	BEEF GROUND	01 _ _ _ _	5# CASE	1.00	L	45.00	18.00	27.00	30.00
444	BEEF GROUND BULK FZ	01 _ _ _ _	LB	1.00	L	210.00	_____	210.00	_____
440	BEEF LIVER SLICED FZ	01 _ _ _ _	LB	1.00	L	34.00	_____	34.00	_____
437	BEEF PATTIES FZ	01 _ _ _ _	LB	1.00	_	400.00	_____	400.00	_____
449	BEEF ROUND FZ	01 _ _ _ _	LB	1.00	_	25.00	_____	25.00	_____
451	BEEF STEAK BRAISING FZ	01 _ _ _ _	LB	1.00	_	25.00	_____	25.00	_____
446	BEEF STEAK RIBEYE 6 OZ FZ	01 _ _ _ _	LB	1.00	_	25.00	_____	25.00	_____
432	BEEF STEWING FZ	01 _ _ _ _	LB	1.00	_	25.00	_____	25.00	_____
542	BROCOLLI SPEARS FZ	01 _ _ _ _	2# BOX	12.00	I	25.00	15.00	10.00	120.00
543	BRUSSEL SPROUTS FZ	01 _ _ _ _	2.5# BOX	12.00	I	25.00	_____	25.00	_____
1727	CARROTS SLICED FZ	01 _ _ _ _	20# BOX	1.00	_	25.00	3.00	22.00	3.00
545	CAULIFLOWER FZ	01 _ _ _ _	2# BOX	12.00	I	25.00	25.00	_____	120.00
507	COD BRD SQUARES 3 OZ	01 _ _ _ _	6# BOX	6.00	I	10.00	10.00	_____	_____
506	COD FILLETS RAW FZ	01 _ _ _ _	5# BOX	10.00	I	_____	_____	_____	_____
505	COD WEDGIES BATTER DIPT	01 _ _ _ _	CASE	1.00	_	16.00	6.00	10.00	_____
539	CORN WHOLE FZ	01 _ _ _ _	2.5# BOX	12.00	I	25.00	18.00	7.00	60.00
49	CRUST PIZZA 14"	01 _ _ _ _	CASE	1.00	_	10.00	2.00	8.00	5.00
521	EGG WHITES FZ	01 _ _ _ _	30 LB	1.00	_	_____	_____	_____	_____
419	EGGS WHOLE FZ	01 _ _ _ _	LB	30.00	_	60.00	25.00	35.00	150.00
3957	FISH TURBOT FILLET UNB FZ	01 _ _ _ _	LB	1.00	_	25.00	10.00	15.00	_____
493	FRANKFURTERS BEEF 10/1 FZ	01 _ _ _ _	LB	1.00	_	143.00	_____	143.00	_____
464	HAM BONED AND TIED FZ	01 _ _ _ _	LB	1.00	_	26.00	_____	26.00	_____

Figure 9–3 *Inventory item status report.*

dry storage areas, and refrigerators indicate where the product should be. The product is issued from the central storeroom to each of these locations in the issue unit. The stock unit indicates whether the item is stored in quantities of the purchase unit or the issue unit.

Lima beans, for example, are received frozen (FZ). Location 01 indicates that they are stored in the freezer. They will be issued in 20-pound boxes and have a secondary packaging in 1-pound boxes. Twenty-five 20-pound boxes are on hand in freezers, but 5 boxes have been committed to production, leaving 20 boxes available. Five boxes have been ordered.

An inventory extension such as that pictured in Figure 9–4 can be generated to calculate a daily value of available inventory so management can accurately assess cash flow needs. The inventory listed is located in the main kitchen in produce cooler two. The item name and number are indicated as well as the unit by which the item is stocked and the number of units on hand. The price per stock unit multiplied times the number of units on hand gives the inventory value.

An example of another valuable computerized inventory report is the inventory variance report shown in Figure 9–5 which allows management to compare projected item usage against actual production usage. Production waste or theft can often be identified in this report. Because such losses can significantly affect the overall profitability of an operation, it is crucial for management to locate the source of the variance and eliminate it immediately. The total value of the variance for the 24 produce items in Figure 9–5 is $22.36. The major items in question are table apples, eggplant, green peppers and baking potatoes. The missing table apples and baking potatoes either spoiled and have been thrown out or have been consumed by staff. The eggplant and green peppers are very possibly being overportioned in the ingredient stage of recipe production.

Recipes

Recipe management is production control that contributes greatly to the consistency of the quantity and the quality of food production. Computer systems can construct on demand standard recipes based on any production volumes. These recipes then provide data for purchase requisitions and preproduction reports.

A computer-generated recipe format for beef stew is shown in Figure 9–6. The top half of the recipe form details supplemental information such as the yield (2.750 gallons), the number of portions (50), and the portion size (10 ounces). The selling price is listed at $1.25, with a portion cost of $.79 and a total recipe cost of $39.478. The prep time, cooking time, equipment needs, service temperature, and kitchen preparation area are also indicated. This recipe format is used as a reference by management to write the production recipe in Figure 9–7.

The bottom half of the recipe lists the ingredients grouped with directions. This section also includes nutritional information, preparation location, and ingredient costing information.

```
REPORT#: 36    * * * CBORD FOODSERVICE MANAGEMENT SYSTEMS * * *        PAGE:   3
OPTION : 8.1.2.        MENU MANAGEMENT SYSTEM - V4.1.35H               MAR 27 90
USER#  : 1              THE CBORD GROUP TRAINING CENTER                0923 HOURS
                             INVENTORY EXTENSION

Unit            : P 1 MAIN KITCHEN
Inventory Date  : 03/31/90
Storage Location: 2 PRODUCE COOLER
-----------------------------------------------------------------------------
Item Name                  Item Units      Stock       Price/      Inventory
                           Nmbr On Hand     Unit        Stk U       Value
-----------------------------------------------------------------------------

APPLES TABLE               405   50.000 LB            0.44          22.00

CABBAGE GREEN              388   55.000 LB            0.27          14.85

CANTALOUPES               409   10.000 LB            1.51          15.10

CARROTS                   393   50.000 LB            0.21          10.50

CELERY                    387   75.000 LB            0.32          24.00

CRANBERRIES               403    2.000 LB            0.95           1.90

CUCUMBERS                 386   25.000 LB            0.67          16.75

EGGPLANT                  416  100.000 LB            1.67         167.00

ENDIVE                    378   12.000 HEAD          0.58           6.96

GARLIC FRESH              413    5.000 LB            2.00          10.00

LEMONS                    412    2.000 CASE         20.00          40.00

LETTUCE ICEBERG           374   90.000 LB            0.42          37.80

LETTUCE ROMAINE           379   50.000 LB            0.74          37.00

LETTUCE SHREDDED          375   10.000 10# BAG       7.20          72.00

MUSHROOMS WHITE           734   25.000 LB            1.22          30.50

ONIONS GREEN              380   60.000 LB            0.28          16.80

ONIONS YELLOW             249    6.000 25# BAG       4.00          24.00

ORANGES                   406    5.000 88/CASE      10.67          53.35

PARSLEY                   391   10.000 LB            0.21           2.10

PEPPERS GREEN             385   25.000 5 LB          6.80         170.00

POTATOES BAKERS           410   75.000 LB            0.24          18.00

POTATOES WHOLE PEELED     425    3.000 30# BAG      12.00          36.00

RADISHES                  423   25.000 LB            1.06          26.50

TOMATOES                  384   50.000 LB            4.66         233.00

TURNIP WHITE              274   10.000 LB            0.55           5.50

-----------------------------------------------------------------------------
```

Figure 9–4 *Inventory extension.*

```
REPORT#: 278   * * * CBORD FOODSERVICE MANAGEMENT SYSTEMS * * *        PAGE:   :
OPTION : 7.5.1.9.4.   MENU MANAGEMENT SYSTEM - V4.1.35Z               SEP 26 9(
                      THE CBORD GROUP TRAINING CENTER                 1944 HOUR:
                          INVENTORY VARIANCE REPORT

Storage Location: 02 PRODUCE COOLER
----------------------------------------------------------------------------------------
Item  Item Name        -Purchase Unit--  --Physical Inventory--  -Calculated Inventory-  ---------- Variance ----------
Nmcr                   Name      Price   Quantity      Cost      Quantity      Cost      Quantity      Cost  -- % --
----------------------------------------------------------------------------------------

405 APPLES TABLE        LB        0.44      420       184.80        425       187.00        -5        -2.20   -1.19

408 AVOCADO             AVOCADO   1.02      316       322.32        310       316.20         6         6.12    1.90

3967 BLUEBERRIES        PINT      4.25       15        63.75         15        63.75         0         0.00    0.00

388 CABBAGE GREEN       LB        0.27      546       147.42        543       146.61         3         0.81    0.55

409 CANTALOUPES         LB        1.51       23        34.73         20        30.20         5         4.53   13.04

393 CARROTS             LB        0.21        9         1.89         10         2.10        -1        -0.21  -11.11

3907 CARROTS            LB        0.21       15         3.15         15         3.15         0         0.00    0.00

387 CELERY              LB        0.32       25         8.00         25         8.00         0         0.00    0.00

403 CRANBERRIES         LB        0.95       40        38.00         40        38.00         0         0.00    0.00

386 CUCUMBERS           LB        0.67       15        10.05         15        10.05         0         0.00    0.00

416 EGGPLANT            LB        1.67      725      1210.75        730      1219.10        -5        -8.35   -(..

378 ENDIVE              HEAD      0.58       15         8.70         15         8.70         0         0.00    0.00

413 GARLIC FRESH        LB        2.00        6        12.00          6        12.00         0         0.00    0.00

412 LEMONS              CASE     20.00        4        80.00          3        60.00         1        20.00   25.00

374 LETTUCE ICEBERG     LB        0.42      575       241.50        575       241.50         0         0.00    0.00

379 LETTUCE ROMAINE     LB        0.74      327       241.98        325       240.50         2         1.48    0.61

375 LETTUCE SHREDDED    10# BAG   7.20       20       144.00         20       144.00         0         0.00    0.00

734 MUSHROOMS WHITE     LB        1.22       26        31.72         25        30.50         1         1.22    3.85

380 ONIONS GREEN        LB        0.28       51        14.28         50        14.00         1         0.28    1.96

249 ONIONS YELLOW       25# BAG   4.00       16        64.00         15        60.00         1         4.00    6.25

406 ORANGES             88/CASE  10.67        4        42.68          4        42.68         0         0.00    0.00

391 PARSLEY             LB        0.21       10         2.10         10         2.10         0         0.00    0.00

385 PEPPERS GREEN       5 LB      6.80        9        61.20         10        68.00        -1        -6.80  -11.11

410 POTATOES BAKERS     LB        0.24      840       201.60        860       206.40       -20        -4.80   -(
```

Figure 9–5   *Inventory variance report.*

```
REPORT#:  5    * * * CBORD FOODSERVICE MANAGEMENT SYSTEMS * * *      PAGE:   1
OPTION : 3.5.1.         MENU MANAGEMENT SYSTEM - V4.1.35H             MAR 16 90
USER#  : 1             THE CBORD GROUP TRAINING CENTER                1131 HOURS
                              STANDARD RECIPE BOOK

------------------------------------------------------------------------------
Recipe Number: 1008        BEEF STEW                          BEEF STEW
------------------------------------------------------------------------------
User Rec #:L-22                    Menu Item  :HEARTY BEEF STEW
Plan Group:01 ENTREES BEEF VEAL & LAMB   Course     :04 ENTREES
Division  :                        Mn:Mx Batch:_____:_____
Recp Yield:   2.750 GAL            Round      :
          ------1------ ------2------   Adv Days   :
# of Ptns :     50.000       33.333   Prep Sched :DDDDDDD
Ptn Desc  :1 CUP       1 1/2 CUP      Prep Time  :1 HR
Ptn Size  :   10.00 OZ     15.00 OZ   Cook Time  :2.5 HR
CalcPtnWgt:   10.40                   Cook Temp  :
Sell Price:    1.25          1.55     Cook Equip :09 TILTING SKILLET
                                      Serve Uten :10 8 OZ LADLE
Prc Chg   :03/16/90     03/16/90      Serve Pan  :02 FULL STEAM PAN 4"
Targ FC_% :                           Yield/Pan  :
Trans Prc :      64.93       97.40    ServTemp   :185F
Ptn Cost  :      0.790       1.180    Prod Unit  :
FIDF Nmbr :                           Prep Area  :01 HOT FOOD
Total Cost:     39.478                Plate Area :
Last Updat:     03/16/90              Pop  Index :
Last Used :        /  /               Pref Flag  :
Used Menu :                           Evap Loss  :
Metric    :                           Cal/Ptn    :
Initials  :NSS                        Raw/Ck/Fill:
Status    :U
Type      :B
Diet Types:
------------------------------------------------------------------------------
FIDF   Ingredient Name              Wgt   Ext  Cost  Nutr  Nutr  R  I Prp Adv FOW  Item
Nmbr   (Instruction -->)   Quantity Unit in lbs Flg  Yld   Yld   ID  F C Area Prp  Cost
------------------------------------------------------------------------------

432   STEWING BEEF          15   LB  *  15      _   1    0.750 13036 Y  1 _  _-_ Y  32.700
  1   1. BROWN BEEF IN TILTING SKILLET.
  1
  0   WATER                 2    QT  *   4      _   1    1     0*    _  _ _  _-_ _   0
715   SALT                  2    TBSP *  0.053  _   1    1     89630 Y  1 _  _-_ _   0.017
710   BLACK PEPPER          2    TSP *   0.013  _   1    1     2030  Y  1 _  _-_ _   0.045
251   WORCESTERSHIRE SAUCE  0.750 CUP *  0.375  _   1    1     -2002 Y  1 _  _-_ _   0.116
 36   BAY LEAVES            2    LEAVES * 0.001 3   1    1     2004  Y  1 _  _-_ _   0.004
413   GARLIC, MINCED    *   2    CLOVES * 0.003 _   1    0.870 11215 Y  1 _  _-_ _   0.005
  1   2. ADD WATER AND SEASONINGS TO MEAT.  COVER AND SIMMER 1 HOUR.  ADD
  1      MORE WATER IF NECESSARY.
  1
425   POTATOES, DICED   *   4    LB  *   4      _   1    1     11367 Y  _ 05 09-1 _  1.400
1727  SLICED CARROTS        3    LB  *   3      _   1    0.900 11125 Y  _ _  _-_ _   1.368
249   ONIONS, DICED     *   1    LB  *   1      _   0.900 0.900 11283 Y  _ 05 09-1 _ 0.232
387   CELERY, DICED     *   1    LB  *   1      _   0.730 0.910 11143 Y  _ 05 09-1 _ 1.206
665   CRUSHED TOMATOES      1    #10 CAN * 6.150 _  1    0.900 11531 Y  _ _  _-_ _   2.273
  1   3. ADD VEGETABLES TO MEAT AND SIMMER 1 1/2 HOURS OR UNTIL VEGETABLES
  1      ARE DONE.
  1
673   FLOUR                 12   OZ  *   0.750  _   1    1     94390 Y  1 _  _-_ Y   0.114
  0   WATER                 1    QT  *   2      _   1    1     0*    _  _ _  _-_ _   0
  1   4. MIX FLOUR AND WATER UNTIL SMOOTH.  ADD TO STEW AND COOK UNTIL
  1      THICKENED.
------------------------------------------------------------------------------
SUBTOTAL NUMBER OF RECORDS PRINTED  24
------------------------------------------------------------------------------
```

Figure 9–6 *Recipe format I.*

```
REPORT#: 90    * * * CBORD FOODSERVICE MANAGEMENT SYSTEMS * * *       PAGE:    1
OPTION : 3.5.8.       MENU MANAGEMENT SYSTEM - V4.1.35H               MAR 16 90
USER#  : 1            THE CBORD GROUP TRAINING CENTER                 1247 HOURS
                             PRODUCTION RECIPE
FUNCTION NAME: MEALS ON WHEELS
          UNIT: MAIN KITCHEN
          DATE: FRIDAY    03/16/90
===========================================================================
1008  BEEF STEW                              YIELD    :    11.00 GAL
---------------------------------------------------------------------------
PORTIONS :     200   10.00 OZ     COOKING TIME : 2.5 HR
PORTION DESC : 1 CUP              COOKING TEMP :
PREP TIME: 1 HR                   COOKING UTEN : TILTING SKILLET
                                  SERVING PAN  : FULL STEAM PAN 4"
PREPARE MAIN BATCH   1 TIME(S)    SERVING UTEN : 8 OZ LADLE
---------------------------------------------------------------------------
      INGREDIENT          ------- MAIN BATCH -------- ------ PARTIAL BATCH ------
                                   QUANTITY                    QUANTITY
---------------------------------------------------------------------------
STEWING BEEF                  60 LBS
   1.   BROWN BEEF IN TILTING SKILLET.

WATER                         2 GAL
SALT                                        1/2   CUP
BLACK PEPPER                  2 TBSP    2          TSP
WORCESTERSHIRE SAUCE                     3         CUP
BAY LEAVES                               8         LEAF
GARLIC MINCED                            8         CLOVES
   2.   ADD WATER AND SEASONINGS TO MEAT.  COVER AND SIMMER 1 HOUR.  ADD
        MORE WATER IF NECESSARY.

POTATOES DICED                16 LBS
SLICED CARROTS                12 LBS
ONIONS DICED                   4 LBS
CELERY DICED                   4 LBS
CRUSHED TOMATOES                         4        #10 CAN
   3.   ADD VEGETABLES TO MEAT AND SIMMER 1 1/2 HOURS OR UNTIL VEGETABLES
        ARE DONE.

FLOUR                          3 LBS
WATER                          1 GAL
   4.   MIX FLOUR AND WATER UNTIL SMOOTH.  ADD TO STEW AND COOK UNTIL
        THICKENED.
```

Figure 9–7 *Recipe format II.*

The format in Figure 9–7 is a production recipe for beef stew. This format lists preparation time (1 hour), cooking time (2.5 hours), the primary piece of kitchen equipment needed for production (tilting skillet), the serving pan, and the serving utensils. The chef needs the equipment information in order to plan the total cooking load for the kitchen and determine if there are enough serving pieces and utensils to accommodate all of the food items being produced for service during that specific period.

A variation on these recipe formats is given in Figure 9–8. This recipe for coleslaw calculates the ingredient needs for different numbers of portions. For example, a yield of 25 portions of coleslaw requires 4 tablespoons and 2 teaspoons of cider vinegar; a yield of 300 portions requires 2 cups. This recipe format is useful when there are very limited directions and the item is prepared on a daily basis.

Production

Successful catering management requires that labor be used to maximum capabilities when available. Unlike restaurant service where preparation is scheduled for every meal service, catering functions are held only by prearrangement. Kitchen preparation staff is not scheduled on a regular basis for preproduction work. As a result it is necessary for the chef and kitchen managers to predetermine production needs, determining when kitchen staff can be used most effectively.

The worksheet in Figure 9–9 forecasts the produce needs for Tuesday, Wednesday, Thursday and Friday, estimating the per pound needs for each item on a daily basis. The worksheet in Figure 9–9 considers the vendors' ordering and delivery schedule, illustrating ordering and delivery dates. It is important to the effective management of an operation's cash flow and inventory control to schedule delivery dates as close to production time as possible. This information next appears on the advance preparation list in Figure 9–10. This report details the production needs for iceberg lettuce, romaine lettuce, and yellow onions to be prepared on Saturday, April 14, 1990, for use on Sunday, April 15, 1990. The form of preparation, the menu items in which the product will be included, and the meal service times are given. In addition the amount issued and the corresponding weight or measure are posted.

The information on the catering production sheet in Figure 8–7 is compiled by the computer in the service summary report in Figure 9–11. This report for luncheon details the production figures for each menu item listed. The production forecast can be compared with the actual portions prepared. Leftover portions are subtracted from the amount prepared to calculate the total number served. If the kitchen ran out of an item, the time at which it did so is recorded. The portion size, portion description, and selling price are also included along with the required serving equipment and utensils. This report is used as a guideline by the kitchen production staff as well as by the service staff. Kitchen production staff can make their work time more productive by following an outline of prepreparation production needs without constantly referring to management for instructions. Service staff can set up the required serving equipment.

Sales Mix

The sales mix application discussed in chapter eight evaluates catering menu items according to their popularity and contribution to sales. The form supplied in Figure 8–8 outlines a sales mix format on which management manually posts the required data. The computer-generated major group sales report in Figure 9–12 analyzes the sales of menu items by category for a given day and over a given period. The quantity sold is valued and the percentage of sales for each major group calculated against total menu sales. In this example

0007-COLESLAW   THE CBORD GROUP   PAGE: 8

PORTION SIZE 1:   4.00 OZ ( )   1/2 CUP   COOKING TIME :   PLAN GROUP : 16
SERVICE PAN :   COOKING TEMP :   PREPARATION TIME: DIVISION   : 0
SERVICE UTENSIL: COOKING UTENSIL: LAST UPDATE: 07/27/88

YIELDS ---> INGREDIENTS	25 PORTIONS 6.3 POUNDS	50 PORTIONS 12.5 POUNDS	100 PORTIONS 25.0 POUNDS	200 PORTIONS 50.0 POUNDS	300 PORTIONS 75.0 POUNDS	400 PORTIONS 100.0 POUNDS	500 PORTIONS 125.0 POUNDS	1000 PORTIONS 250.0 POUNDS
0097 CABBAGE	4 LBS	8 LBS	17 LBS	34 LBS	50 LBS	67 LBS	84 LBS	168 LBS
0154 MAYONAISE	1/4 1GAL	1/2 1GAL	3/4 1GAL	1 2/3 1GAL	2 1/2 1GAL	3 1/4 1GAL	4 1GAL	8 1GAL
0053 CIDER VINEGAR	4 TBSP 2 TSP	9 TBSP 2 TSP	1 CUP	2 CUP	1 QT	1 1/4 QT	1 1/2 QT	3 QT
0163 SUGAR	2 TBSP 1/2 TSP	4 TBSP 1 TSP	8 TBSP 2 TSP	1 CUP	2 CUP	2 CUP	3 CUP	1 1/4 QT
0176 MILK	1 2/3 CUP	3 1/4 CUP	1 QT 2 1/2 CUP	3 1/4 QT	1 GAL 3 CUP	1 GAL 2 1/2 QT	2 GAL	4 GAL

DIRECTIONS:

1. SHRED CABBAGE.
2. COMBINE CABBAGE WITH REMAINING INGREDIENTS.

Figure 9–8 Recipe format III.

```
REPORT#: 33    * * * CBORD FOODSERVICE MANAGEMENT SYSTEMS * * *        PAGE:   2
OPTION : 7.1.7.8.      MENU MANAGEMENT SYSTEM - V4.1.35H              MAR 23 90
USER#  : 1             THE CBORD GROUP TRAINING CENTER                1952 HOURS
                       FORECAST ORDER WORKSHEET

Production Unit: 1  MAIN KITCHEN                      Order Date : MONDAY   04/09/90
                                                     Vendor     : 12 COSTA PRODUCE
----------------------------------------------:------:------:------:------:------:------:------:--------:--------
                                        : 04/10 : 04/11 : 04/12 : 04/13 :      :      :      :
Vendor   FIDF Food Item Name    Purchase: TUE   : WED   : THU   : FRI   :      :      :      :
Order #  Nmbr                   Unit    : Amount: Amount: Amount: Amount: Amount: Amount: Amount :Total   : Cost
-------- Alternate Vendor       PU/Price:       :       :       :       :      :      :      :
----------------------------------------------:------:------:------:------:------:------:------:--------:--------
V-823    388 CABBAGE GREEN      LB          10     43      9     35                                97    26.19
                                0.27
V-956    387 CELERY             LB          19     22     33    126                               200    64.00
                                0.32
V-018    378 ENDIVE             HEAD        23     17     19     72                               131    75.98
                                0.58
F-890    413 GARLIC FRESH       LB                                                                  0     0.00
                                2.00
V-408    374 LETTUCE ICEBERG    LB          87     72     91    298                               548   230.16
                                0.42
V-397    379 LETTUCE ROMAINE    LB          30     21     23     88                               162   119.88
                                0.74
V-628    249 ONIONS YELLOW      25# BAG      2             1                                        3    12.00
                                4.00
F-837    406 ORANGES            88/CASE      5      2             6                                13   138.71
                                10.67
V-713    391 PARSLEY            LB                               3                                  3     0.63
                                0.21
V-231    425 POTATOES WHOLE PEELED 30# BAG  11      2      6     30                                49   588.00
                                12.00
V-755    384 TOMATOES           LB          17      5     21     37                                80   372.80
                                4.66
                                                                                          TOTAL      1628.35
```

Figure 9–9   *Forecast order worksheet.*

```
REPORT#: 35    * * * CBORD FOODSERVICE MANAGEMENT SYSTEMS * * *       PAGE:   4
OPTION : 7.1.7.6.        MENU MANAGEMENT SYSTEM - V4.1.35H            MAR 27 90
USER#  : 1               THE CBORD GROUP TRAINING CENTER              1355 HOURS
                         ADVANCE PREPARATION LIST


Production Unit: 1 MAIN KITCHEN              Prep Date: SATURDAY  04/14/90
                                            Prep Area: VEGETABLE PRE PREP


...............................................................................
Food Item ...................
    Preparation Technique
          ..............For use in............  ..... Production ----   Issue Amount  ..... Recipe Amount .....
               Recp# Recipe Name              Date     Meal
...............................................................................
LETTUCE ICEBERG
    CLEAN CORE AND TEAR

          331 TOSSED GREEN SALAD         04/15/90 2 LUNCH      69.61  HEADS    29 LBS
          331 TOSSED GREEN SALAD         04/15/90 3 DINNER     40.82  HEADS    17 LBS

    TOTAL CLEAN CORE AND TEAR                                 110.43  HEADS    47 LBS
    CLEAN CORE AND LEAF

          384 CHEF'S SALAD               04/15/90 3 DINNER      1.65  HEADS           11    OZS

    TOTAL CLEAN CORE AND LEAF                                   1.65  HEADS           11    OZS
    CUT INTO 8 WEDGES

          330 LETTUCE WEDGE SALAD        04/15/90 3 DINNER     28.79  HEADS    12 LBS

    TOTAL CUT INTO 8 WEDGES                                    28.79  HEADS    12 LBS

    ISSUE TOTAL FOR LETTUCE ICEBERG    (ITEM#: 374)BIN#0010   141     HEADS
...............................................................................
LETTUCE ROMAINE
    CLEAN CORE AND TEAR

          331 TOSSED GREEN SALAD         04/15/90 2 LUNCH      46.15  HEADS    15 LBS
          331 TOSSED GREEN SALAD         04/15/90 3 DINNER     27.69  HEADS     9 LBS

    TOTAL CLEAN CORE AND TEAR                                  73.84  HEADS    24 LBS

    ISSUE TOTAL FOR LETTUCE ROMAINE    (ITEM#: 379)BIN#0250    74     HEADS
...............................................................................
ONIONS YELLOW
    DICED

          1008 BEEF STEW                 04/15/90 0 ALL MEALS   0.13  25# BAG   3 LBS
          1002 TACOS                     04/15/90 3 DINNER      0.09  25# BAG   2 LBS
          1002 TACOS                     04/15/90 3 DINNER      0.18  25# BAG   4 LBS
          404 POTATO SALAD               04/15/90 3 DINNER      0.13  25# BAG   3 LBS
       TOTAL    3 DINNER                                        0.40  25# BAG   9 LBS

    TOTAL DICED                                                 0.53  25# BAG  12 LBS
    MINCED

          410 FRENCH DRESSING            04/15/90 0 ALL MEALS   0.04  25# BAG          15    OZS

    TOTAL MINCED                                                0.04  25# BAG          15    OZS

    ISSUE TOTAL FOR ONIONS YELLOW      (ITEM#: 249)BIN#0170     0.57  25# BAG
...............................................................................
-------------------------------------------------------------------------------
NOTES: 1. ISSUE TOTALS ARE ROUNDED
```

Figure 9–10   *Advance preparation list.*

```
REPORT#: 28   * * * CBORD FOODSERVICE MANAGEMENT SYSTEMS * * *      PAGE:   3
OPTION : 7.1.5.1.6.   MENU MANAGEMENT SYSTEM - V4.1.35H             MAR 20 90
USER#  : 1            THE CBORD GROUP TRAINING CENTER               1448 HOURS
                      SERVICE SUMMARY REPORT

                                                          Cy-Mo-Wk:  0000
  Unit  : 2   CAFETERIA               Day :SUNDAY  04/15/90      Cust Cnt: 525
                                      Meal:2  LUNCH             Act Cust: _____
-------------------------------------------------------------------------------
-- Recipe --              Serving Utensil   ------------Portions------------   Time    Ptn Size  Sell
Nmbr Name                 Serving Pan       Fcst Prepared - Leftover= Served   Ran Out Ptn Desc  Price
-------------------------------------------------------------------------------
  1  BRK FRUITS AND JUICES
 596 FRUIT CUP                              352<_____>-<_____>=<_____> <_____>   5.00   0.60
                          FRUIT DISH                                              1/2 CUP
 790 TOMATO JUICE COCKTAIL                  158<_____>-<_____>=<_____> <_____>   5.00   0.75
                                                                                 5 OZV
  4  ENTREES
 896 BAKED HAM            TONGS             294<_____>-<_____>=<_____> <_____>   6.00   1.85
                          FULL STEAM PAN 2 1/2"                                   6 SLICES
  94 ROAST TURKEY                           131<_____>-<_____>=<_____> <_____>   6.00   1.55
                                                                                 6 SLICES
1008 BEEF STEW            8 OZ LADLE          79<_____>-<_____>=<_____> <_____>  15.00   1.55
                          FULL STEAM PAN 4"                                       1 1/2 CUP
  5  STARCHES
 229 POTATOES AU GRATIN                      257<_____>-<_____>=<_____> <_____>   6.00   0.55
                          DISPOSABLE HALF PAN 4"                                  1/2 CUP
 226 MASHED POTATOES                         268<_____>-<_____>=<_____> <_____>   6.00   0.55
                          1 GALLON BAG                                            1/2 CUP
  6  VEGETABLES
 255 GREEN BEANS PARISIENNE                  331<_____>-<_____>=<_____> <_____>   5.00   0.65
                          1 GALLON BAG                                            1/2 CUP
 910 CAULIFLOWER AU GRATIN SOLID SPOON       147<_____>-<_____>=<_____> <_____>   5.00   0.55
                          DISPOSABLE HALF PAN 4"                                  1/2 CUP
  7  SALADS
 331 TOSSED GREEN SALAD                      399<_____>-<_____>=<_____> <_____>   2.00   0.45
                          SMALL SALAD BOWL                                        1 CUP
 410 FRENCH DRESSING                         399<_____>-<_____>=<_____> <_____>   1.00   0.25
                                                                                 1 OZV
  8  BREADS
 924 DINNER ROLLS                            289<_____>-<_____>=<_____> <_____>   4.00   0.55
                          COOKIE BAG                                              2 ROLLS
  9  DESSERTS
 457 LEMON CHIFFON PIE                        236<_____>-<_____>=<_____> <_____>   3.50   0.75
                          9" PIE PAN                                              1/6 PIE
 500 ANGEL FOOD CAKE                         105<_____>-<_____>=<_____> <_____>   1.25   0.60
                                                                                 1/13 CAKE
 10  BEVERAGES
 865 MILK                                    446<_____>-<_____>=<_____> <_____>   8.00   0.55
                                                                                 1 CONTAINER
 858 COFFEE                                  289<_____>-<_____>=<_____> <_____>   8.00   0.35
                                                                                 1 CUP
 11  CONDIMENTS
 776 IND CREAMERS                            656<_____>-<_____>=<_____> <_____>   0.10   0.00
 217 IND PEPPER                              289<_____>-<_____>=<_____> <_____>   0.05   0.00
 748 IND SALT                                341<_____>-<_____>=<_____> <_____>   0.03   0.00
-------------------------------------------------------------------------------
```

Figure 9–11 *Service summary report.*

```
---------------------------------------------------------------------------------
 MAJOR GROUP SALES REPORT              MICROS 4700 VERSION 3.00 SYSTEM          02-SEP-88  05:53 PM    Page   1
 ALL                                            RESTAURANT                                    C: PRIMARY DATABASE
---------------------------------------------------------------------------------
 EXAMINE          POSTED 02-Sep-88 05:28pm   CURRENT RESET 0002 02-Sep-88 02:32am   TO-DATE RESET 0001 01-Sep-88 02:35am

                             CURRENT TOTALS                          TO-DATE TOTALS
                     ------------------------------------   ------------------------------------
 Grp  Description     Qty     %Qty     Total    %Total       Qty     %Qty     Total    %Total
                     Sold    Sold      Sold      Sold        Sold    Sold      Sold      Sold

   1  APPETIZERS       50    17.99    173.29    18.67         75    13.25    270.91    14.76
   2  LIGHT ENTREES   108    38.85    539.50    58.13        228    40.28  1,130.60    61.58

        Subtotal      158    56.83    712.79    76.81        303    53.53  1,401.51    76.34

  11  DESSERTS         11     3.96     31.57     3.40         21     3.71     68.32     3.72

        Subtotal       11     3.96     31.57     3.40         21     3.71     68.32     3.72

  16  BEER             27     9.71     51.30     5.53         49     8.66     93.10     5.07
  17  WINE             14     5.04     56.88     6.13         22     3.89     79.96     4.36
  18  BEVERAGES        68    24.46     75.50     8.14        171    30.21    193.00    10.51

        Subtotal      109    39.21    183.68    19.79        242    42.76    366.06    19.94

        Total Sales   278             928.04                 566            1,835.89
```

Figure 9–12 *Major group sales report.*

11 desserts were sold, representing 3.96 percent of the quantity sold for the period posted. Revenues from dessert sales totaled $31.57, or 3.40 percent of total sales posted.

The family group sales report in Figure 9–13 breaks this information down further into family groups such as soups, salads, and sandwiches.

Costing

Costing is an important function of any menu program. Unless sales prices reflect accurate product costs then forecasted profits will not be achieved and revenue will not be available to meet ongoing budget needs. Accurate costing begins with purchasing. Up-to-date prices must be available for each food item for management to monitor cost fluctuations on a daily and weekly basis. The product cost sheet in Figure 9–14 lists current purchasing information for meat items. The unit of issue, purchase unit, and weight are listed as well as the inventory on hand. The purchase unit price multiplied times the number on hand is the replacement value on the current stock of this item. The sheet also contains the average purchase price for this item and the average value of the current stock. The total purchases of this product within the report period are listed as PTD $. The cost of goods represents the value of the amount of the food item used during the report period.

```
FAMILY GROUP SALES REPORT              MICROS 4700 VERSION 3.00 SYSTEM        02-SEP-88  05:53 PM   Page   1
ALL                                              RESTAURANT                                C: PRIMARY DATABASE
---------------------------------------------------------------------------------------------------------
EXAMINE           POSTED 02-Sep-88 05:28pm   CURRENT RESET 0002 02-Sep-88 02:33am   TO-DATE RESET 0001 01-Sep-88 02:35am

                              CURRENT TOTALS                              TO-DATE TOTALS
                    -------------------------------------    -------------------------------------
Grp  Description       Qty     %Qty      Total   %Total        Qty     %Qty      Total    %Total
                      Sold     Sold       Sold     Sold        Sold     Sold      Sold      Sold

   2  DINING RM APPTZR    13     4.68     68.79     7.41         22     3.89     120.41     6.56

        Subtotal         13     4.68     68.79     7.41         22     3.89     120.41     6.56

   3  SOUPS              37    13.31    104.50    11.26         53     9.36     150.50     8.20
   4  SALADS             28    10.07    170.80    18.40         55     9.72     326.85    17.80
   6  SANDWICHES         59    21.22    270.70    29.17        121    21.38     558.25    30.41

        Subtotal        124    44.60    546.00    58.83        229    40.46   1,035.60    56.41

   7  EGGS               21     7.55     98.00    10.56         52     9.19     245.50    13.37

        Subtotal         21     7.55     98.00    10.56         52     9.19     245.50    13.37

  20  DESSERTS           11     3.96     31.57     3.40         21     3.71      68.32     3.72

        Subtotal         11     3.96     31.57     3.40         21     3.71      68.32     3.72

  30  BEVERAGES          68    24.46     75.50     8.14        171    30.21     193.00    10.51

        Subtotal         68    24.46     75.50     8.14        171    30.21     193.00    10.51

  32  BOTTLED BEER       27     9.71     51.30     5.53         49     8.66      93.10     5.07

        Subtotal         27     9.71     51.30     5.53         49     8.66      93.10     5.07

  36  HOUSE WINE         13     4.68     39.74     4.28         21     3.71      62.82     3.42
  37  BTLD WINE-CHAMP.    1     0.36     17.14     1.85          1     0.18      17.14     0.93

        Subtotal         14     5.04     56.88     6.13         22     3.89      79.96     4.36

      Total Sales       278             928.04                566            1,835.89
```

Figure 9–13 *Family group sales report.*

For example, 235 pounds of inside round corned beef were purchased for $2.90 per pound. The average price per pound is $3.08 indicating a savings of 18 cents per pound or a total of $42.30 on the total inventory.

				Replace
on hand		PU price		value
235	×	2.90	=	681.50

				WGT AVG
on hand		WGT AVG		value
235	×	3.087	=	725.47

```
REPORT#: 144   * * * CBORD FOODSERVICE MANAGEMENT SYSTEMS * * *          PAGE:    1
OPTION : 7.5.1.9.6.     MENU MANAGEMENT SYSTEM - V4.1.35Z               SEP 26 90
                      THE CBORD GROUP TRAINING CENTER                   0909 HOURS
                             PRODUCT COST SHEET
```

PRODUCT GROUP: 01 MEAT

Inv Item Name	Issue Unit	PU Wgt	Purch Unit	On Hand	Pu Price	Replace Value	Wgt Avg Price	Wgt Avg Value	Purchs PTD $	Cost of Goods
469 BEEF CORNED INSIDE RND FZ	LB	1	LB	235	2.90	681.50	3.087	725.47	182.75	77.31
3909 BEEF GROUND	5# CASE	5	5# CASE	27	7.20	194.40	7.302	197.16	199.20	146.05
444 BEEF GROUND BULK FZ	LB	1	LB	220	1.29	283.80	1.299	285.69	286.80	51.82
440 BEEF LIVER SLICED FZ	LB	1	LB	80	0.89	71.20	0.832	66.53	30.40	12.44
437 BEEF PATTIES FZ	LB	1	LB	320	1.59	508.80	1.548	495.49	353.80	193.69
449 BEEF ROUND FZ	LB	1	LB	55	3.24	178.20	3.108	170.93	111.15	46.61
451 BEEF STEAK BRAISING FZ	LB	1	LB	45	1.90	85.50	1.871	84.18	47.50	28.06
446 BEEF STEAK RIBEYE 6 OZ FZ	LB	1	LB	100	3.29	329.00	3.389	338.87	220.15	101.60
432 BEEF STEWING FZ	LB	1	LB	95	0.92	87.40	0.833	79.09	30.45	41.61
498 BOLOGNA ALL BEEF	LB	1	LB	40	1.59	63.60	1.380	55.22	36.75	13.80
493 FRANKFURTERS BEEF 10/1 FZ	LB	1	LB	255	0.79	201.45	0.733	186.89	54.30	40.19
464 HAM BONED AND TIED FZ	LB	1	LB	70	2.39	167.30	2.366	165.62	169.25	59.13
458 HAM CANNED	5 LB CAN	5	5 LB CAN	25	14.29	357.25	15.003	375.08	526.15	300.08
459 LAMB LEG BNLS FZ	LB	1	LB	30	3.24	97.20	3.133	93.98	79.70	31.31
494 PORK BACON SLICED FZ	LB	1	LB	30	2.29	68.70	2.283	68.49	80.00	91.31
491 PORK CHOPS C-CUT 5 OZS FZ	LB	1	LB	30	2.89	86.70	2.862	85.86	73.60	57.24
462 PORK LOIN BNLS FZ	LB	1	LB	75	3.29	246.75	3.198	239.87	153.55	143.95
499 SALAMI HARD	LB	1	LB	70	1.39	97.30	1.287	90.08	33.25	25.71
465 SAUSAGE BREAKFAST LINK FZ	LB	1	LB	65	1.29	83.85	1.149	74.67	54.45	22.97
275 VEAL CUTLETS	LB	1	LB	65	6.79	441.35	6.845	444.90	250.15	68.43
467 VEAL CUTLETS BRD FZ	LB	1	LB	35	3.29	115.15	3.151	110.30	115.15	126.07
468 VEAL ROAST BNLS FZ	LB	1	LB	55	4.19	230.45	4.102	225.61	84.40	41.04
TOTAL(S)						4676.85		4659.98	3172.90	1720.42

SUBTOTAL NUMBER OF RECORDS PRINTED 22

Figure 9–14 *Product cost sheet.*

This report is used to assist in determining the preferred method of valuing inventory. WGT AVG is most often used because it is less affected by market price fluctuations.

Menu selection for business catering functions is often left to catering management. The information posted on the alphabetic menu planner report in Figure 9–15 allows management to quickly review current food costs, selling prices, and food cost percentages for major menu items and make selections on the basis of an item's contribution to overall profit. In this report two portion sizes are offered for each menu item.

The information from the menu planner is consolidated onto the menu postcost report form in Figure 9–16. Management can evaluate the sales of individual menu items and identify items and menu categories that need adjustment. For example, 131 portions of roast turkey were forecasted at $1.55 per portion for total sales of $203.05. The cost for this item was projected at $.89 per portion, resulting in a food cost percentage of 57.42 percent. The gross margin on this item is $.66 per portion or $86.46 total.

```
REPORT#: 66     * * * CBORD FOODSERVICE MANAGEMENT SYSTEMS * * *        PAGE:    1
OPTION : 4.4.           MENU MANAGEMENT SYSTEM - V4.1.35H                MAR 16 90
USER#  : 1              THE CBORD GROUP TRAINING CENTER                  1408 HOURS
                       ALPHABETIC MENU PLANNER


Menu-Planning Group: 01 ENTREES BEEF VEAL & LAMB
-----------------------------------------------------------------------------------------------
-- Recipe --              Portion  Selling Portion  Gross   Food  Portion Selling Portion  Gross   Food
Nmbr Name                 Size 1   Price 1 Cost 1   Margin 1 Cost%1 Size 2  Price 2 Cost 2  Margin 2 Cost%2
-----------------------------------------------------------------------------------------------

1008 BEEF STEW          _ 10.00 OZ  1.25    0.790   0.460   63.20   15.00   1.55   1.180    0.370   76.13

  16 BEEF STROGANOFF    _  7.50 OZ  1.75    1.070   0.680   61.14   12.00   2.25   1.710    0.540   76.00

  55 BRAISED BEEF CUBES _  6.00 OZ  1.50    0.680   0.820   45.33   12.00   2.00   1.360    0.640   68.00

  66 BRAISED LIVER WITH ONIONS _ 6.00 OZ 1.25 0.290 0.960  23.20    6.00   1.55   0.290    1.260   18.71

 278 BREADED VEAL       _  5.00 OZ  2.55    2.001   0.549   78.47    5.00   2.75   2.001    0.749   72.76

  71 CORNED BEEF        _  4.00 OZ  2.20    1.193   1.007   54.23    6.00   2.65   1.790    0.860   67.55

  31 GRILLED STEAK      _  4.50 OZ  2.50    2.290   0.210   91.60    4.50   2.95   2.290    0.660   77.63

  44 HOME STYLE POT ROAST _ 6.00 OZ 2.20   0.738   1.462   33.55   12.00   2.75   1.476    1.274   53.67

 218 ROAST LAMB         _  4.00 OZ  1.85    1.188   0.662   64.22    6.00   2.25   1.782    0.468   79.20

  51 STEAK STRIPS SMOTHERED IN ONIONS _ 7.00 OZ 2.00 0.570 1.430 28.50 7.00 2.55 0.570 1.980 22.35

  52 SWISS STEAK WITH BROWN GRAVY _ 8.00 OZ 2.20 0.750 1.450 34.09 8.00 2.50 0.750 1.750 30.00

 928 VEAL PARMESAN      _  6.00 OZ  2.55    2.057   0.493   80.67    6.00   2.75   2.057    0.693   74.80

-----------------------------------------------------------------------------------------------
SUBTOTAL NUMBER OF RECORDS PRINTED 12
-----------------------------------------------------------------------------------------------
```

Figure 9–15 *Alphabetic menu planner.*

```
REPORT#: 124   * * * CBORD FOODSERVICE MANAGEMENT SYSTEMS * * *      PAGE:   2
OPTION : 7.1.5.2.5.     MENU MANAGEMENT SYSTEM - V4.1.35H           MAR 23 90
USER#  : 1               THE CBORD GROUP TRAINING CENTER            2145 HOURS
                         CONTROLLABLE FOOD COST ANALYSIS
                          MENU POSTCOST CONSOLIDATION

Day : SUNDAY  04/15/90
Meal : 2 LUNCH

----------------------------------------------------------------------------------------------
-- Recipe --            ---Portions---- ----Per Portion----  -------------Totals-----------------  ---------Per Customer-------
Nmbr Name               Prepped Sold Sales  Cost  Margin     Sales     Cost   Cost%    Margin     Items  Sales   Cost   Margin
----------------------------------------------------------------------------------------------
  790 TOMTO JUC CK        160:  158  0.75  0.107  0.643      118.50   16.906  14.27   101.59       0.301  0.226  0.032   0.194
  596 FRUIT CUP           360:  355  0.60  0.165  0.435      213.00   58.575  27.50   154.43       0.676  0.406  0.112   0.294
                        --------------                      ------------------ ----------------   ------ ------------- -------
TOTAL BRK FRUITS AND JUICES 520:  513                        331.50   75.481  22.77   256.02       0.977  0.632  0.144   0.488

   94 ROAST TURKEY        200:  125  1.55  0.758  0.792      193.75   94.750  48.90    99.00       0.238  0.369  0.180   0.189
  896 BAKED HAM           300:  290  1.85  1.151  0.699      536.50  333.790  62.22   202.71       0.552  1.022  0.636   0.386
 1008 BEEF STEW            85:   78  1.55  0.580  0.970      120.90   45.240  37.42    75.66       0.149  0.230  0.086   0.144
                        --------------                      ------------------ ----------------   ------ ------------- -------
TOTAL ENTREES            585:  493                           851.15  473.780  55.66   377.37       0.939  1.621  0.902   0.719

  226 MSHD POTATO         268:  268  0.55  0.161  0.389      147.40   43.148  29.27   104.25       0.510  0.281  0.082   0.199
  229 AU GRAT POT         260:  257  0.55  0.188  0.362      141.35   48.316  34.18    93.03       0.490  0.269  0.092   0.177
                        --------------                      ------------------ ----------------   ------ ------------- -------
TOTAL STARCHES           528:  525                           288.75   91.464  31.68   197.28       1.000  0.550  0.174   0.376

  910 CAULI AU GRN        160:  155  0.55  0.262  0.288       85.25   40.610  47.64    44.64       0.295  0.162  0.077   0.085
  255 GR BEAN PARI        331:  331  0.65  0.110  0.540      215.15   36.410  16.92   178.74       0.630  0.410  0.069   0.341
                        --------------                      ------------------ ----------------   ------ ------------- -------
TOTAL VEGETABLES         491!  486                           300.40   77.020  25.64   223.38       0.926  0.572  0.146   0.426

  331 TOSSED SLD          375:  355  0.45  0.090  0.360      159.75   31.950  20.00   127.80       0.676  0.304  0.061   0.243
  410 FRENCH DRSG         399:  355  0.25  0.057  0.193       88.75   20.235  22.80    68.52       0.676  0.169  0.039   0.130
                        --------------                      ------------------ ----------------   ------ ------------- -------
TOTAL SALADS             774:  710                           248.50   52.185  21.00   196.32       1.352  0.473  0.100   0.373

  924 DINNER ROLLS        300:  275  0.55  2.055 -1.505      151.25  565.125 373.64  -413.88       0.524  0.288  1.076  -0.788
                        --------------                      ------------------ ----------------   ------ ------------- -------
TOTAL BREADS             300:  275                           151.25  565.125 373.64  -413.88       0.524  0.288  1.076  -0.788

  457 LMN CHFN PIE        250:  249  0.75  2.951 -2.201      186.75  734.799 393.47  -548.05       0.474  0.356  1.400  -1.044
  500 ANGL FOOD CK        100:   98  0.60  2.138 -1.538       58.80  209.524 356.33  -150.72       0.187  0.112  0.399  -0.287
                        --------------                      ------------------ ----------------   ------ ------------- -------
TOTAL DESSERTS           350:  347                           245.55  944.323 384.57  -698.77       0.661  0.468  1.799  -1.331

  858 COFFEE              289:  289  0.35  0.107  0.243      101.15   30.923  30.57    70.23       0.550  0.193  0.059   0.134
  865 MILK                446:  446  0.55  0.120  0.430      245.30   53.520  21.82   191.78       0.850  0.467  0.102   0.365
                        --------------                      ------------------ ----------------   ------ ------------- -------
TOTAL BEVERAGES          735:  735                           346.45   84.443  24.37   262.01       1.400  0.660  0.161   0.499

  776 CREAM IND           656:  656  0.00  0.014 -0.014        0.00    9.184   0.00    -9.18       1.250  0.000  0.017  -0.017
  164 SUGAR IND           394:  394  0.00  0.013 -0.013        0.00    5.122   0.00    -5.12       0.750  0.000  0.010  -0.010
  187 SUGAR SUB IN        184:  184  0.00  0.013 -0.013        0.00    2.392   0.00    -2.39       0.350  0.000  0.005  -0.005
  217 PEPPER IND          289:  289  0.00  0.006 -0.006        0.00    1.734   0.00    -1.73       0.550  0.000  0.003  -0.003
  748 SALT IND            341:  341  0.00  0.003 -0.003        0.00    1.023   0.00    -1.02       0.650  0.000  0.002  -0.002
                        --------------                      ------------------ ----------------   ------ ------------- -------
TOTAL CONDIMENTS        1864: 1864                             0.00   19.455   0.00   -19.44       3.550  0.000  0.037  -0.037

                        --------------                      ------------------ ----------------   ------ ------------- -------
----------------------------------------------------------------------------------------------
NOTES: 1. PTN COUNTS MARKED WITH '*' ARE ACCOMPANIMENTS NOT INCLUDED IN PTN COUNT TOTALS
```

Figure 9–16 *Menu postcost consolidation.*

Accounting

The wide variety of information required for accounting can be compiled from appropriate software applications used in daily operations. An example of one such report is the product cost financial statement in Figure 9–17. It presents the cost and flow of foods within a given period, essential information for a profit and loss statement. In the case of meat, the beginning inventory was valued at $3,207.45 on January 1, 1990. Between that date and September 25, 1990, additional purchases of beef were made totaling $4,773.80. The inventory in stock on September 25 was valued at $2,014.36. Calculations indicate that the cost of meat sold between January 1 and September 25 was $5,966.89. The value of the average inventory on any given day was $2,610.91. The inventory of meat during this period turned over 2.29 times or approximately every 16 weeks.

```
REPORT#: 277   * * * CBORD FOODSERVICE MANAGEMENT SYSTEMS * * *        PAGE:    1
OPTION : 7.5.5.1.        MENU MANAGEMENT SYSTEM - V4.1.35Z              SEP 26 90
                       THE CBORD GROUP TRAINING CENTER                 1028 HOUPS
                        PROD COST FINANCIAL STATEMENT
                        ORGANIZED BY PRODUCT GROUP

Period      : 01/01/90 - 09/25/90
-------------------------------------------------------------------------------------
Group                                   Beginning            Returns/   Ending   Cost of   Average    Turn
                                        Inventory Purchases  Transfers  Inventory   Goods  Inventory   over
-------------------------------------------------------------------------------------
25 SUBASSEMBLIES                         4365.58  13873.50    -42.60    4873.78  13322.70   4619.68    2.88
26 COMMISSARY                           11239.40   2402.10   -574.00   10874.04   2193.46  11056.72    0.20
SUBTOTAL FOR:                           --------- --------- --------- --------- --------- ---------  ---------
  UNSPECIFIED ACCT CODE ( 0) UNSPECIFIED GROUP CODE 15604.98 16275.60 -616.60 15747.82 15516.16 15676.40 0.99

 1 MEAT                                  3207.45   4773.80      0.00    2014.36   5966.89   2610.91    2.29
 2 FISH                                  1888.90   1435.76   -399.60    1730.25   1194.81   1809.57    0.66
 3 POULTRY                                223.55   8475.00      0.00     318.42   8380.13    270.99   30.92
 4 DAIRY                                 2601.40  11692.67   -669.90    7839.38   5784.79   5220.39    1.11
 5 PRODUCE                               1053.61   6458.80      0.00    1435.27   6077.14   1244.44    4.88
 6 BAKERY                                1319.61   2892.75   -197.20     782.22   3232.94   1050.92    3.08
 7 GROCERIES                            14038.01   7876.00      0.00   11787.73  10126.28  12912.87    0.78
 8 BEVERAGES                             1792.01   6984.40      0.00    1386.62   7389.79   1589.31    4.65
13 BAKERY PRODUCTS                        872.73   5918.50      0.00     784.29   6006.94    828.51    7.25
14 COMMISSARY RECIPES                      27.00    860.00      0.00      86.00    801.00     56.50   14.18
SUBTOTAL FOR:                           --------- --------- --------- --------- --------- ---------  ---------
  1910-941 ( 15) FOOD                   27024.27  57367.68  -1266.70   28164.54  54960.71  27594.40    1.99

11 PAPER                                    3.00   2056.00      0.00       8.00   2051.00      5.50  372.91
SUBTOTAL FOR:                           --------- --------- --------- --------- --------- ---------  ---------
  1911-941 ( 16) NON FOOD                   3.00   2056.00      0.00       8.00   2051.00      5.50  372.91

 9 ALCOHOL                                224.75    278.69      0.00      62.93    440.51    143.84    3.06
SUBTOTAL FOR:                           --------- --------- --------- --------- --------- ---------  ---------
  1912-941 ( 17) ALCOHOL                  224.75    278.69      0.00      62.93    440.51    143.84    3.06

                                        ========= ========= ========= ========= ========= =========  =========
TOTAL                                   42857.00  75977.97  -1883.30   43983.29  72968.38  43420.15    1.68
                                        ========= ========= ========= ========= ========= =========  =========
-------------------------------------------------------------------------------------
```

Figure 9–17 *Product cost financial statement.*

Dinner in the
Circular Dining Room
Appetizers

Chilled Apple Cider
Grape Cocktail with Champagne   Florida Citrus Sunburst Plate
Hors D'Oeuvre Plate "Du Garde Manger"
Hot Scallop Mousse with Lobster Sauce
House Smoked Norwegian Salmon Garni ($1.50 Surcharge)
Chilled Louisiana Shrimp Cocktail ($3.50 Surcharge)

Soups

Game Consomme with Wild Mushrooms and Cheese Straws   Iced Fruit Soup
Creamy Tomato Soup with Orange and Ginger

Salads

Boston Bibb Lettuce, Red Oak Leaves and Mache, Hazelnut Vinaigrette
Tossed Salad
Cottage Cheese on Fruit Compote
Dressings
Hotel Hershey's Own Lo-Cal, No Cholesterol Salad Dressing
Hershey   French   Blue Cheese   Russian   Caesar   Vinaigrette

Specialties of the Day

BAKED FILET OF BROOK TROUT "NEWPORT"
With Herbed Crumb, Sauce Bearnaise and Red Bliss Potato

LOUISIANA PRAWNS IN CREOLE SAUCE
Served in Cumin Rice Ring, Buttered Snow Peas

SAUTEED CALF'S LIVER WITH BACON AND ONIONS
Madeira Sauce, Parisienne Potatoes
Zucchini Boat with Ratatouille

CHARBROILED BREAST OF CHICKEN
With Apricot Honey Glaze
Served on Bed of Wild Rice, Buttered Snow Peas and Broiled Tomato

MEDALLION OF BEEF AND LAMB WITH HERB "JUS LIE"
Parisienne Potatoes, Ratatouille and Snow Peas

ROAST FILET OF BEEF PERIGUEUX
With Truffle Red Wine and Shallot Sauce
Parisienne Potatoes and Snow Peas

Available for all guests at an additional charge

FILET MIGNON SAUCE BEARNAISE (8 Ounce) $3.75
NEW YORK SIRLOIN STEAK MAITRE D'HOTEL (10 Ounce) $2.50
CHATEAUBRIAND BOUQUETIERE (FOR TWO) $10.00
BROILED ROCK LOBSTER TAIL $9.25
SURF AND TURF COMBINATION $9.25

Special Dietary Requirements Accommodated
Limited Kosher Meals Available

MONDAY, NOVEMBER 5, 1990

Figure 9–18   *Graphic menu design. (Courtesy of Hershey Hotel, Hershey, PA.)*

Word Processing and Desktop Publishing

Word processing is a computer application used almost universally by businesses. Letters, reports, databases, client files, and personnel records are just a few of the many functions performed daily by word processing systems. Catering sales management can take advantage of available programs in a variety of ways.

Catering sales efforts can be greatly enhanced by computerized client file listings. Names of clients who hold functions regularly can be accessed on a trace file system that will call client names to the attention of catering management on a weekly or monthly basis.

A word processor provides much flexibility in creating letters and forms. Format letters can be constructed with personalized clauses and messages inserted into the body of the letter. Mailing lists and labels can also be generated. In addition, many of the control forms shown in chapter eight can be formatted using word processing systems.

Desktop publishing programs can be used to create effective menu packages. Partially preprinted menu forms can be completed on a laser printer. Newsletters, menu inserts, and brochures for direct mail campaigns are just a few of the marketing applications for desktop publishing programs.

Graphic menu designs can be developed using a variety of software programs. The menu design in Figure 9–18 shows the inside page layout for a menu created with a desktop publishing program and generated by a laser printer. The program allows the operator to choose among several options for paper selection, stock coating, and color.

Summary

The commonalities of volume production and service between retail catering operations and institutional/business and industry operations allow for the application of software systems specifically designed for volume feeding.

Computers provide catering management with a valuable tool for achieving efficiency and profitability. A wide variety of software programs offering a range of report facilities and capabilities are available. Foodservice operations expanding into the catering business will find that many of these programs are compatible with their existing computer hardware systems. Even smaller catering operations can benefit from computerized menu management.

The success of catering foodservice businesses is greatly enhanced by using software programs in the areas of purchasing, inventory, production forecasts and analyses, sales mix, costing, and accounting. Word processing has numerous applications, including sales files and letter formats. Desktop publishing software programs can assist marketing efforts with the production of newsletters, brochures, and menu package design.

10

Catering Marketing

Marketing is the key to the continued expansion of the catering segment of the foodservice industry. The Bureau of Food Service Research states that the real growth forecasted for this segment of the industry is accounted for by "the ability of caterers to adapt to increasing demands from the general public. Their extensive product line and broad service appeal conforms to the changing ways in which consumers eat out. What other foodservice segments are now getting involved in, caterers continue to capitalize on in the 1990's."[1]

The principal goals of marketing are to recognize the trends in cuisine, entertainment, and other catering concepts that shape customer needs and develop products or services in response to those needs. This process is known as the marketing cycle. The flexibility to respond to a wide variety of customer needs is one of the main reasons for the growth of catering businesses.

The success of a catering business depends on management's ability to evaluate not only the profitability of catering functions but also the level of customer satisfaction. Customer response is an accurate gauge of the performance of a business. Both positive and negative feedback can help a catering business determine areas that are favorable for development.

The Marketing Cycle

The American Marketing Association defines marketing as follows:

> Marketing is the process of planning and executing the conception, pricing, promotion, and distribution of ideas, goods, and services to create exchanges that satisfy individual and organizational objectives.[2]

The process of achieving these objectives is called the marketing cycle. It encompasses the general marketing plan for a business as well as specific issues, products, and ideas. In the marketing cycle, as outlined in Figure 10–1, customer needs are identified, a product or service is developed to satisfy those needs, customer interest in the product or service is created, and the success of these efforts is measured against both financial goals and customer reactions. The ability of catering services to adapt to customer demands with an extensive product line and broad service appeal produces dynamic and profitable results.

Identify Customer Needs

Customer needs are shaped by demographic and social trends. The ability to perceive these trends and apply them to a catering service expands marketing opportunities. Trends contributing to the current growth in catering opportunities are the demographic increases in two-income families, working mothers, and the age of the overall population. These three factors, combined with increased retail food costs have created a trend toward prepared food items.

1.

Identify customer needs

4.   *2.*

Measure financial   *Create a product*

success and customer   *or service in response*

satisfaction   *to customer needs*

3.

Develop

customer interest

Figure 10–1 *Marketing cycle.*

Customers will often choose to purchase pre-prepared food items when they perceive that the cost of retail food, including the indirect cost of preparation time, becomes close to or equals the price of pre-prepared products. These satisfy the two major priorities of foodservice in the 1990s: convenience and time management.

Recent surveys of the foodservice industry confirm that concerns for healthy eating also continue to have an impact on the buying habits of the American public. In the graph in Figure 10–2 over 45.8 percent of the households surveyed are very concerned with nutritious eating and over 51 percent somewhat concerned, for a combined total 96.8 percent of those surveyed.

Foodservice operations in every segment of the industry are responding to this customer need. Fast-food operators such as McDonald's are creating nutritious menu items that are low in fat, salt, and carbohydrate content. Restaurant associations across the United States have been joining with local hospitals and associations such as the American Cancer Society and the American Heart Association to create healthy dining programs in their cities.

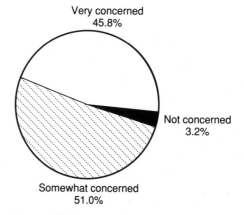

Figure 10–2 *Nutritious eating graph.*
(Source: R& I's 1990 Tastes of America Study.)

Create a Product or Service

The needs for convenience and nutrition create marketing opportunities for new pre-prepared food products and new services. Catering operations can develop menus for on- or off-premise dining as well as take-home food items for retail food outlets. The dietary department of the local medical center is usually willing to assist foodservice operators in implementing a healthy dining program in the community. A good resource for nutritional menu development is *A Nutrition Guide for the Restaurateur* published by the National Restaurant Association.

Nutritious meals that are also conveniently pre-prepared for take-home or delivery service are an important extension of many foodservice operations. Catering services can develop delivery service for a selected group of menu items on an à la carte basis with a minimum purchase specified. As a convenience, the luncheon menu selection in Figure 10–3 is offered for takeout or office delivery to local businesses from Monday through Friday. The Tex-Mex menu featured in Figure 10–4 offers five *Platillos Lite*. The selections offer a variety of poultry, seafood, and meat items in a regional cuisine theme for take-home and delivery service. Customers can also order items from the general menu.

Formal catering functions provide further marketing opportunities to develop healthy and nutritious menus. The challenge in this example was to create a wedding dinner for both vegetarians and meat-eaters. A compromise was reached so that chicken could appear on the menu. The menus in Figure 10–5 and Figure 10–6 were submitted in answer to this customer need.

Develop Customer Interest

Customer interest for catering functions is developed through a combination of advertising and in-house promotions. The broad range of clients served by catering operations necessitates the use of a variety of promotional vehicles. Hotel and conference facilities have the ability to post display boards advertising new catering services. Mailing brochures to everyone on a customer list is one of the most effective ways of advertising special features and promotions. The four-panel brochure in Figure 10–7 promotes the delivery service of complete holiday menus priced on a per person basis. The presentation of the items on these menus on "ready to serve trays" responds to the customer need for time-saving convenience. Figure 10–8 promotes beverage sales of wine by the glass and by the bottle. Customers may elect to serve only one glass of wine with the main course or may provide a specified number of bottles to be served until consumed.

Evaluate Success

The success of a catering menu is measured by customer response. Interest from guests attending the function is one indication. Another is requests from clients who plan business functions on an ongoing basis for additional

LUNCH MENU
SERVED FROM 11 TO 5

NUMERO UNO

Beef Burrito topped with chili con questo served with rice and beans. **$5.50**

NUMERO DOS

Choice of enchilada-beef, chicken, or cheese, choice of taco-beef or chicken. Served with rice. **$5.50**

NUMERO TRES

Bean chalupa, cheese enchilada ranchera, and rice. Served with guacamole. **$5.50**

NUMERO CUATRO (LUNCH FAJITAS)

A lunch sized portion of beef or chicken fajitas, served with rice, guacamole and tortillas. **$6.50**

NUMERO CINCO

Beef enchilada topped with chili con carne, cheese taco topped with queso. Served with rice. **$5.50**

NUMERO SEIS (POLLO MESQUITE)

Mesquite grilled chicken breast served with rice, ranchera sauce and guacamole salad. **$6.95**

NUMERO SIETE

One spinach and cheese enchilada topped with sour cream or ranchera sauce. Served with rice, black beans and guacamole. **$4.95**

NUMERO OCHO

Black beans and chicken served on a large flour tostada topped with lettuce, tomatoes, cheese and sour cream. **$4.95**

NUMERO NUEVE

Two soft tacos with spicy beef or chicken, lettuce, tomatoes, and cheese. Served with choice of soup or beans. **$5.50**
With beef or chicken fajita. **$6.50**

NUMERO DIEZ

Mesquite grilled filet of red fish served with sauteed mexican squash. **$6.50**

Figure 10–3 *Takeout luncheon menu. (Courtesy of El Chico Corporation, Dallas, TX.)*

ENSALADAS

CHALUPA GRANDE Spicy beef or chicken, lettuce, guacamole, sour cream and cheese served in a flour tortilla shell served with rice and black bean soup. **$6.75** with beef or chicken fajita. **$7.75**

FAJITA SALAD A large bowl filled with beef or chicken fajita, lettuce, tomatos, guacamole, cheese, carrots and celery. Served with your favorite dressing. **$7.50** with shrimp. **$8.50**

POLLO EN LA CONCHA A flour tortilla shell filled with spicy chicken topped with sour cream sauce and Monterey Jack cheese and baked in a shell. Served with rice, black bean soup and guacamole. **$6.75**

SOPAS

SOPA DE TORTILLA Chicken, avocado pieces, and tortilla strips smothered in a spicy tortilla broth. Served with sour cream and cheese. **$4.75**

BLACK BEAN SOUP A unique blend of black beans, onion, bell pepper, and spices. Served with sour cream and topped with pico de gallo. **$4.50**

Figure 10–3 *(continued)*

PLATILLOS LITE
(low fat and no salt, oil, or sugar)

GILBERT'S FAJITAS $9.45

Seasoned with lime, black pepper, and garlic, mesquite grilled and served with grilled onions and bell peppers, sliced avocado, tossed salad, and corn tortillas.

CHICKEN FAJITAS $9.45

Fresh chicken breast seasoned with lime, black pepper, and garlic, mesquite grilled and served with grilled onions and bell peppers, sliced avocado, tossed salad, and corn tortillas.

HUACHINANGO AL MESQUITE $12.95

Fresh filet of fish seasoned with lime, black pepper, and garlic, mesquite grilled and served with a tossed salad and sliced avocado.

CAMARONES DE LA PARRILLA $12.95

Mesquite grilled shrimp served with grilled onions and bell peppers, sliced avocado, tossed salad, and corn tortillas.

STEAK TAMPICO $9.95

Premium outside skirt steak seasoned with garlic and black pepper. Served with grilled green onions, tossed salad, and sliced avocado.

Figure 10–4 *Convenient nutritious menu. (Courtesy of El Chico Corporation, Dallas, TX.)*

As Your Guests Arrive, They Will Be Offered Tiny
Punch Cups Full of Steaming Spiced Apple Cider

Hors D'Oeuvres to Be Passed

Lacy Potato Pancakes Topped with a Dollop of Dilled Creme Fraiche and Smoked Salmon
Phyllo Triangles Oozing with Melted Mozzarella, Sun Dried Tomatos and Fresh Herbs

For the Buffet

Cranberry Sauteed Chicken - Chicken Breast Pieces
Sauteed with Shallot Butter and Fresh Cranberries
Spinach Strudel with Madiera Mushroom Sauce
Wild Rice Studded with Toasted Hazelnuts
Broccoli Souffle Ring Filled with Creamed Chestnuts
Winter Greens with Roquefort Vinaigrette
Poppy Seed Knot Rolls and Tiny Sweet Potato Muffins
Sweet Butter

* * *

"Gift Box Wedding" Cake
Chocolate Dipped Strawberries
Freshly Brewed Coffee
Cream and Sugar

For the Bar

Lemons and Limes
Bar Fruit
Orange Juice

Figure 10–5 *Wedding menu I. (Courtesy of Ridgewell's Caterers, Bethesda, MD.)*

Hors D'Oeuvres to be Passed

Golden Phyllo Pockets Plumped with Sauteed Wild Mushrooms and Herbs

Vegetable Tempura with Ginger Soy Scallion Dipping Sauce

Pink Shrimp Wrapped with Crisp Snow Peas

For the Buffet

Sauteed Chicken Piccata - Chicken Sauteed with Lemon, Capers, Parsley and Butter

A Selection of Pastas Prepared before Your Guests Including Spinach Filled Agnolotti
Tossed with Morsels, Plum Tomatoes, Pine Nuts and Finished with Cognac

Tri-colored Fusilli with Creamy Garlic Panna Romana
and Your Guests' Choice of the Following Toppings:
Sweet Garden Peas,
Prosciutto Ribbons,
Freshly Grated Parmesan and
Sauteed Broccoli Florets

Figure 10–6   *Wedding menu II. (Courtesy of Ridgewell's Caterers, Bethesda, MD.)*

*Braised Leeks and Glazed Baby Carrots with
Their Tops Sprinkled with Freshly Chopped Parsley*

*Whole Wheat Rosemary Rolls
Italian Panini
Sweet Butter*

*Beautiful Mascarpone Wreath Layerd with Lingon Berries and Lime Marmalade
Imported Gingersnap Crackers*

*Luscious Fresh Fruit Display Featuring Plump Driscoll Strawberries,
Sun Ripend Casaba and Cantaloupe, Freshly Cut Hawaiian Pineapple,
Clusters of Frosty Green and Black Grapes and Emerald Kiwi Slices
Warm Chocolate Frangelico Sauce*

Beautiful Moist Carrot Wedding Cake Filled and Frosted with Cream Cheese Icing

*Freshly Brewed Coffee, Cream and Sugar
English Teas*

For the Bar

*Lemons and Limes
Bar Fruit
Orange Juice*

Figure 10–6   *(continued)*

Special Holiday Menus

MENU I
Santa's Snack

Layered Tex Mex Terrine
Tortilla Chips
Cheese Torte with
Lime and Lingonberry Preserves
Gingersnaps
Holiday Crudite
Confetti Dip
Ribbon tied Brioche filled
with Brandied Pate
Toasted French Bread Medallions
Tutti Frutti Scones
with Virginia Sugar Cured Ham
Honey Mustard
Corn Molasses Rolls
with Smoked Turkey
Peppered Horseradish Cream
Colorful Assortment
of Christmas Cookies

...

Minimum of 25 people
10.00 per person
No Substitutions Please
All Items Presented on Ready to Serve Trays

MENU II
Claus and Effect

Charcuterie Display of Sliced Turkey,
Rare Roast Beef, Kentucky Ham,
Domestic Cheeses and Holiday Garnishes
Bearnaise Mayonnaise
Honey Mustard
Trio of Fusilli Pasta
with Black Olives, Feta Cheese,
Sun Dried Tomatoes and Sausage
Tuscan Focaccia Bread
Rye Rolls
Knotted Milk Rolls
Holiday Vegetable Wreath
Three Herb Dip
Spicy Guacamole
Tostada Chips
Smoked Salmon Christmas Tree
Bagel Chips
Fumei Spiced Nuts

...

Minimum of 25 people
15.00 per person
No Substitutions Please
All Items Presented on Ready to Serve Trays

MENU III
It's a Wonderful Life

Pumpkin Muffins
stuffed with Smithfield Ham
Mustard Cream
Cranberry Scones
plumped with Sliced Turkey
Apple Chutney
Smoked Salmon Napoleon
Wreath of Chicken Almond Mousse
Holiday Brie crusted with Pistachios
Champagne Crackers
French Bread Medallions
Vegetable Christmas Tree
Red Pepper Dip
Angel Hair wrapped Crocquembouche
Shortbread Stars
Kris Kringle Cookies

...

Minimum of 25 people
17.00 per person
No Substitutions Please
All Items Presented on Ready to Serve Trays

MENU IV
The Groaning Board

Maple Glazed Turkey Display with a
Wreath of Della Robbia Fruit
Apple Ginger Butter
Sage Finger Rolls
Chive Croissants with Tarragon Cream
and Perfectly Pink Roast Beef
Clove Studded Tennessee Ham
Lingonberry Preserves
Orange Muffins
Marinated Dill Shrimp
A Selection of Sliced Smoked Sausages,
Hungarian Pastramis, Imported and
Domestic Cheeses, Relishes and Olives
Honey Mustard
Bearnaise Mayonnaise
Russian Raisin Pumpernickel Bread
Water Crackers
Maryland Crab and Horseradish Dip
Pita Crisps

...

Minimum of 25 people
22.50 per person
No Substitutions Please
All Items Presented on Ready to Serve Trays

Figure 10-7 Promotional brochure I. (Courtesy of Ridgewell's Caterers, Bethesda, MD.)

IDER VALLEY   TEMECULA   DRY CREEK VALLEY   CARNEROS   NAPA VALLEY   ALEXANDER VALLEY   TEMECULA   DRY C

LLEY   ALEXANDER VALLEY   TEMECULA   DRY CREEK VALLEY   CARNEROS   NAPA VALLEY   ALEXANDER VALLEY   TEM

Figure 10–8   *Promotional brochure II. (Courtesy of Westin Galleria, Houston, TX.)*

proudly features
the premium wines of

CLOS DU BOIS

	Glass	*Bottle*
Chardonnay, Calcaire Vineyard, 1989 Elegant, complex and rich with pear, honey and vanilla flavors.	$5.75	$23.00
Chardonnay, Flintwood Vineyard, 1988 Very crisp on the palate with silky smoothness and excellent structure.	$6.25	$25.00
Sauvignon Blanc, Alexander Valley, 1989 Clean, fruity aroma of citrus, melon and pear; medium body and a refreshing finish.	$4.25	$17.00
Cabernet Sauvignon, 1988 Rich in flavor, deep in color and smooth on the palate with complex, lingering flavors of berries and chocolate.	$4.95	$20.00
Marlstone, Alexander Valley, 1986 Succulent, generous personality and deep flavors; full body and long finish. A complex wine with lots of finesse.	$7.50	$30.00

Figure 10–8   *(continued)*

functions incorporating the same menu theme. The financial success of promotions such as those featured in Figure 10–7 and Figure 10–8 can be directly measured by the resulting volume of sales.

Cuisine, Entertainment, and Concept Trends

Trends as they relate to catering menu management reflect changes in the patterns of customer requests for catering services. For many years wedding receptions were planned strictly along the lines of formal sit-down dinner-dances or cocktail receptions. However, the past 15 years have witnessed a recognizable trend away from the traditional patterns for wedding reception plans, toward entertainment and cuisine themes in a wide variety of settings and formats.

Corporate and conference or convention functions have undergone significant changes in format as concepts and entertainment have been built into what were once simple meal functions. From Mardi Gras parades to Texas hoedowns (see Figure 10–9), entertainment and regional cuisines combine to produce theme parties with enthusiastic attendees. This enthusiasm translates into contributions for community causes and interest in catered business functions.

The menu in Figure 10–10 features the buffet dinner menu for a *Moonshine Jamboree* highlighting regional southern cuisine. The decoration package provided for the function includes country shacks and stills to house the bars, the facade of the front porch of a country house for the bandstand, a dance floor surrounded by split-rail fencing, checkered table cloths, costumed servers, appropriate table centerpieces, and jelly-jar glasses on the bar. Entertainment packages offer country western bands and entertainers in a range of prices. Additional services can include costumes for attendees, portrait photographers, and carnival game booths.

Catering function attendees in New Orleans are treated to a Mardi Gras parade complete with a 40-piece marching band with motorcycle escort, Mardi Gras floats, and costumed royal court members. Decorations and entertainment are combined with a creole cuisine buffet in the menu package in Figure 10–11. The set for the French Quarter pictured in Figure 10–12 can be used to provide authentic decoration for a wide variety of catering functions.

Concepts and themes can also be worked into small off- and on-premise catering menus. For example, the meeting breaks shown in Figure 10–13 can be packaged in baskets, boxes, bags, and other colorful containers for delivery to offices and conference centers.

Many catering firms and hotels provide services that include equipment rental and the design and setup of large off-premise functions. Figure 10–14 illustrates the set-up for a dinner for 250 that was held in a Jewish synagogue. The walls and ceiling are draped in fabric with coordinated chair covers and table cloths. In Figure 10–15 buffet tables are set up around a large tiered anniversary cake. The hall is decorated with balloon sculptures highlighting the ceiling span. Finally, an ice rink is the setting for the dinner for 1000 at the Houston International Festival in honor of the Prince of Japan (see

Figure 10–9 *Texas hoe-down theme function. (Courtesy of Westin Galleria, Houston, TX.)*

Cole Slaw with Mayonnaise

Marinated Bean Salad

Potato Salad

Mountain Grown Vegetable Salad

Pickled Okra and Baby Corn

Marinated Scroodle Salad

Tossed Greens with Choice of Dressing

Platter of Sliced Tomatoes

Variety of Cold Meats and Cheeses

Ham, Smoked Turkey, Garlic Sausage

Caraway Cheese, Cheddar Cheese, Monterey Jack

Condiments

From the Chafing Dishes:

Barbecued Pork Spare Ribs

Fried Spring Water Catfish

Tartar Sauce

Southern Fried Chicken

Smoke Honey Glazed Pork Loin

Texas Beef Round Carved by Chef

String Green Beans

Squash Casserole

Au Gratin Potatoes

Hush Puppies

Biscuits and Corn Muffins

Hot Cobbler with Fruits in Season

Bread and Butter Pudding

Assorted Pies

Watermelon Boats with Bourbon Marinated Fruits

Upside Down Cake

Choice of Beverage

Figure 10–10 *Moonshine Jamboree theme menu. (Courtesy of Opryland Hotel, Nashville, TN.)*

CARNIVAL KREWES

Kings and queens in elaborate dress, colorful parade floats, sparkling beads and trinkets and, the crowning touch, Carnival cuisine fit for royalty.

Imagine rooms filled with balloons, Mardi Gras heads, a Dixieland Band and elaborate parade floats. Imagine authentic kings and queens parading in their finery and throwing doubloons and other favors to your guests. Motorcycles appearing with lights and sirens screaming, followed by the thundering sounds of a 40-piece marching band. Crown your honored guests king and queen of the evening. Truly a night to remember.

MENU

Carving Station

Whole Standing Steamship Round Of Beef, Au Jus Accompanied By A Mild Horseradish Sauce And Pee Wee Rolls

Seafood Bar

Chilled Louisiana Jumbo Shrimp

Fresh Bayou Oysters On The Half Shell

Spicy Cracked Crab Claws Or

Crawfish
(Seasonal)

The Above Served With Cocktail Sauce, Remoulade Sauce, White Horseradish, And Lemon Wedges
Displayed In Decorative Pirogues

Mirrors Of Decorative And Imported Cheeses Garnished With Whole Fresh Fruit, Carr Water Wafers And Thinly Sliced French Bread
Miniature Louisiana Muffelettas

New Orleans Famous Filé Gumbo With Rice

Louisiana Seafood Creole

Hot Hors D'Oeuvres

Fresh Mushroom Caps Stuffed With Lump Crab Meat

Breast Of Chicken Tempura

Grilled Andouille And Boudin Sausages

Battered Artichoke Hearts

Fried Dill Pickle Chips

Delicate Beignets Dusted With Powdered Sugar
Fried In Room

Café Au Lait

ENTERTAINMENT

Seven-piece dance/variety band

Parade to consist of:
• Forty-piece marching band
• Two motorcycle police escorts
• Ten Royal Court members in full costume
• Revelers, tossing beads and doubloons
• Two mini-Mardi Gras floats
• Two 10-foot-tall walking figures
• Two costumes for honored guests
• Complete sound and stage lighting and follow spots for parade.

Entertainment Cost:
$8,000

DECORATIONS

Entrance:
The entrance of the ballroom will be lined with four large urns filled with assorted helium balloons of purple, green, and gold Mardi Gras colors.

Ballroom Area:
Placed around the ballroom to depict the festive Mardi Gras atmosphere will be
• Four large wicker baskets filled with towering balloons
• Fifteen individual clusters. All balloons will be the assorted Mardi Gras colors of purple, green, and gold
• Three decorative 5 x 5 ft. papier-mâché Mardi Gras heads will be placed in the ballroom to emphasize the bigger than life attitude of Mardi Gras

Entertainment Area:
Suspended over the entertainment stage is a three dimensional jeweled crown, draped with flowing gold lamé and satins, forming the backdrop of the stage.
Decorations Cost:
$6,000

Figure 10–11 *Carnival Krewes theme party package. (Courtesy of New Orleans Hilton, New Orleans, LA.)*

Figure 10–12   *French Quarter set.*

SPECIAL MEETING BREAKS

SMB - 1 JUNK FOOD BREAK
Assorted Candy Bars to include:
Baby Ruths, Snickers, Milky Ways, M&Ms (Plain & Peanut),
3 Musketeers, Goo Goo Bars, and Peanut Butter Cups.

Assorted Hostess Cakes to include:
Cup Cakes, Twinkies, Sno Balls, Ding Dongs, and Susi Qs

Assorted Soft Drinks
$6.00

SMB - 4 LET'S GET THE MEETING POPPING
Variety of Fresh-Popped Corn to include:
Nacho Cheese, Pizza, Sour Cream and Onion, and Caramel

Assorted Soft Drinks
Coffee, Tea, Decaffeinated Coffee
$6.00

SMB - 7 ALMOST BREAKFAST
Selection of Chilled Juices
Assorted Breakfast Bakeries to include:
Danish, Croissants, and Blueberry Muffins
Preserves and Butter
Sliced Fresh Fruits

Choice of Beverage
$6.50

SMB - 2 CHOCOLATE BREAK
Chilled Chocolate Milk
Chocolate-Dipped Strawberries
Petite Chocolate Eclairs
Assorted Chocolate Cookies
Displays of Sacher Tortes and Chocolate Mousse Tortes
Freshly Brewed Coffee served with Shaved Chocolate
and Whipped Cream

Assorted Soft Drinks
$7.50

SMB - 5 MAKE-YOUR-OWN-SUNDAE BAR
Chocolate, Vanilla, and Strawberry Ice Cream
Chocolate Sauce, Strawberry Sauce, Whipped Cream,
Chocolate Sprinkles, and Crushed Nuts
Assorted Cookies

Coffee and Soft Drinks
$6.50

SMB - 3 DOWN HOME BREAK
Assorted Chilled Juices
Fresh Strawberries with Brown Sugar and Fresh Cream
Country Style Sausage Biscuits and Ham Biscuits
Sliced Coffee Cakes and Cinnamon Rolls

Choice of Beverage
$8.25

SMB - 6 HEALTH FOOD BREAK
Selection of Chilled Juices
Granola Bars
Assorted Fruit Yogurts
Dried Apples, Apricots, Pears, and
Bananas with Prunes, Raisins, and Toasted Granola
Banana Bread, Zucchini Bread, Blueberry Muffins

Choice of Beverage
$6.75

SMB - 8 HOT CHOCOLATE BREAK
Hot Chocolate
Chocolate Chips
Chocolate Blocks
Whipped Cream
Chocolate Sprinkles
Chocolate Cocoa Beans
Cookies

Coffee, Tea, Decaffeinated Coffee
$6.75

(PLUS 17% SERVICE CHARGE AND 7.75% SALES TAX)

Figure 10–13   *Theme meeting packages. (Courtesy of Opryland Hotel, Nashville, TN.)*

Figure 10–14   *Banquet dinner setup. (Courtesy of Westin Galleria, Houston, TX.)*

Figure 10–15   *Anniversary celebration setup. (Courtesy of Westin Galleria, Houston, TX.)*

Figure 10–16 *Dinner for 1,000. (Courtesy of Westin Galleria, Houston, TX.)*

Figure 10–16). Large metal sculptures in red were hung from the ceiling. The imperial colors of gold and red highlighted the decorations.

Off-premise catering has become a major source of business for large catering firms. The PGA Golf Championship was serviced through a village of tents representing its corporate sponsors (see Figure 10–17). In order to carry out this function for 20,000 guests, the design graphics department for the catering firm creates a technical and operational layout. (see Figure 10–18). Color-coded keys identify sponsor locations, as well as satellite kitchens, warehouses, freezers, and dumpsters.

Menus for these off-premise events are developed around menu items that can be preprepared at satellite locations or fully prepared on site. Consideration is given to items that can withstand adverse weather conditions and lengthy holding times. The menus for the PGA function were coordinated to create as much preparation duplication as possible while still providing individual corporate sponsors with customized cuisine themes.

Pricing Packages

Packaging catering services into one price for customers can provide additional sources of revenues and profit by capturing a percentage of the income that would otherwise go to outside contractors such as florists, photographers, and musicians. The function package most common to catering services is the wedding reception. The wedding reception plan in Figure 10–19 is a three-hour function featuring an open bar and hors d'oeuvre buffet. The per person

Figure 10-17 *Design layout. (Courtesy of Ridgewell's Caterers, Bethesda, MD.)*

216

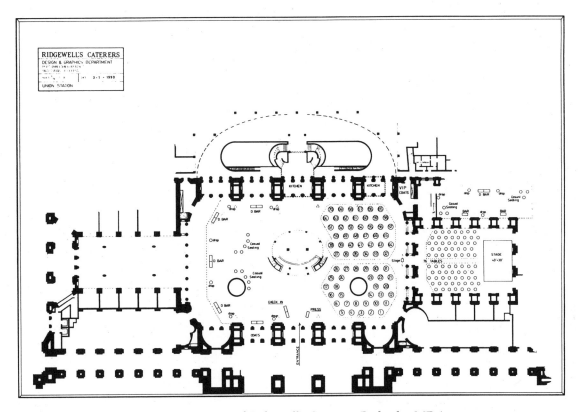

Figure 10–18 *Design layout. (Courtesy of Ridgewell's Caterers, Bethesda, MD.)*

price is $43.50 including 16 percent gratuity. The package price breaks down as follows:

Hors d'oeuvres	$ 19.00
Wedding Cake	2.00
Champagne toast	1.00
3-Hour open bar	12.00
Coffee	1.00
Complimentary parking	2.50
Subtotal	$ 37.50
16% gratuity	6.00
Total per person	$ 43.50

The package plan has been developed to include all the services offered directly by the catering operation. Customers have the option to arrange for flowers, a photographer, music, and limousine service on their own. However, the catering operation can make agreements with local businesses to include the cost of one or more of these services in the overall per person package price.

"1991"

WEDDING RECEPTION PLAN

(Recommended for Mid-Afternoon)

$43.50 including gratuity

BAR SERVICES

Continuous (3 Hours) Open Bar Offering Premium Brands

TOAST

French Gratien and Meyer Brut Champagne

HORS D'OEUVRES BUFFET

Deepfried Shrimp, Cocktail Sauce
Tenderloin Kabobs, Bearnaise
Mushroom Caps, Beef
Chicken Nuggets in Beer Batter, Pineapple Sauce
Salami Coronets – Stuffed Devilled Egg – Chicken Salad Bouchees
Assorted Finger Sandwiches
(Beef on Whole Wheat – Turkey on White – Tuna Salad on Whole Wheat Bread)
Assorted Cheese Trays, Fruit Center, Crackers
Cheddar Cheeseballs in Almonds, French Bread
Fresh Vegetable Garden Bowl with Curry Dip

WEDDING CAKE

Traditional Pound Cake – Swiss Chocolate Cake – Hazelnut or Almond Nut Cake
Selection of Ornaments
Wedding Cake Knife

Demitasse Coffee (Silver Urn Service)
Complimentary Parking at Hotel Carpark
Special Valet Parking for Bridal Party
Cloakroom Attendant
Silver Candelabras – Buffet Table
Professional Guidance Throughout Reception
Choice Color Linen: White, Off-White or Pink
Special Overnight Value Rates for out-of-town guests
Complimentary Suite for Bride and Groom at a Nearby Hotel

Room Rental (if applicable)
Gold Ballroom, for less than 150 Guests – $250.00
du Barry Room, for less than 100 Guests – $150.00

Figure 10–19 *Wedding reception package plan. (Courtesy of Hotel DuPont, Wilmington, DE.)*

In this example, optional costs are calculated per person for a reception with 200 guests. The flowers include two centerpieces for the hors d'oeuvre table ($100), bud vases for each of the cocktail tables ($200), and flowers for the reception table ($20), for a total of $320.

$$\$320 \div 200 = \$1.60 \text{ per person}$$

The services of a photographer are included by selecting one of the package options offered by the participating studio. Here a wedding photography package priced at $2,000.00 is included in the reception package price.

$$\$2,000.00 \div 200 = \$10.00 \text{ per person}$$

A four-piece band for a three-hour reception might be priced at $600.00

$$\$600.00 \div 200 = \$3.00 \text{ per person}$$

Limousine service for the bride from her home might be priced at $150.00

$$\$150.00 \div 200 = \$.75 \text{ per person}$$

The per person cost for optional services and for this total wedding package is:

Flowers	$ 1.60
Photographer	10.00
4-piece band	3.00
Limousine service	.75
Total optional services per person	$ 15.35
Wedding reception services per person	$ 43.50
Total per person plus tax	$ 58.85

The participating services have lowered their costs in order to guarantee this source of business. The catering service also charges a percentage for their efforts into the cost of optional services. In the preceding example, if the catering service is receiving 15 percent of the optional service charges then $2.30 per person, or $460, will be added to the total revenue for the function. This marketing strategy takes advantage of the customer need for time-saving convenience taking over the responsibility of arranging for these extra services, contracts, and payments. Package pricing has the further advantage of allowing the catering service to control the quality of optional services, assuring the customer that the entire function will run smoothly.

Equipment and tent rentals, though initially costly to stock, can be profitable for catering services who specialize in off-premise catering. Figure 10–20 is only a partial listing of serving pieces, tables, and specialty items offered for rental by a large catering business.

Serving Pieces

Glass Items

Pitcher	1.50
Finger Bowl	.35
Salad on the Side	.55
Glass Bowl 1 Qt./2 Qt./4 Qt.	1.00/1.75/2.25
Creamer & Sugar Set	1.30
Ash Tray	.35

Specialty Items

Table Lighting

3-Light Candelabra	7.50
5-Light Candelabra	10.25
Candlestick—Tall/Short	2.50
Grecian Candlestick 10"/6"	6.00/5.00
Votive Clear/Frost	2.00/2.50
Williamsburg Globe	5.75
Candleholder/Star	.30

Chafing Dishes & Small Stoves

6 qt. Chafer (Copper)	45.00
2 gal. Round Chafer (Copper)	60.00
2 gal. Oval Chafer (Copper)	60.00
2 gal. Rectangular Chafer (Copper)	60.00
1 gal. Square Chafer (Copper)	40.00
2 qt. Round/Pyrex	12.50
3 qt. Round/Pyrex	15.00
4 qt. Rectangular/Round	30.00
4 qt. Oval/Deluxe	30.00
5 qt. Oval	23.00
2 gal. Round	30.00
2 gal. Rectangular	30.00
2 gal. 2 Compartment Rectangular	30.00
2 gal. Sterno Grill	30.00
Wok	28.00
2½ gal. Round Deluxe	60.00
5 qt. Waterbath	28.00
Gas mini-stove/single burner	20.00
Gas mini-stove/double burner	22.50

Incidentals

Red/Blue Runners 4'x12'	34.00
Screens	17.00
Ceramic Mug—Soup/Coffee	.80
Coffee Maker—55 cups	11.25
Carving Rack/Tray/Set	4.50/9.00/2.50
Carving/Cheese Board	5.50
Tub—Plastic/Metal	2.00
Trash Can	3.50
Table #. Stand—Short/Med/Tall Set	2.00
Ice Glow—Sm./Med./Lg.	22.50/28.00/31.50
BBQ Grill—Sm./Lg.	46.00/73.00
with Rotesollie	100.00

Figure 10–20 *Equipment rental chart. (Courtesy of Ridgewell's Caterers, Bethesda, MD.).*

Specialty Items

Incidentals cont'd.

Charcoal (20#)/Fluid	7.50/5.50
Coat Rack (cap. 40)	18.00
Hangers (wire)	n/c
Ropes/Stansions (ea.)	11.50
Wicker Basket/Tray	3.00
Carrier—Small/Large	18.75/23.00
Sheet Pan	2.00
Lg. Stove & Gas	34.00
Ice Bucket	6.00

Disposable Items

Trash Can Liners	1.00
Coat Checks (per 100)	4.75
Gas fuel cans	4.50
Paper Cocktail Napkins (per pkg.)	1.50
Inquire about our new colors	
Paper Napkins—Dinner/Luncheon	
(per pkg.)	3.25/2.50
Paper Doilies—3"/12" (per pkg.)	2.50
Candles—18"/Cylinder	1.25/8.00
Sterno—Small/Large	1.50/2.00
Plastic Mug	.22
Styrofoam Cup	.12
Plastic Glass—Highball	.17
Plastic Glass—Old Fashioned	.17
Plastic Punch Cup	.17
Plastic Stemware—Champagne/Wine	.22
Plastic Knife	.12
Plastic Fork	.12
Plastic Spoon	.12
Plastic Service Spoon/Fork	3.25
Plastic Dinner Plate	.17
Plastic Luncheon Plate	.17
Plastic Bread & Butter Plate	.17
Disposable Platter	2.50
Paper Cloth 2x3 yds.	3.50

Tables

30" x 30" (seats 4)	4.00
30" x 5' (seats 6)	6.25
30" x 6' (seats 8)	7.25
3' x 4' (seats 6)	6.50
3' x 5' (seats 6)	6.75
3' x 6' (seats 8)	7.75
3' x 8' (seats 10)	8.00
4' x 4' (seats 8)	7.50
4' x 6' (seats 10)	8.50

Figure 10–20 *(continued)*

Creative catering firms can use subcontractors to gain the flexibility necessary to provide a wide variety of theme parties. The catering service featured in Figure 10–21 uses a simple format to offer a wide range of theme parties and services to their customers using subcontractors to supplement equipment and supplies. This small firm operates out of a warehouse and kitchen facility with one retail food outlet.

The cuisine theme menus in Figure 10–22 offer an interesting selection of menu items appropriate to some of the theme party ideas listed in Figure 10–21. Italy, Japan, France, Morocco, and Vietnam are just a few of the national cuisines that offer opportunities for entertainment and concept functions.

Measuring Customer Satisfaction

The level of satisfaction of the guests attending catering functions is difficult to evaluate. Therefore the most satisfactory method of accessing the success of a function is to ask the primary planning contact to complete a customer comment form. The comment form should include a section for each segment of events within the total function. For example, the breakdown of a dinner-dance would be as follows:

Segment I	Reception
Segment II	Dinner
Segment III	Dance

The customer comment form in Figure 10–23 outlines the appropriate questions that should be asked in order to effectively evaluate customer satisfaction. The results of this comment form allow management to identify areas of service, production, and facilities that need to be improved, changed, or repaired. Sometimes the customer will mention staff whose performance is to be commended.

Summary

The objectives of marketing, identifying customer needs, and developing products and services are important to the continued success of catering businesses. Catering services must possess the flexibility to respond to a wide variety of customer needs. Marketing opportunities are created by customer needs that are identified for product or service development.

Entertainment and concept packaging provide dynamic and profitable ways to expand catering services. Decorations, entertainment, and cuisine themes combine to create festive settings for business and social functions.

Package pricing of food, beverages, and services responds to customer needs for time-saving convenience in planning catering functions.

Kathy and Peter Callahan

(215) 296-7769
FAX 640-0940

93 E. Lancaster Avenue
Paoli, PA 19301

Strafford Farmers Market
Strafford, PA 19087

SPECIAL EFFECTS BY GOURMET EXPRESS

The use of Ethnic Food Stations are a popular alternative to the traditional Cocktail Party or Buffet Dinner. The following list outlines some of the more popular ideas for food stations.

Individual Menus available upon request.
Theme Parties Available.

Sushi
Filet
Smoked Salmon
Thai/Vietnamese
Caviar with or without Frozen Vodka in Flowered Ice Blocks
Raw Bar
Californian
Tex Mex
Italian
Greek
Indonesian Rice Table
Meditteranean
Carribean
Oriental (Japanese and Chinese)
French
Morrocan
Regional American
Cajun, Creole
Pasta
Stir Fry
Grilling, Charcoal, Mesquite, Wine Vines, or Oak

The following is a list of the kinds of parties that we cater:

Sit Down Dinners, Cocktails, Buffet Dinners, Station Parties, Galas, Fundraisers, Weddings, Theme Parties, Garden Parties, Picnics, Barbecues, Open Houses, Brunches, Bar Mitzvah, and Bat Mitzvah

We offer Full Service including:

Staff, Rental Equipment, Bar Set Up, Tenting, Valet, Location of Party Sites, Security, Flowers and Decorations, Music, Wedding Consultation, Liquor Subcontracting, and more......

Figure 10–21 *Theme party services. (Courtesy of Gourmet Express Caterers, Paoli, PA.)*

ITALY

Veal Fennel Sausage Grill

Roast Loin of Pork with Rosemary and Sage
Red Onion Marmalade

Bruschetta

Seafood Salad of Squid, Mussels,
Shrimp, Grilled Swordfish,
Onions and Peppers Marinated in
Trattoria Vinaigrette

Risotto with Portabello Mushrooms,
Chianti Wine, Garlic and Saffron

Assorted Antipasti

JAPAN

Negimaki—Beef Tenderloin Marinated and
Grilled with Scallions

Ebi Shiitake Mushrooms Stuffed with
Savory Shrimp Filling

Sushi Bar

Sashimi to Include Chirashi, Maguro and Futomaki
Soy Sauce
Wasabi

Harumaki—Japanese Spring Rolls Stuffed with
Chicken, Shrimp and Fresh Vegetables

THE FRENCH COUNTRYSIDE

Emincee of Rabbit with a Concassee of
Tomatoes, Spring Onions and Herb Provencale

Frog Legs à la Lyonnaise

Pork and Goose Rillette

Selections of Specialty French Cheeses
Crusty French Breads in Shapes of Farm Animals
Baguettes
Petit Pain

MOROCCO

Roast Chicken wth Lemon and Olives

Butterflied Leg of Lamb
Infused with Fresh Herbs and Citrus

Couscous Salad—Perfumed with Turmeric, Cumin,
Coriander and Ginger

Byesar—Fava Bean Dip,
A Moroccan Version of Hummus

Khboz Moroccan Bread—Hearty Flatbread
Encased with Aromatic Seeds

SWITZERLAND

Kirsch Torte—Meringue with Kirsch Flavored
Sponge Cake

Swiss Dacquoise—Hazelnut Meringue,
Chocolate Mousse and Raspberry Cream

Engadiner Nuss Torte—with
Caramel Walnut Filling

Country Fruit Tart Marguerite
Scalloped Puff Pastry Layered with
Creamy Custard and Seasonal Fresh Fruits

Zwetschgen Plum Strips

Perfect Pear Tart

Peach Charlotte with Spun Caramel

Delicate Caramelized Mille Feuille Loops

Swiss Chocolate Candies

Figure 10–22 *International cuisine theme menus. (Courtesy of Ridgewell's Caterers, Bethesda, MD.)*

```
CATERING CUSTOMER COMMENT FORM
_____

CUSTOMER NAME: _____

DATE OF FUNCTION: _____
TYPE OF FUNCTION: _____

Please indicate your level of satisfaction with the following
points regarding your recent function with us. Your comments
will help us to answer the needs of our customers and identify
areas for improvement. We sincerely appreciate your taking the
time to complete this comment form:
_____

LOCATION:
1. Accessible to your guests:_____
2. Clean and attractive:_____
_____
SERVICES:
1. Bar and beverage services: _____

2. Reception or cocktail service: _____

3. Main Meal Service: _____

4. Courtesy level of wait staff: _____

5. Audio Visual Equipment if supplied: _____

6. Entertainment if supplied: _____
   _____
   _____

7. Quality of food service: _____
   _____

_____
MANAGEMENT:
1. Function arrangements and follow through: _____
   _____
2, Billing: _____
_____
ADDITIONAL COMMENTS: _____
_____
_____
_____

Thank you for your comments. Please feel free to call me and discuss
any of the aspects of your function with me.
                                        Sincerely,
```

Figure 10–23 *Customer comment form.*

Measuring the level of customer satisfaction for catering functions is best done by following up with a customer comment form. Catering functions generally consist of two or more segments, each requiring a critique of services for evaluation by management.

Endnotes

1. *Source*: 1991 Foodservice Forecast, Bureau of Foodservice Research, *Restaurant & Institutions Magazine*, 1990.
2. American Marketing Association, 1985.

Bibliography

Apicius, *Cookery and Dining in Imperial Rome*. Edited by Joseph Dommers Vehling, New York: Dover Publications Inc., 1977.

Bardi, James A. *Computer Assisted Hospitality Management Applications: A Study of Selected Hosteliers, Restauranteurs and Caterers in Pennsylvania 1989*. CHRIE Conference, Washington D.C., 1990.

Booth, Letha. *The Williamsburg Cookbook*. Williamsburg, VA: The Colonial Williamsburg Foundation. 1975.

Brillat-Savarin, Jean Anthelme. *The Physiology of Taste*. Edited by M. F. K. Fisher. San Francisco: North Point Press, 1986.

Bureau of Foodservice Research. "1991 Foodservice Forecast." *Restaurants and Institutions Magazine, Special Report*, 1990.

Cannon, Poppy, and Patricia Brooks. *The Presidents' Cookbook*. U.S.A.: Funk & Wagnalls, 1968.

Carter, Susannah. *The Frugal Colonial Housewife*. Edited by Jean McKibbin. Garden City, NY: Dolphin Books, 1976.

Chefs of ARA Fine Dining. *A Taste For All Seasons*. Boston: The Harvard Common Press, 1990.

Combes, Steven. *Restaurant French*. 2d ed. London: Barrie & Jenkins Ltd., 1974.

Delfakis, Helen, Nancy L. Scanlon, and Janis B. VanBuren. *Food Service Management*. Cincinnati: South-Western, 1991.

Editors of American Heritage. *The American Heritage Cookbook and Illustrated History of American Eating and Drinking*. New York: American Heritage Publishing Company, 1964.

Gisslen, Wayne. *Professional Cooking*. 2d ed. New York: John Wiley & Sons, 1989.

Glasse, Hanna. *The Art of Cookery Made Plain and Easy*. Yorkshire, England: S. R. Publishers.

Hale, William Harlan. *The Horizon Cookbook and Illustrated History of Eating and Drinking through the Ages*. New York: American Heritage Publishing Company, 1968.

Harris, Margaret A. *Banquets*. Nashville, TN: Broadman Press, 1937.

Harrison, Molly. *The Kitchen in History*. New York: Charles Scribner's Sons, 1972.

Kimball, Marie. *Thomas Jefferson's Cookbook*. Richmond, VA: The University Press of Virginia, 1976.

Kinnear, Thomas C., and Kenneth L. Bernhardt. *Principles of Marketing*. Glenview, IL: Scott, Foresman, 1983.

Klapthor, Margaret Brown. *The First Ladies Cookbook*. New York: Parents' Magazine Press, 1966.

Kotschevar, Lendal H. *Management by Menu*. 2d ed. New York: W. C. Brown, 1987.

Kotschevar, Lendal H. *Quantity Food Processing*. 2d ed. New York: John Wiley & Sons, 1975.

Life Saving Training for Alcohol Serving Professionals. New York: Insurance Information Institute, April 1988.

Lincoln, Anne H. *The Kennedy White House Parties*. New York: The Viking Press, 1967.

McLaughlin, Jack. *Jefferson and Monticello*. New York: Henry Holt & Co., 1988.

Millar, Jack. *Menu Pricing and Strategy*. Boston: CBI Publishers, 1980.

Montagné, Prosper. *The New Larousse Gastronomique*. New York: Crown Publishers Inc., 1961.

Nograd, Robert M., ed. *Culinary Arts IV*. Providence: P.A.R. Inc., 1985.

Nykiel, Ronald A. *Marketing in the Hospitality Industry*. New York: Van Nostrand Reinhold, 1983.

Old Mr. Boston Deluxe Official Bartenders Guide. Boston: Mr. Boston Distiller Corporation, 1979.

Roberts, Laura. "Dining at the John Brown House." *Rhode Island Historical Society: Information for Tour Guides*. Providence, RI: Rhode Island Historical Society, 1980.

Root, Waverly, and Richard de Rochemont. *Eating in America*. New York: William Morrow & Co., 1976.

Rysavy, Francois, and Francis S. Leighton. *A Treasury of White House Cooking*. New York: G. P. Putnam's Sons, 1972.

Sass, Lorna J. *To the King's Taste*. New York: Metropolitan Museum of Art, 1975.

Scanlon, Nancy L. *Marketing by Menu*. New York: CBI Publishers, 1985.

Scanlon, Nancy L. *Marketing by Menu*. 2d ed. New York: Van Nostrand Reinhold, 1990.

Sherry, John E. H. *Legal Aspects of Foodservice Management*. New York: John Wiley & Sons, 1984.

Showman, Richard K. et al., eds. *The Papers of General Nathanael Greene*. Volume III, *October 1778 to May 1779*. Chapel Hill: University of North Carolina Press, 1983.

Simmons, Amelia. *American Cookery*. Grand Rapids, MI: William B. Eerdmans Publishing Company, 1965.

Szathmary, Louis. *American Gastronomy*. Chicago: Henry Regnery Co., 1974.

Tannahill, Reay. *Food in History*. New York: Stein & Day, 1973.

Thomas, Gertrude I. *Food of Our Forefathers*. Philadelphia: F. A. Davis Co., n.d.

Toulouse-Lautrec, H., and Maurice Joyant. *The Art of Cuisine*. New York: Holt, Rinehart & Winston, 1966.

Tschirky, Oscar. *"Oscar" Of The Waldorf's Cook Book*. New York: Dover Publications Inc., 1973.

Ziemann, Hugo, and F. L. Gillette. *The White House Cookbook*. New York: The Saalfield Publishing Co., 1906.

Index